# ANGLES
## ON THE ENGLISH-SPEAKING WORLD

VOLUME 3

*Romantic Generations:
Text, Authority and Posterity
in British Romanticism*

Editor: Lene Østermark-Johansen

# ANGLES
# ON THE ENGLISH-SPEAKING WORLD

VOLUME 3

*Romantic Generations:*
*Text, Authority and Posterity*
*in British Romanticism*

Editor: Lene Østermark-Johansen

MUSEUM TUSCULANUM PRESS
UNIVERSITY OF COPENHAGEN
2003

Published for
The Department of English,
University of Copenhagen

\*

EDITORIAL BOARD

DORTE ALBRECHTSEN          RUSSELL DUNCAN

LENE ØSTERMARK-JOHANSEN

BOOK REVIEW EDITOR
CHARLES LOCK

\*

*Angles on the English-Speaking World* is published once a year by the Department of English at the University of Copenhagen. Issues are thematic and contain a balance of articles from local and international contributors. *Angles* is intended as a lively forum for a broad range of literary, linguistic, cultural and historical studies from various theoretical standpoints.

\*

Articles for consideration and all editorial communication should be sent in three copies to:
Angles on the English-Speaking World
University of Copenhagen, Department of English
Njalsgade 128-132, bygning 24, DK-2300 Copenhagen S, Denmark

Business communications, including subscriptions and orders for reprints, should be addressed to the publishers:

MUSEUM TUSCULANUM PRESS
Njalsgade 92, DK-2300 Copenhagen S, Denmark
www.mtp.dk

\*

Cover design by Henrik Maribo based on a hand-coloured engraving entitled *Monde dans une tête de fou* (ca. 1590). Bibliothèque nationale de France.

Set by Anna Henneberg and Sanne Larsen

Printed in Denmark by KOPI SERVICE at the Faculty of Humanities,
University of Copenhagen

© 2003 MUSEUM TUSCULANUM PRESS &
ANGLES ON THE ENGLISH-SPEAKING WORLD
New Series, volume 3

ISBN 87-7289-860-7
ISSN 0903-1723

# CONTENTS

List of Plates ........................................................................... 7

Editor's Preface ...................................................................... 9

Pernille Strande-Sørensen
Authentication of National Identity:
Macpherson and Burns as Editors of Scottish Ballads ....... 11

Charles Lock
Those Lips: on Cowper (*Ekphrasis* in Parentheses) ............ 27

Robert W. Rix
William Blake and the Prophetic Marketplace .................... 47

Ian Duncan
Hume, Scott, and the 'Rise of Fiction' ................................... 63

Andrew Bennett
Poetry and Ignorance .............................................................. 77

Peter J. Manning
Home Thoughts From Abroad:
Wordsworth's 'Musings Near Aquapendente' ..................... 93

Peter Simonsen
Self Generations:
On Wordsworth's Frontispiece Portraits .............................. 113

Karsten Engelberg
Poetic Laments of P. B. Shelley:
Conventions, Familiar Mysteries, and Critical Responses .... 129

Lene Østermark-Johansen
Victorian Angles on Blake:
Reading the Artist's Head in the Late Nineteenth Century .... 141

Reviews

Glen Cavaliero: Lis Christensen,
*Elizabeth Bowen: The Later Fiction* ............................................................ 165

Michael West: Russell Duncan and David J. Klooster, editors,
*Phantoms of a Blood-Stained Period:*
*The Complete Civil War Writings of Ambrose Bierce* ................................ 167

Clara Juncker: Justin D. Edwards,
*Gothic Passages: Racial Ambiguity and the American Gothic* ................... 170

Abstracts ........................................................................................ 173

Notes on Contributors ............................................................... 177

Forthcoming Issues ..................................................................... 179

# LIST OF PLATES

1. Dietrich Heins, *Anne Cowper, née Donne* (1703-1737), oil on copper, 13 x 16 cms, c. 1723. Private Collection ............................ 45

2. The first authorised frontispiece portrait of Wordsworth. Engraved in 1836 by W. H. Watt from the portrait taken by H. W. Pickersgill in 1832. Published in *The Poetical Works of William Wordsworth. A New Edition* 6 Vols (London: Edward Moxon, 1836). Reproduced by kind permission of The British Library (shelfmark 11611.b.11-16) ............................ 116

3. The second authorised frontispiece portrait of Wordsworth. Engraved in 1845 by W. Finden from the bust made by F. Chantrey in 1820. Published in *The Poems of William Wordsworth. A New Edition* Vol. I (London: Edward Moxon, 1845). Reproduced by kind permission of The British Library (shelfmark 11632.ee.5 fp) ............................ 117

4. William Blake, *Self-portrait caricature*, pencil, before 1809. Reproduced from David Erdman and Donald Moore (eds), *The Notebook of William Blake. A Photographic and Typographic Facsimile* (Oxford: Clarendon Press, 1973), p. [N67] ............................ 149

5. William Blake, *Self-caricature as Cancer*, pencil, 16.5 x 11.4 cm, c. 1820. Reproduced from *Drawings of William Blake: 92 Pencil Studies* ed. and intr. Geoffrey Keynes (New York: Dover Publications, 1970), no. 70 ............................ 149

6. William Blake, *Socrates*, pencil, 31.1 x 20.2 cm, c. 1820. Reproduced from Robert N. Essick and Donald Pearce (eds), *Blake in his Time* (Bloomington and London: Indiana University Press, 1978), pl. 77 ............................ 149

7. William Blake, *Jerusalem*, plate 93. Reproduced from G. E. Bentley Jr, *The Stranger from Paradise: A Biography of William Blake* (New Haven and London: Yale University Press, 2001), p. 313 ............................ 151

8. Engraving by C. H. Jeens after John Linnell, *Portrait of William Blake* (1861). Frontispiece to Vol. I of Alexander Gilchrist, *Life of William Blake, "Pictor Ignotus."* With Selections from his Poems and Other Writings, 2 vols (London and Cambridge: Macmillan & Co., 1863). Reproduced by kind permission of the British Library (shelfmark 10825.e.g) ........................................ 152

9. Engraving by Schiavonetti after Thomas Phillips, *Portrait of William Blake* (1807). Frontispiece to Vol. II of Alexander Gilchrist, *Life of William Blake, "Pictor Ignotus."* With Selections from his Poems and Other Writings, 2 vols (London: Macmillan & Co., 1880). Reproduced by kind permission of the British Library (shelfmark 2408.g.5/2) ......................................... 155

10. Tatham, *William Blake in Youth and Age* (1830). Frontispiece to Vol. I of Edwin John Ellis and William Butler Yeats, *The Works of William Blake. Poetic, Symbolic, and Critical*, 3 vols (London: Bernard Quaritch, 1893). Reproduced by kind permission of the British Library (shelfmark TCK.11.bb) ....................... 159

11. James Deville, phrenological cast of William Blake's head (1823). Frontispiece to Edwin J. Ellis, *The Real Blake: A Portrait Biography* (London: Chatto & Windus, 1907). Reproduced by kind permission of the British Library (shelfmark 10852.dd.15) ..................................................................... 161

# EDITOR'S PREFACE

Unlike the first two volumes of *ANGLES on the English-Speaking World*, this special issue does not originate in a set of conference papers. The idea of compiling a collection of essays on Romanticism emerged from the unusually strong concentration on Romantic studies among the graduate students of the English Department a couple of years ago. This volume places their work in the context of distinguished international scholars of greater seniority, scholars who have become academic contacts through conferences and assessment committees, and whose contributions I am very pleased to be able to include alongside the works of local contributors.

The Romantic generations of the title of this volume thus strike a number of different chords: generations of scholars in Romantic studies; conventional divisions of Romantic poets into first, second and possibly third generations; the self-generative aspect of Romanticism; the awareness of poetic reputation and the image and afterlife of the poet. The collection spans just over a hundred years, from the 1780s to the 1890s, and while not in any way attempting to define Romanticism or raise issues of periodization the volume allows for the continued existence of Romantic features right until the end of the nineteenth century.

Poetry looms large in this issue of *ANGLES*; apart from Ian Duncan's essay on 'Hume, Scott, and the "Rise of Fiction",' all the other essays are in some way concerned with the Romantic poet and his poetry. The Romantic poet is thus represented as a collector and editor of ballads, as a political radical and printmaker, as other to himself, essentially ignorant of the process of poetic composition, as a rival and collaborator with other poets, or as a poet long dead, the subject of successive generations of poetic lament. The boundaries between poetry and the visual arts is explored in a couple of the essays; indeed, the rivalry between portraiture and literature pervades no less than three of the contributions, and no matter whether the subject of inquiry is the image of the poet or the image of the poet's mother, the Romantic poet displays a high degree of self-consciousness with respect to both literary and visual media. Romantic generations generate both selves and others in poetry and portraiture.

Lene Østermark-Johansen

# AUTHENTICATION OF NATIONAL IDENTITY: MACPHERSON AND BURNS AS EDITORS OF SCOTTISH BALLADS

Pernille Strande-Sørensen

Macpherson and Burns are among the most famous names of eighteenth-century Scottish literary history. Macpherson's success was founded on the Gaelic poetry of the Highlands, which he, in 1760, published in a collection entitled *Fragments of Ancient Poetry*, which struck a chord among the urbane readers of the Scottish Enlightenment.[1] In the following years, Macpherson produced a series of translations of Gaelic poetry, now commonly known as the poems of Ossian.[2] Although investigations into the matter were not initiated until after Macpherson's death in 1796,[3] the authenticity of Macpherson's translations was subjected to criticism in the 1770s, and Macpherson was called upon to produce textual evidence of the Gaelic originals. A generation later, in 1786, Burns shot to fame with his first publication, *Poems, Chiefly in the Scottish Dialect*, published in Kilmarnock. The anthology attracted attention from the Edinburgh literati, and an Edinburgh edition followed in 1787 to much acclaim.[4] Burns, after having spent a season as the Edinburgh literary super-star of 1787, moved back to Dumfriesshire, where he lived until his death in 1796.

Both Macpherson and Burns have become inextricable parts of Scottish literary heritage: since the Ossianic Controversy of the 1770s, Macpherson has had a somewhat tarnished reputation, which contrasts with Burns's sanctified status as a national icon. For almost two hundred years, 'Macpherson' has, to literary critics, been synonymous with lack of originality and authenticity.[5] However, this situation has changed in the last 15 years, as scholars have begun to place Macpherson and the poems of Ossian within a cultural, literary, and epistemological context in order to study this quintessentially eighteenth-century phenomenon and its impact and influence on literature in the following hundred years.[6]

Despite the major differences between the works of Macpherson and Burns, several interesting coincidences occur when addressing their respective works on Scottish balladry. As will be argued, Macpherson and Burns have much in common regarding the editing and treatment of traditional vernacular poetry: both carried out their works on Scottish balladry, Gaelic and Scots respectively, within the parameters of the Enlightenment, and both of them operated with an editorial rationale which relied on the concept of authenticity for its validation. It may appear strange to emphasize the authentication of national identity as that which most closely links Macpherson and Burns as eighteenth-century editors of Scottish balladry. After all, authenticity is the very element on which Macpherson's scholarly and editorial credibility foundered. In this essay it will be argued that both Macpherson and Burns place authentication of national identity as the validating factor of their contributions to Scottish balladry. However, their means of authentication and conceptions of national identity vary greatly: Macpherson, as will be argued, is, in his conceptions of authentication and national identity, firmly embedded in an eighteenth-century linear mode of thought, whereas Burns's ideas of national identity and the authentication thereof challenge the linearity of empirical, representational thought, despite taking their points of departure in this prevalent mode of conception.

The eighteenth-century study of ballads was an integrated part of the empiricist inquiry of the Enlightenment.[7] The study of vernacular traditional narrative verse was but one aspect of the overwhelming interest in antiquities which followed in the wake of the scientific revolution of the seventeenth century.[8] Following the writings of, among others, Locke, Newton, and Descartes, interest and intellectual inquiry into the nature and origin of the human condition gained momentum in the eighteenth century. Historiography – the study of the origins of Man as both an individual and a social creature – in the eighteenth century rested on its ability to ascertain absolute certainty regarding its object of study.[9] As will be discussed below, interest in the ballad, by way of the manuscript, very early in the eighteenth century became an integrated part of historiography. However, the scientific empiricist means of experiment and experience ensuring absolute certainty in analysis were not readily transferable to the field of historiography and balladry. Though attempts were made to uphold empiric ideals of science within the study of ballads, the ubiquitous elements of fiction and poetry in the ballads constantly threatened to undermine these ideals and consequently devalue the study.[10]

By making the validity of the ballad completely dependent on its presence within an ancient manuscript, scholars and editors in the early eighteenth century tried to circumvent the problems caused by incorporating fiction into the study of history. Ballads provided a vernacular counterpart to Classical epic poetry, and, consequently, to the eighteenth-century scholar held the promise of a national vernacular epic tradition, rivalling those of ancient Greece and Rome. The interest in ballads as historical representations was a direct result of what Haywood terms 'the cult of the ancient manuscript.'[11]

Within eighteenth-century historiography, the manuscript was revered as the absolute empirical unit of knowledge next to Man himself, and the primary concern of eighteenth-century ballad-scholars was to authenticate the manuscript rather than its contents.[12] Orally transmitted ballads and their printed counterparts on broadsheets, however, held very few attractions to the antiquarian. These types of ballads were not considered examples of a glorious historic past, but of modern plebeian vulgarity.[13] Initially, only historical ballads were of interest, as they were considered the most 'authentic.'[14] However, even the most detailed versified account of a battle – or cattle raid – still possessed an uncomfortable affinity with the vulgar fiction of traditional ballads and broadsheets, and these types of balladry could under no circumstances be tolerated within the study of history, as Bishop Percy's apologetic 'Dedication to the Countess of Northumberland' suggests:

> [T]hese poems are presented to your *Ladyship*, not as labours of art, but as effusions of nature, shewing the first efforts of ancient genius, and exhibiting the customs and opinions of remote ages: of ages that had been almost lost to memory, had not the gallant deeds of your illustrious ancestors preserved them from oblivion.[15]

The concept of authenticity became one of the most dominating aspects of the study of ballads in the eighteenth century, because of the necessity to evaluate several types of ballads. Unfortunately, no standard definition as to *what* the concept of authenticity entailed had been articulated, and each editor could, in principle, define the concept of authenticity at his own discretion. In other words, the eighteenth-century editor of antiquities and editor of ballads had no other method with which to exclude undesirable representations from his inquiry, except his own judgment. David Hume, whose *Treatise* well argues about the epistemological pit-falls, describes the situation of the scholar thus:

> When we are convinc'd of any matter of fact, we do nothing but conceive it, along with a certain feeling, different from what attends the mere *reveries* of the imagination. And when we express our incredulity concerning any fact, we mean, that the arguments for the fact produce not that feeling. Did not the belief consist in a sentiment different from our mere conception, whatever objects were presented by the wildest imagination, wou'd be on equal footing with the most establish'd truths founded on history and experience. There is nothing but the feeling of sentiment to distinguish one from the other.[16]

Macpherson was not the first to use Highland material; some years prior to the publication of *Fragments*, Jerome Stone published an English translation of a Gaelic ballad.[17] However, it was Macpherson's *Fragments* which catapulted Gaelic poetry into the world. Recent research indicates that *Fragments* probably is the collaborative work between Macpherson and Hugh Blair – Macpherson's most enthusiastic supporter and sponsor. Blair also wrote the Preface to the anonymously published *Fragments*.[18] Macpherson had managed to combine the eighteenth-century nostalgia for the primitive and corresponding interest in the Sublime with the narrative songs of his childhood, thus creating a package which at the same time articulated contemporary literary taste with insight into a culture, alien yet familiar.[19]

As demonstrated by, among others, Derick Thomson, Fiona Stafford, Howard Gaskill, Nick Groom, and Ian Haywood, Macpherson's editorial treatment of his Gaelic source material does not differ radically from contemporary conventions.[20] Most ballad-editors considered their source material corrupt and 'broken,' and, in order to restore the ballads to their authentic original state, extensive interpolation and revision were considered an absolute necessity.[21] It is therefore interesting that though Dr Johnson 'believed [Macpherson] to be an Impostor,' his reasons for doing so rest almost exclusively on the fact that Macpherson availed himself of oral rather than written sources.[22] Johnson's main objections to the poems of Ossian are centred on the alleged mode of Macpherson's source material, rather than on Macpherson's manipulations of his sources. Macpherson's translations were rooted in an oral and, to the English, alien culture. In *Journey to the Western Isles*, Johnson makes his opinion regarding the ability of Gaelic to produce poems such as those attributed to Ossian quite clear:

> Of the Earse language, as I understand nothing, I cannot say more than I have been told. It is the rude speech of a barbarous people, who had few thoughts to express, and were content, as they conceived grossly, to be grossly understood. After what has been lately talked about Highland Bards, and Highland genius, many will startle when they are told, that the Earse never was a written language; that there is not in the world an Earse manuscript a hundred years old; and that the sound of Highlanders were never expressed by letters.[23]

The criticism against Macpherson was, ironically, partly his own fault. Throughout the prefaces and forewords to his translations, Macpherson continuously stresses the authenticity of the poems as well as his own editorial integrity. This type of emphasis may be regarded as a natural response to criticism, but the concept of authenticity in the English version of the poems of Ossian is emphasized prior to any public criticisms. In the Preface to *Fragments*, the reader is assured that '[t]he public may depend on the following fragments as genuine remains of ancient Scottish poetry,' and that '[t]he translation is extremely literal.'[24] In Macpherson's subsequent defences of the poems of Ossian, it is interesting to note that the concept of authenticity, exclusively, is addressed as a phenomenon of antiquarianism. Macpherson draws attention to the historical value of his translations, and plays down the poetic and literary qualities of the translations:

> The story of the poem is so little interlarded with fable, that one cannot help thinking of the genuine history of Fingal's expedition, embellished by poetry. In that case, the compositions of Ossian are not less valuable for the light they throw on the ancient state of Scotland and Ireland than they are for their poetical merit.[25]

When Johnson's criticism is compared to Macpherson's response, it is interesting to note that the dispute between them takes place on two different levels. Johnson argues that the poems of Ossian have to be forgeries because they are supposed to be *written* in Gaelic. Macpherson does not respond to this point of argument. Instead, he is focused on establishing an historical reality within which the existence of traditional Gaelic epic poetry may be justified:

> The Caracul of Fingal is no other than Caracalla, who, as the son of Severus, the Emperor of Rome, whose dominions were extended almost over the known world, was not without reason called in the poems of Ossian, *The Son of the King of World*. The space of time between 211, the year Severus died, and the beginning of the fourth century, is not so great, but Ossian the son of Fingal, might have seen the Christians whom the persecution under Dioclesian [sic] had driven beyond the pale of the Roman empire.[26]

Though he claimed to have an ancient manuscript in his possession, Macpherson's primary argument regarding the validity of the poems of Ossian is based on establishing the existence of Ossian, rather than the authentication of his poetry.[27] It may be argued that Johnson, in his criticism of the poems of Ossian, does not differentiate between discourse and text, whereas Macpherson, in his response to Johnson, does not differentiate between author and text. Within Macpherson's reasoning, the authenticity of Ossian is extended to include Macpherson's own translations.

In order to comprehend the logic of Macpherson's argument, it is necessary to look at the eighteenth-century method of historiography. As mentioned above, the study of history in the eighteenth century was modelled on the developments following the scientific revolution in the seventeenth century. The method and quality of the work of the Enlightenment historian relied, almost exclusively, on the transparency and order of historical representations.[28] Hume writes:

> 'Tis obvious all this chain of argument or connection of causes and effects, is at first founded on those characters or letters, which are seen and remember'd, and that without the authority either of the memory or the senses, our whole reasoning wou'd be chimerical and without foundation. Every link in the chain wou'd in that case hang upon another; but there wou'd not be anything fix'd to one end of it, capable of sustaining the whole; and consequently there wou'd be no belief nor evidence.[29]

In order for an antiquarian work to have any value, it had to be rooted in fact. As ballads became included in antiquarian studies, the need to differentiate between fact and fiction became imperative in order to uphold the validation of the object of study and also of the study itself. With the inclusion of balladry into the field of antiquities, the antiquarian suddenly becomes an integral part of the study: someone who not only had to conduct the analysis according to scholarly conventions but also has exclusive privileges to differentiate and define data.[30] The editor, as Hume describes him, has to be 'virtuous':

> To have a sense of virtue, is nothing but to *feel* a satisfaction of a particular kind from the contemplation of a character. The very *feeling* constitutes our praise or admiration. [...] We do not infer a character to be virtuous because it pleases: But in feeling that it pleases after such a particular manner, we in effect feel that it is virtuous. The case is the same as in our judgments concerning all kinds of beauty, and tastes and sensations.[31]

As the scarcity of ancient manuscripts in Gaelic made it difficult for Macpherson to found his translations 'on those characters or letters, which are seen and remember'd,' his argument had to circumvent the importance placed on written material in eighteenth-century antiquarian analysis. In other words, Macpherson has to produce evidence of a representation of ancient Gaelic epic poetry which trumps written representation: Ossian himself. It is in his attempt to sustain this argument that Macpherson rearranges 'this chain of argument or connection of causes and effect,' consequently shifting the focal point of controversy from that of authenticating written representation to authenticating the author. In other words, Macpherson eliminates the aspect of validity of oral sources in antiquarianism from the discussion, and consequently, Johnson's objections remain ignored. Within Macpherson's line of argument then, the validity of his translations becomes completely dependent upon the authentication of Ossian's existence. Ossian's existence, however, is established by arguing that the well-known Irish bard Oisín was, in fact, Scottish rather than Irish. Macpherson, interestingly, bases his argument on the reputed antiquity of the Caledonian language:

> The dialect of the Celtic tongue, spoken in the north of Scotland, is much more pure, more agreeable to its mother language, and more abounding with primitives, than that now spoken, or even that which has been writ for some centuries back, amongst the most unmixed part of the Irish nation. A Scotchman, tolerably conversant in his own language, understands an Irish composition, from that derivative analogy which it has to the *Galic* of North-Britain. An Irishman, on the other hand, without the aid of study, can never understand a composition in the *Galic* tongue. – This affords a proof, that the *Scotch Galic* is the most original, and, consequently, the language of a more antient and unmixed people.[32]

Macpherson's argument suspends the aspect of authentication within a circular line of argumentation which at no point addresses the initial objection to the authenticity of the poems of Ossian: their alleged oral transmission. Within Macpherson's argument, the authenticity of his translations is established by creating an argument of Ossian being Scottish. The implications of Macpherson's argument well illustrate Hume's concerns: at no point in his argument does he produce any external evidence, but rests contentedly in his own 'feelings.'

Whereas the poems of Ossian were validated by authentication of their historical origins and their status as the autographed creations of Ossian, Burns's work on ballads marks a shift of the focal point of validation of ballads. It will be argued that Burns's primary view of balladry is not that of versified history but of living culture. This view forms a stark contrast to the prevailing late eighteenth-century and early nineteenth-century views of ballads as relics of an ancient past. Balladry as a specimen of contemporary plebeian culture in the early nineteenth century was not commercially viable; balladry as a representation of an ancient noble Scottish *poiesis* was – something to which Walter Scott's best-selling collection *Minstrelsy of the Scottish Border* is a testimony.[33] Though the position of ballads within the study of antiquities had been problematic since the days of Macpherson, interest in ballads had by no means diminished when Robert Burns, in 1787, became involved with James Johnson and his production of *The Scots Musical Museum*.[34] Johnson's work was a serialized collection which Burns considered to be a 'Work [that] will outlive the momentary neglects of Idle Fashion & defy the teeth of Time.'[35]

Burns continued his commitment to the *Museum* until his death, and in 1792 he also began to contribute to George Thomson's *Select Collection of Scottish Song*.[36] Burns was not oblivious to the various aspects of antiquarian value of Scottish balladry, but they were, nevertheless, of minor importance to him, as stated in the following extract of a letter he wrote to Thomson in 1792:

> Let me tell you, that you are too fastidious in your ideas of Songs & ballads. – I own that your criticisms are just – the Songs you specify in your list have, *all but one,* the faults you remark in them – but who shall mend the matter? – Who shall rise up & say 'Go to, I will make a better!' – […] Your observation as to the aptitude of Dr. Percy's ballad, to the air Nanie O, is just. – It is, besides, perhaps, the most beautiful Ballad in the English language. – But let me remark to you, in the sentiment & style of our Scottish airs, there is a pastoral simplicity, a something that one may call, the Doric style & dialect of vocal music, to which a dash of our native tongue & manners is particularly, nay peculiarly apposite.[37]

Shortly before his death, Burns had declared to Thomson that he wished his contributions in the *Museum* and *Select Collections* to be published independently as a book.[38]

Burns never published a collection of songs and ballads in his own name as editor, and, officially, Burns's contribution to Scottish song and balladry is restricted to the aspect of collection. Nominally then, the editorial discourses of the *Museum* and the *Select Collection* belong to either James Johnson or George Thomson, whereas the balladic discourse belongs to Burns. In fact, as demonstrated by Burns's correspondence with the two editors, he *was* the general editor of the *Museum*, and argued with Thomson for appropriation of the editorial discourse of the *Select Collection*. In Burns's letters to Johnson, very little is mentioned about the ballads and songs, thus indicating that Johnson printed the songs and ballads the way Burns wanted it.[39] Thomson, however, as Burns's letters to him suggest, proved to have somewhat different ideas about the nature and style of Scottish song:

> If you mean, my dear Sir, that all the Songs in your Collection shall be Poetry of the first merit, I am afraid you will find difficulty in the undertaking more than you are aware of. – There is a peculiar rhythmus in many of our airs, and a necessity of adapting syllables to the emphasis, or what I would call the *feature notes*, of the tune that cramps the Poet, & lays him under almost unsuperable difficulties. – For instance, in the air, 'My wife's a wanton wee thing,' if a few lines, *smooth & pretty*, can be adopted to it, it is all you can expect.[40]

It is the Scottish qualities of lyrics, as well as tunes, which constitute Burns's editorial rationale: fidelity to the Scottish vernacular poetic discourse, not those of an ideal genre or historiography. When Burns first became engaged in the work on the *Museum*, the Scottish quality of the topic was emphasized:

> An Engraver [Johnson] in this town [Edinburgh] has set about collecting and publishing all the Scotch Songs, with the Music, that can be found. Songs in the English language, if by Scotchmen, are admitted; but the music must all be Scotch.[41]

Burns's 'enthusiastic attachment to the Poetry & Music of Caledonia' found a compliant outlet in Johnson's publication. Thomson, however, was not as discriminate about the music being Scots. Thomson, who wished to publish a collection of song specifically targeted to a female audience, expressed a completely opposite attitude towards Scottish song than Burns's. Thomson may be viewed as the stereotypical Anglicised song-collector of the late eighteenth century, and many of his suggestions to Burns relate to the Anglicisation of Burns's material. Despite Burns's initial promise to Thomson in which he assures his editor that Burns

> may have an opportunity of suggesting any alteration that may occur to [Burns] – [...] 'tis in the way of [Burns's] trade – still leaving [Thomson] the undoubted right of Publishers, to approve, or reject, at [Thomson's] pleasure in [Thomson's] own publication,[42]

he tried, persistently, to enlighten Thomson on the nature of Scottish song:

> 'One day I heard Mary say' – is a fine Song; but for consistency's sake, alter the name 'Adonis' – Was there ever such banns published, as a purpose of marriage between *Adonis* & *Mary*? – These Greek & Roman pastoral appellations have a flat, insipid effect in a Scots song.[43]

Burns worked from an assumption that it was not possible to separate the lyrics from their tunes.[44] His work on ballads and songs are not works of restoration or excavation, but on the alignment of tune and lyric. The beauty and importance of traditional Scottish music are mentioned in almost every letter in which Burns mentions the topic of song, as is his project of complementing already existing tunes with appropriate Scots lyrics. In a letter, Burns describes how important music is to his work of composition:

> [...] – I do not know the air; & untill I am compleat master of a tune, in my own singing, (such as it is) I never can compose for it. – My way is: I consider the poetic Sentiment, correspondent to my idea of the musical expression then chuse my theme; begin one Stanza; when that is composed, which is generally the most difficult part of the business, I walk out, sit down now & then, look out for objects in Nature around me that are in unison or harmony with the cogitations of any fancy & workings of my bosom; humming every now & then the air with the verses I have framed [...].[45]

Burns used different signatures to differentiate between the songs in the *Museum*: 'Z,' 'X,' 'R,' 'B,' and 'M,' occasionally followed by the post-script 'Written for this work by Robert Burns.'[46] However, as Donald A. Low writes in a note to no. 212 in the *Museum* in *The Songs of Robert Burns*, Burns's editorial comments were not always trustworthy:

> Burns comments on this song, 'This air is the march of the Corporation of Tailors. The 2nd and 4th stanzas are mine.' (*Notes* 43) He [Burns] has in fact brought together and given fresh meaning to two fragments of traditional song.[47]

Burns's editorial discourse differentiates between original traditional songs and his own revisions and rewritings. The notes which Burns uses to introduce his songs are not protestations of editorial integrity, nor are they claims that the songs published be originals or restored originals. In other words, in Burns's official editorial discourse, no conceptions of an ideal or original text to which the published song is an approximation exist. In the 'Introduction' to *The Songs of Robert Burns*, Low discusses the complex nature of Burns's signatures. Using 'My Luive is like a Red, Red Rose' as his example, Low argues that Burns may, deliberately have understated his personal contribution to the song. In 1794, Burns submitted 'My Luive is like a Red, Red Rose' to Urbani's *A Selection of Scots Song*; however, at the time he was also involved with Johnson's *Museum* and Thomson's *Collection*, and, not wishing to offend either Johnson or Thomson, Low argues, 'it [conceivably] occurred to [Burns] that there was likely to be less objection to a song collected by him than one avowedly written by him.'[48] Low argues that Burns's contribution to 'My Luive is like a Red, Red Rose' is made more complicated because almost every line of the song has been found in songs and ballads printed in chapbooks. It is possible, as Low argues, that Burns has picked whatever he could from already existing material, both oral and printed, and then, subsequently arranged his collage into a harmonious mosaic pattern.[49]

As discussed in, among others, Thomas Crawford's *A Study of Poems and Songs, Society and the Lyric,* McCue's 'Burns, Women, and Song,' and Mary Ellen Brown's *Burns and Tradition*, the relationship between Burns's creations and the traditional material is very complicated.[50] McCue emphasizes how the matter of song in the eighteenth century, whether revised, collected, or written, is characterized by the phenomenon of sharing tunes, phrases, and sources, and thus 'it is often impossible [...] to *account for the development of the song.*'[51] It is primarily in the collaborative work with Thomson that Burns discloses his attitudes towards the relationship between source material and the finished, edited product. In contrast to Thomson, Johnson printed whatever Burns sent him, and, consequently, little information is available as to what Burns's conception of Scottish song in the *Museum* is, except for the printed product. Matters are different in Thomson's *Collection*. Their differences in conceptions of Scottish song force Burns to articulate how he regards Scottish song and the editing thereof. In a letter to Cunningham, Burns discusses the problems of 'My Luive is like a Red, Red Rose':

> I would, to tell the fact, most gladly have seen it in our Friend's [Thomson's] publication; but though I am charmed with it, it is a kind of Song about which I know we would think very differently. It is the only species of Song about which our ideas disagree. – What to me, appears simple and wild, to him, & I suspect to you likewise, will be looked on as the ludicrous & the absurd.[52]

As Burns discovered in his dealings with Thomson, the determination of the exact nature of a Scots song, depended on who was in control of the editorial discourse, and the correspondence between the two often resembles a war over the coveted discourse. It is ironic that it is, primarily, in the dialogue with an editor, who insists on being an editor, that Burns's editorial discourse is articulated most strongly. It also suggests that the interaction between balladic and editorial discourses, which constitutes the ballads and songs as particularly Scottish, though active, in the case of Burns, is suppressed and subversive – 'buccaneering' – and accessible only through intertextual studies of Burns's collected writings, songs, poems, notebooks and letters.

Burns is not interested in engaging in a balladic discourse *on* Scottish song and balladry. Rather, he wishes to engage *in* Scottish balladic discourse. Instead of being presented as parts of a critical or historiographic discourse, Burns's songs and ballads are produced as parts of a poetic discourse. The balladic discourse of Burns's songs is, in all its aspects, lyrical and tonal, a continuation of an already existing oral discourse. Burns differs significantly from contemporary ballad-editors, because he, at the time when he begins his contributions to the *Museum* and the *Select Collection*, does not differentiate ontologically between revising and rewriting songs. To Burns, the most important thing is not whether the songs and ballads be restored to whatever former glory they possessed, but that the poetic, balladic discourse of *Scotland* be presented in its most supreme manifestation; this he makes clear to Thomson at the very beginning of their collaboration:

> Àpropos, if you are for *English* verses, there is, on my part, an end of the matter. – Whether in the simplicity of *the Ballad*, or the pathos of *the Song*, I can only hope to please myself in being allowed at least a sprinkling of our native tongue. [...] [I]f I am to be called on for my strictures & amendments – I say, amendments; for I will not *alter* except where I myself at least think that I *amend*.[53]

In light of the previous discussion, it is then possible to argue that Burns, in concurrence with Macpherson, also employs the concept of authentication as a means of validation. However, as mentioned above, there is one significant difference between the two. Burns's method of editing ballads does not differ significantly from that of Macpherson. Both editors revise and interpolate extensively in order to approximate a ballad ideal, in which the concept of authenticity is central. Burns argues that he will alter only where he can *amend*; however, he is, in his unofficial, private discourse (articulated in his letters and commonplace books), quite frank about the extent of revision and interpolation needed to make the songs appropriate for publication.[54] As Burns's communications with Thomson testify, Burns also operates with an editorial ideal. In contrast to Macpherson, though, Burns's ideal is not textual. Burns does not, at any point in his letters, notes and comments, explicitly state that his goal is to recreate the particularities of an ancient specific song. On the contrary, Burns begins his work with a song, which may or may not be rooted in oral tradition, which may or may not be already printed, and he then constructs his song, either by borrowing phrases and chorus from other songs (or versions) or by writing new words to the song himself.[55] Compared to the method employed by Macpherson, Burns's method is not unique. Macpherson too constructs his epic from a collage of versions.[56] Both collectors claim that their songs and ballads are authentic representations of a Scottish national identity. In the case of Macpherson, this authenticity is based on alleged historical evidence. By arguing that Ossian is Scottish – and therefore authentic – the poetry ascribed to Ossian as well as Macpherson's translations are included in this argument of authenticity. In other words, Macpherson's conception of national identity and authentication is a thing that once established is permanent, and whose authority automatically is conferred on subsequent representations, regardless of their present manifestations. Burns, on the other hand, does not regard national identity as a permanent fixture which, once established, may be subjected to all sorts of manipulations, whilst retaining its authenticity. Rather, the question of national identity, as expressed in traditional songs and ballads, is negotiable, and necessitates an address with each individual manifestation. Whereas Macpherson, in his editorial efforts, is engaged in the recreation of a specific autographed text, the authentication of the 'lost' epic poem of Ossian, the focal point of Burns's work on Scottish song and balladry centres on the creation and continuation of an authentic national discourse – an authentic Scottish discourse.

## Notes

[1] Cf. Edmund Burke, *A Philosophical Enquiry into the Origins of the Ideas of the Sublime and Beautiful* (1759) ed. Adam Phillips (Oxford: Oxford University Press, 1992); Samuel H. Monk, *The Sublime – A Study of Critical Theories in XVIII-Century England* (New York: Modern Language Association of America, 1935).

[2] Following the publication of *Fragments*, Macpherson issued the following autographed translations of Gaelic poetry: *Fingal* (1761/62), *The Works of Ossian* (1765): *Fingal* (1765), *The Works of Ossian* (1765): *Temora*, and *The Poems of Ossian* (1773).

[3] In 1796, a committee was set up by the Highland Society of Scotland to investigate the extent of editorial interpolation in Macpherson's translations. The committee concluded that though Macpherson had not followed the original Gaelic sources closely in his translations, characters, plots and episodes were in congruence with the Gaelic material. Cf. Fiona Stafford, 'Introduction' in *The Poems of Ossian and Related Works*, ed. Howard Gaskill with an Introduction by Fiona Stafford (Edinburgh: Edinburgh University Press, 1996), p. xiii.

[4] The Kilmarnock edition of *Poems* was sold in 612 copies, and became very popular

in Ayrshire. The Revd. George Lawrie introduced Dr Thomas Blacklock to Burns's poetry, and Blacklock, in turn, introduced Burns to the Edinburgh literati, among them Hugh Blair, and he also suggested that Burns publish an Edinburgh edition of *Poems*. Cf. *The Poems and Songs of Robert Burns*, ed. James Kinsley, Vol. III, Commentary (Oxford: Clarendon Press, 1968), pp. 976-977; Letter 125 in *The Letters of Robert Burns*, Second Edition, ed. G. Ross Roy, 2 vols. (Oxford: Clarendon Press, 1985), vol. I, pp. 133-146.

5. In 'Introductory Remarks on Popular Poetry' (1830), in *Sir Walter Scott's Minstrelsy of the Scottish Border*, ed. T. F. Henderson (1902), 4 vols. (Detroit: Singing Tree Press, 1968), vol. IV, p. 43, Walter Scott writes about John Pinkerton that he 'with a boldness, suggested perhaps by the success of Mr. Macpherson, [...] included, within a collection amounting to only twenty-one tragic ballads, no less than five, of which he afterwards owned himself to have been altogether, or in great part, the author.'

6. Among others: Fiona Stafford, *The Sublime Savage. A Study of James Macpherson and The Poems of Ossian* (Edinburgh: Edinburgh University Press, 1988); *Ossian Revisited* ed. Howard Gaskill (Edinburgh: Edinburgh University Press, 1995); Josef Bysveen, *Epic Tradition and Innovation in James Macpherson's Fingal*, Studia anglistica Upsaliensia 44 (Uppsala: Uppsala University Press 1982); Paul deGategno, *James Macpherson* (Boston: Twayne, 1989); Kirstine Louise Haugen, 'Ossian and the Invention of Textual History' in *Journal of the History of Ideas*, vol. 59:2 (1998), pp. 309-328; Ian Haywood, *The Making of History. A Study of the Literary Forgeries of James Macpherson and Thomas Chatterton in Relation to Eighteenth-Century Ideas of History and Fiction* (London: Associated University Presses, 1986).

7. Cf. Haywood.

8. Cf. *The Origins and Nature of the Scottish Enlightenment*, eds R. H. Campbell and Andrew S. Skinner (Edinburgh: John Donald Publishers, 1982); Anand D. Chitnis, *The Scottish Enlightenment. A Social History* (London: Croom Helm, 1980); *Eighteenth-Century Scotland. New Perspectives*, eds T. M. Devine and J. R. Young (East Linton: Tuckwell Press, 1999).

9. Cf. David Hume, *A Treatise of Human Understanding* (1740). Second Edition with text revised and notes by P. H. Nidditch. Analytical Index by L. A. Selby-Bigge (Oxford: Clarendon Press, 1978).

10. Cf. Haywood, pp. 19-24.

11. Ibid., pp. 19-21.

12. Hume, p. 146.

13. Cf. A. B. Friedman, *The Ballad Revival. Studies in the Influence of Popular on Sophisticated Poetry* (Chicago: University of Chicago Press, 1961); Natascha Würzbach, *The Rise of the English Street-Ballad 1550-1650*. Trans. from the German *Die englische Strassenballade 1550-1650* (1981). European Studies in English Literature (Cambridge: Cambridge University Press, 1990).

14. Haywood, p. 21.

15. Thomas Percy, *Reliques of Ancient English Poetry* (1765) (Berlin: 1893), p. 5.

16 Hume, p. 458.
17 Stafford, pp. 63-65; Derick Thomson, *The Gaelic Sources of Macpherson's Ossian*, Aberdeen University Studies no. 130 (Edinburgh: Oliver and Boyd, 1951), p. 6.
18 Cf. Kirstine Louise Haugen.
19 Cf. Stafford, pp. 61-76.
20 Cf. Thomson. Macpherson's interpolations and revisions can be viewed as continuations of the attempts of Classical philologists to retrieve lost original works – either by restoration or reconstruction – and the problems Macpherson encountered with his Gaelic sources may be compared to the problems faced by Classical and Biblical scholars of the eighteenth century. Cf. Macpherson, 'A Dissertation' in *The Poems of Ossian and Related Works*, p. 216.
21 Haywood, pp. 15-25.
22 Samuel Johnson, *A Journey to the Western Islands of Scotland*, ed. Allan Wendt (Cambridge: The Riverside Press, 1965), pp. 81-89.
23 Ibid., p. 86.
24 Preface to *Fragments* in *Ossian and Related Works*, p. 5.
25 Preface to *Fingal* in *Ossian and Related Works*, p. 37.
26 'A Dissertation Concerning...' in *Ossian and Related Works*, p. 47.
27 Macpherson, 'A Dissertation Concerning...,' p. 51: 'let it suffice therefore that, after a peregrination of six months, the translator collected from tradition, and some manuscripts, all the poems in the following collection [...].'
28 Hume, p. 146.
29 Ibid., p. 83
30 Ibid., p. 458.
31 Ibid., p. 471 [italics in original].
32 Macpherson, 'A Dissertation,' pp. 216-17.
33 Within a year of its publication, *The Minstrelsy of the Scottish Border* (1802) sold 800 copies. A year later, in 1803, an additional thousand copies were sold. In 1812, the fifth three-volume edition was issued, representing a total sale of ten thousand copies. Cf. Edgar Johnson, *Sir Walter Scott: The Great Unknown*, 2 vols (London: Hamish Hamilton, 1970).
34 *The Scots Musical Museum* (1787-1803).
35 Letter 288, in *Letters* vol. I, p. 339.
36 *Select Collection of Original Scottish Airs* (1793-1818).
37 Letter 511 in *Letters* vol. II, p. 153.
38 Letter 695 in *Letters* vol. II, p. 380.
39 Cf. Donald A. Low, Introduction. *The Songs of Robert Burns*, ed. Donald A. Low (London: Routledge, 1993), pp. 12-18.
40 Letter 514, *Letters* II, p. 157.
41 Letter 147 A, *Letters* I, p. 169.
42 Letter 507, *Letters* II, p. 149.
43 Letter 557, *Letters* II, p. 380.
44 Letter 586, *Letters* II, pp. 239-48.

[45] Ibid.
[46] Low, p. 27.
[47] 'The taylor fell thro' the bed, thimble an' a'.' *The Songs of Robert Burns*, p. 365.
[48] Low, p. 24. Kirsteen McCue, 'Burns, Women, and Song' in *Robert Burns and Cultural Authority*, ed. Robert Crawford (Edinburgh: Edinburgh University Press, 1997) pp. 42-43.
[49] Low, pp. 22-32.
[50] Cf. Thomas Crawford, *Burns. A Study of the Poems and Songs* (Stanford CA: Stanford University Press, 1965); Thomas Crawford, *Society and the Lyric – a study of the song culture of eighteenth-century Scotland* (Edinburgh: Scottish Academic Press, 1979); Mary Ellen Brown, *Burns and Tradition* (London: Macmillan Press, 1984); McCue.
[51] McCue, p. 52-53 [italics in original].
[52] Letter 593A in *Letters* vol. II, pp. 258-59.
[53] Letter 507 in *Letters* vol. II, pp. 148-49.
[54] In September 1793 Burns writes to Thomson about suggested alterations: 'Your idea, "honour's bed," is, though a beautiful, a hacknied idea; so, if you please, we will let the line stand as it is. – I have altered the Song as follows. – [...]. NB. I have borrowed the last stanza from the common Stall edition of Wallace. –' Letter 584 in *Letters* vol. II, p. 337-38.
[55] Letter 586, to Thomson, in December 1793 provides a very detailed account of Burns's editorial rationale, *Letters* II, pp. 239-48.
[56] In 'A Dissertation,' p. 215, Macpherson writes of *Temora* that '[t]he story of the poem [...] enabled me to reduce the broken members of the piece into the order in which they now appear. For the ease of the reader, I have divided it myself into books, as I had done before with the poem of *Fingal*.'

# THOSE LIPS: ON COWPER
# (*EKPHRASIS* IN PARENTHESES)

CHARLES LOCK

Mowbray, threatened with exile from his motherland and from the use of his mother-tongue:

> My native English, now I must forgo ....
> Within my mouth you have enjailed my tongue,
> Doubly portcullised with my teeth and lips ....[1]

Mowbray's speech carries a peculiar form of iconic significance, which might be termed 'performative iconicity.' As the apostrophic 'O' opens our mouth (MOwbray) to match the letter's shape, so the word *lips* closes them and bring release. 'O' can be iconic of a ring or a hole or a globe, and of the mouth in the act of vocalizing the phonetic value: in studies of iconicity this letter has received more attention than any other – with the possible exception of 'I.'[2] The vernacular link, in English, between lips and their pronunciation, as likewise between teeth and theirs, is established by Shakespeare. Chaucer's Prioress, who 'leet no morsel from her lippes fall,' and whose 'overlippe wyped she so clene,' is not so labially conscious, because the Middle English 'lippes' is bisyllabic: only in modern English does the word's speaker enjoy the sudden plosive release of *lips*.

After Mowbray's lament, *lips* becomes an iconic word, an articulated icon in whose voicing the motion of the lips is made visible. *Lips* is, in English, the only word, therefore, that is both metaphorically and metonymically associated with the vocal or oral feature that is involved in its production. *Teeth* is the only rival: it places the strongest emphasis (of any English word?) on the distinctively English 'th' sound in which the tongue is used to expel air around the teeth: it is the only English sound in which the tongue exceeds the limit set by the teeth. The tongue points to and pushes against and beyond that which it names: the deontic meets the dontic.[3] Mowbray certainly feels his tongue enjailed behind the double portcullis of both teeth and lips, and makes us thus aware of our own tongue and its performances: while the teeth are enunciated by an action of release, the lips are spoken by and through closure. The mouth is figured as a fortress.

Of all words, it is *lips* that most makes visible what it names, in closing and opening the mouth. Lips are not visible, not obviously so, when the mouth is open, and is kept open. So Lessing writes in his *Laocoön* of 1766:

> The mere wide opening of the mouth – apart from the fact that the other parts of the face are thereby violently and unpleasantly distorted – is a blot in painting and a fault in sculpture.[4]

The mouth as O forms part of Lessing's argument in setting forth the aesthetic principles of modernity: that the poet can represent actions in time, while the painter or sculptor can represent bodies in space. The two practices, Lessing insists, cannot be mixed or brought together in a single work because 'the co-existence of the physical object comes into collision with the consecutiveness of speech.'[5] To depict in space an open mouth is to frustrate the expectation that the mouth is giving voice to words, or a cry, which could be heard only in time, successively.

In establishing the separate spheres of the plastic and temporal arts, Lessing posed a particular challenge for that mode of literary representation known as *ekphrasis*. The debate about the *Laocoön* sculpture focussed attention on the silence of the plastic arts. Most portraits, it can be observed, differ from the *Laocoön* in that they show their sitter with the mouth shut, that is, with the facial features undistorted. Yet Lessing insists that the central figure of the *Laocoön* group is not crying out, even though his mouth is open, and even though, in the non-plastic art of poetry, Virgil describes him as crying out.

Traditionally, Lessing notes, *ekphrasis* arranges the spatially contiguous elements of the face, or of the body, in a consecutive order of words: 'as the signs of speech are arbitrary, so it is perfectly possible that by it we can make the parts of a body follow each other just as truly as in actuality they are found existing side by side.'[6] This is *ek-phrasis*, a telling out. Yet the poet, Lessing continues, though he could trace out the parts of the body in a consecutive order, from head to toe, will prefer to isolate particular parts, and is under no obligation to mention every part.

And where better for *ekphrasis* to begin than with the lips, whose closed state requires that the subject be spoken for, as she will not speak for herself? Lessing cites Anacreon's ekphrastic song in which the image of his beloved is so artfully drawn that he believes that it is no image but the girl herself. He then addresses her (or himself?): 'Keep your gaze away lest the self, bereft, suppose she speaks.'[7] As Lessing glosses the lines: 'He does not see the image, he sees herself and believes that she is just about to open her lips in speech.' The authority of Anacreon is invoked as a model for poets of Lessing's own day, for it confesses and distinguishes the limitations of both language and painting. By way of contrast Lessing moves from Anacreon to Homer, 'from whom we can scarcely once learn that Helen had white arms and beautiful hair'; Homer avoids describing Helen's surpassing beauty, and allows us instead to hear the words of the Trojan elders, who acknowledge that for one as beautiful as this, it is worth fighting the war.[8] Yet, eschewing Homer's caution, 'Zeuxis painted a Helen and had the courage to set under it those famous lines of Homer in which the enchanted Elders confess their emotions. Never were painting and poetry drawn into a more equal contest.'[9] The story is told precisely in order to enhance the reputation of Zeuxis, to claim that his skill was so great that he could accomplish in paint what Homer chose to avoid in poetry.

Yet the judgement of posterity must be forever deferred, because no painting from Zeuxis's hand has survived from antiquity. And while many sculptures have survived, none of those extant can be ascribed to Praxiteles, the acknowledged master among the Greeks. It is Praxiteles whom Leontes must have in mind when, in the fifth act of *The Winter's Tale*, he does not address but asks of the statue of Hermione:

> What fine chisel
> Could ever yet cut breath?

Paulina responds, threateningly, that if he succumbs to the temptation to kiss the statue, Leontes will himself become painted:

> The ruddiness upon her lip is wet.
> You'll mar it if you kiss it, stain your own
> With oily painting.[10]

This sculpted woman is not beautiful, for her face is, in Leontes' word, 'wrinkled.' Paulina explains:

> So much the more our carver's excellence,
> Which lets go by some sixteen years, and makes her
> As she lived now.

The 'carved' statue is so lifelike that the woman depicted is believable, whereas the image painted by Zeuxis is of a woman of surpassing and unmatched beauty. In *The Winter's Tale* we might say that *ekphrasis* itself meets its match, that the 'most equal contest' between poetry and the plastic arts is not resolved but dissolved in favour (on stage) of the living person represented by the supposed statue. There can be no disclosure like this on the page.

*Ekphrasis* tends to rely for its success on the absence of what it describes, whether the 'living person' of Helen, or the Shield of Achilles, or the Temple of Mars in Chaucer's 'Knight's Tale.' Could we see the object described, we might well find wanting its verbal representation. Horace's famous ode 'exegi monumentum aere perennius' boasts that the poet's words will outlive the apparently more durable memorials of iron and bronze; it is a claim for the triumph of *ekphrasis* over its plastic rivals. The plastic arts will not endure to challenge the verbal descriptions by which, indeed, they will be known to posterity.

After the establishment of the British Museum, in 1753, English poets could no longer assume that works of plastic art would not endure. The confidence displayed by Horace in the staying power of poetry was to be undermined by the expectation that, henceforth, works of art might last as long: sculptures would survive intact, not in the ruined state of the *Laocoön*; the paintings of Raphael would last as those of Zeuxis had not. As late as 1767, one year after Lessing's *Laocoön*, Thomas Morrison addressed to Joshua Reynolds 'A Pindarick Ode on Painting,' in which the poet pleads that paintings by Reynolds might be saved for posterity:

> Spare, Oh! Time, these colours; spare 'em,
> Or with thy tend'rest touch impair 'em:
> At least, for some few centuries space,
> Shine they with unlessen'd grace!

Yet Morrison concludes, in a late flourish of Horatian confidence, that his poems will outlast the plastic works of Reynolds:

> In the long course of rolling years,
>   When all thy labour disappears,
> Yet shall this verse descend from age to age,
>   And, breaking from oblivion's shade,
> Go on, to flourish while thy paintings fade![11]

Another poem addressed to Reynolds, just fourteen years later, registers the shift: William Cowper retorts that the works of Reynolds, 'whose art sublime Gives perpetuity to Time,' will 'survive, And in unfading beauty live.'[12]

***

Cowper's confident riposte to Morrison was to be amply justified within a few years. John Johnson, known as 'Johnny of Norfolk,' visited his cousin William Cowper in January 1790; this was the first contact that Cowper had had with any of his maternal relatives in twenty-seven years. Johnson at once encouraged his aunt, Anne Bodham, to send to Cowper a portrait of Anne's aunt, Cowper's mother.[13] Ann Cowper, née Donne, had been born in 1703 and died in 1737: more than fifty years after his mother's death, William Cowper received a portrait of whose very existence he had known nothing. To Lady Hesketh, on 26 February 1790, he wrote:

> I am delighted with Mrs. Bodham's kindness in giving me the only picture of my own mother that is to be found, I suppose, in all the world. I had rather possess it than the richest jewel in the British crown, for I loved her with an affection that her death 52 years since has not in the least abated. I remember her too, young as I was when she died, well enough to know that it is a very exact resemblance of her.[14]

To John Johnson, on 28 February 1790, Cowper reiterates the point about his memory and his reliability as witness to the accuracy of the portrait: 'I am perhaps the only person living who remembers her, but I remember her well, and can attest, on my own knowledge, the truth of the resemblance.'[15] And to the donor, his cousin Anne Bodham, whose gift accompanied her very first letter to him, Cowper wrote on 27 February:

> The world could not have furnish'd you with a present so acceptable to me.... I received it the night before last, and view'd it with a trepidation of nerves and spirit somewhat akin to what I should have felt had the dear Original presented herself to my embraces. I kissed it and hung it where it is the last object that I see at night, and, of course, the first on which I open my eyes in the morning. She died when I had completed my sixth year, yet I remember her well and am an ocular witness of the great fidelity of the Copy.[16]

We note that the painting is itself not the original, but the copy of the sitter: Cowper's mother is the 'Original,' against which the portrait must be matched. To another correspondent, Cowper writes on March 12:

> I have lately received, from a female Cousin of mine in Norfolk, whom I have not seen these thirty years, a picture of my own mother. She died when I wanted two days of being six years old, yet I remember her perfectly, find the picture

a strong likeness of her, and because her memory has been ever precious to me, have written a poem on the receipt of it: a poem which, one excepted, I had more pleasure in writing, than any that I ever wrote.[17]

According to Peter Simonsen the poem prompted by this gift 'may represent the very first attribution of immortality to an *actual* painting in English literary history.'[18] It would seem that all the objects of well-known ekphrastic verses have disappeared. The gamble of *ekphrasis*, the Horatian faith that the poem will outlive the plastic work, had thus been impressively vindicated.

The opening apostrophe of Cowper's poem contains those iconic sounds voiced and mouthed by Mowbray:

> Oh that those lips had language!

The *oh* and the *lips* make the speaker conscious of his own voicing. It is, we might say, an apostrophe that sums up *ekphrasis*: the giving or lending of voice, only to regret that that which is dumb will remain dumb still, that a borrowed voice can never be re-appropriated, can never be given away or returned. Voice belongs to person, inalienably, and can exist neither in its owner's absence, nor after its owner's death; by contrast, the image is a property of the plastic arts, and is entirely independent of persons. 'Twas mine, 'tis his, as Cowper's cousin might have said. The likeness of an image is materially independent of the 'Original': the image survives the death of the sitter, and can change hands, whether as commodity or as heirloom.

Cowper does not enumerate the various parts of his mother's portrait, nor offer any sort of description. The poem is concerned solely with Cowper's subjective reaction. Where the ekphrastic poem usually inspires in the reader an envious wish that I too could have seen that image, and that I too might have the chance to test my descriptive skills, this poem offers no help to the reader who has not seen the portrait, nor any description that would be superfluous to one who has. Given that the significance of the portrait inheres entirely in the relation of sitter to poet, the reader cannot think of occupying the same optical space as the poet. This portrait is not a work of art destined to hang in a gallery; it is an object of personal devotion, painted with no great skill, and of concern to us now only because of Cowper's poem.

The portrait is not described; its conventional features – lips, eyes, face, smile – are invoked without particularity by simple and unsurprising demonstratives: 'those lips' (line 1), 'those dear eyes' (line 7), 'that face' (line 17), 'that maternal smile' (line 27) and (somewhat less predictably) 'this mimic show of thee' (119). These are the only references to pictorial detail in a poem of 121 lines. Line 3 repeats a phrase from line 1, and reads 'Those lips are thine – thy own sweet smiles I see –' which suggests a series of his mother's smiles recollected from the poet's childhood. For the 1808 edition, however, an emendation was made: 'thy own sweet smile I see –.'[19] This restores the conventional ekphrastic: the difference between *smile* – to be seen in the portrait by any viewer – and *smiles* – recollected only by the poet – is the difference between the objective demands of *ekphrasis* and the subjective summons of memory. The suppression of the plural is not casual.

Cowper's poem is an outcry that laments a silence: our focus is on the lips, that part of the portrait which most needs the supplement of the voice. Lips serve as synecdoche for the mother, and as metonymy for voice:

> Those lips are thine – thy own sweet smiles I see –
> The same that oft in childhood solaced me –
> Voice only fails, else, how distinct they say –
> Grieve not, my child, chase all thy fears away!

'Voice only fails': thus succinctly, the new status of *ekphrasis* as supplement. One might object that the poem need not be classified as ekphrastic at all, because there is no attempt to present the picture in words. The poem supplements the picture in order to honour, and to present (by making present) the living 'original' of which the portrait is a copy. Such an objection can be answered by the remarkable parenthetical apostrophe, addressed to the art that makes present the intelligence of the mother's eyes:

> The meek intelligence of those dear eyes
> (Blest be the Art that can immortalize,
> The Art that baffled Time's tyrannic claim
> To quench it) here shines on me still the same.

This parenthesis works most forcefully as what Cobbett was to call an 'interrupter.'[20] But before we discuss the particular significance of that interruption, we must digress, on the topic of parentheses.

*But I Digress* (1991) is a brilliant account by John Lennard of the use of parentheses in English poetry. However, it pays little attention to the deployment of parentheses in verse of the late eighteenth century. An elliptical leap from Pope and Swift to Coleridge omits much of significance. Lennard's Chapter 4, 'A Philosophy of Moonshine,' looks at lunulae (the little moons that surround this) within and about which the moon is described. His proof-text is (of course) Coleridge's 'Dejection: An Ode':

> For lo! the New-moon winter-bright!
> And overspread with phantom light,
> (With swimming phantom light o'erspread
> But rimmed and circled by a silver thread)....

In parentheses (as in much else) Coleridge has a precursor, in James Thomson's *Seasons*. Though composed as early as the 1720s, the poem displays a very different texture from the works of Pope or Swift. Typographical exuberance is absent, and in the entirety of *The Seasons*, some 5,500 lines, there are (in my scanning of the 1746 text) no more than eight instances of parentheses. Ample reason, then, to omit Thomson from Lennard's story, except that each use is exemplary of a visual pun, an iconic play:

>                               The daw,
> The rook, and magpie, to the grey-grown oaks
> (That the calm village in their verdant arms,
> Sheltering, embrace) direct their lazy flight.[21]

This is a startling interruption, of those which stand firm against those that fly, yet the syntax is not interrupted but only a little disrupted: it makes its way right through the first lunula, so that what is in parentheses is a relative clause and not (as is usual) an independent clause. And the typographical marks of parenthesis embrace the village in imitation of the oaks. The further inwardly concentric embrace, by commas, of '*arms*, Sheltering, *embrace*' is almost redundant, as a signature is: see my cleverness, and see me acknowledging your admiration.

Of the other parenthetical instances in *The Seasons*, we note here only two. The first offers its gift to Coleridge:

>                          Meanwhile the moon,
> Full-orbed and breaking through the scattered clouds,
> Shows her broad visage in the crimsoned east.
> Turned to the sun direct, her spotted disc
> (Where mountains rise, umbrageous dales descend,
> And caverns deep, as optic tube descries)
> A smaller earth, gives all his blaze again....[22]

Here is exquisite typographical wit: what can (through the telescope) be descried within the spotted disc of the moon is described for us within the broken disc of the lunulae (smaller moons).

Our final example, concerning the unexpected and interruptive nature of earthquakes:

> Thus a proud city, populous and rich,
> Full of the works of peace, and high in joy,
> At theatre or feast, or sunk in sleep
> (As late, Palermo, was thy fate) is seized
> By some dread earthquake....[23]

In parentheses words slumber; the enclosed clause does not interrupt what is going on around it, but rather the clause itself gets swept away, all unknowing, a victim of syntactic inattention.

The least obtrusive use of parentheses is to hold a *dixit* or indication of a speaker, not paratextually but within the metre. There is just one example of this in *The Seasons*:

> As when of old (so sung the Hebrew bard)
> Light, uncollected, through the Chaos urged
> Its infant way....[24]

This is not innocuous. For *dixit* or 'so sung' or 'thus spake' are treated as frames for speech: they are part of the metre but not part of the vocalization. Two instances from Pope:

> 'Now turn to diff'rent sports (the Goddess cries)'
> ...
> 'Hold (cry'd the Queen) a Cat-call each shall win...'[25]

The typographical convention allows the lunulae to serve as quotation marks in reverse (as it were), to set apart those words not spoken aloud. In the passage from Thomson we hear Moses, 'the Hebrew bard,' singing of the Creation, and specifically of light: noiselessly it makes its 'infant' or *unspeaking* way through the Chaos.

In parentheses, notating a silence, or a suspension of voice, a disparity is inserted between rhythm and sound. And the misfit between voicing and metre becomes only more haunting when the phrases within lunulae may be sung aloud. The *Olney Hymns*, composed by Cowper and John Newton, abound in parentheses:

> 'Lord (he prayed) remember me
> When in glory thou shalt be:'
> 'Soon with me (the Lord replies)
> Thou shalt rest in Paradise.'[26]

One may sing 'Lord remember me' but it is hard to think of singing, congregationally, 'Lord he prayed remember me.' How is one (or the many) supposed to sing a parenthesis? No less challenging to the economy of voice and metre are those parentheses which seem to be commentaries or asides:

> The woman, who for water came
> (What great events on small depend)[27]

Sometimes parentheses are concessive, and require a softened if not muted voice, or they might be silent (or whispered) modifications of what has been proclaimed aloud. From a hymn of Cowper's:

> Lord, I believe thou hast prepar'd
> (Unworthy though I be)....[28]

In the following instance, two functions of the parenthesis are evident in consecutive lines; the first a *dixit*, the second a stage-whispered injunction:

> 'I am (saith Christ) your glorious head,
> (May we attention give)'[29]

Lunulae may signal a change of volume, a shift from public declamation to intimate confession, or whispered aside. The most extraordinary instance occurs in the most famous of all the *Olney Hymns*:

> Amazing Grace! (how sweet the sound!)
> That sav'd a wretch like me![30]

What is in parenthesis is subdued, and inhibits full vocalization. The parenthetical marks bracket the muted or unspoken, separate the unspoken from the spoken, or sung.

The riddle – how to sing a parenthesis? – should not be too quickly solved. We note that hymns at this date (at least in the Church of England) were not written for congregational singing. Like other texts of the late eighteenth century (such as novels), they were intended for private meditation, silent or softly-voiced reading. Cowper's recent editors write: 'The collection as Newton published it [in 1779] is strikingly deficient in any concession to the singing of hymns.... There is no trace of music in *Olney Hymns*; no tunes, no names of tunes, not even the indication of long metre, short metre, and so on, which appear in contemporary collections and which would help an accompanist to choose a suitable tune.'[31]

In the late eighteenth century a new sort of reading practice emerges – neither public declamation nor silent meditation – in which parenthetical marks serve as guides to vocalization for readers, either solitary or within a small group. This practice, of reading neither silently nor loudly, can be associated with these hymns, with a kind of domestic verse not for public proclamation, with certain types of novel, and with the solitary reading of plays: all are scored or notated by parentheses.

To take seriously, to *heed* the parenthesis in 'Amazing Grace,' is to be vertiginous in hearing. The opening words 'Amazing Grace' rhyme on the long *a* and sibilant (*aze/aze*), and elide the *g* from *ing* to *gr*. Then, in parenthesis '(how sweet the sound)' yields more sibalance, rather as non-lexical sibalance ('*shhh!*') can counsel silence: the sibalance of 'how sweet the sound' exhorts us in four syllables to silence, the better to hear the sound in the four syllables of *amazing grace*. This is silent commentary, not placed in the margin but embedded within the text and within the metre. To recall Lessing, a contemporary of Newton and Cowper, we might now wonder whether sound and silence – the phonetic and iconic claims of text – were ever drawn into a more equal contest than in the line 'Amazing Grace! (how sweet the sound!).' When reading, insofar as it loses voice, is silenced, it changes the very constitution of the literary text, and makes the text resistant precisely to those properties – of temporality and sequentiality, of non-plasticity – that Lessing would confer exclusively on poetry. With silent reading, or reading in which silence plays a role, the look of the page begins to take on the life of its own space: space matters, as do the printer's marks that are not intended for, nor accessible to vocalization; and it is in and around and by means of parentheses that textual space is most made visible, made most to matter.

One of the functions of parenthesis in the late eighteenth century is as an indication of silence in the midst of speech (plenty of examples could be proffered from novels of the period). We can now extend the significance that Simonsen reads into the parenthesis in Cowper's poem. (Our digression on parentheses is thus drawing to a close.) It is precisely within parentheses, Simonsen notes, that Cowper inverts the conventional trope of *ekphrasis*, familiar since Horace, and attributes immortality not to his poem but, rather, to the portrait itself, and 'seems to suggest that poem and portrait may complement one another.'[32] By enclosing the attribution of immortality within parentheses, Cowper pays his tribute in muted fashion: the lunulae enact and enforce a mimetic tribute to the *silence* of the plastic arts.

That Cowper had thought much about parentheses is evident from a letter to the Revd. William Unwin, of 27 April 1782:

> I remember your making an observation while here on the subject of Parentheses, to which I acceded without limitation. But a little attention will convince us both that they are not to be universally condemned. When they abound, and when they are long, they both embarrass the sense, and are a proof that the Writer's head is cloudy, that he has not properly arranged his matter, or is not well skilled in the graces of expression. But as Parenthesis is ranked by Grammarians among the figures of Rhetoric, we may suppose they had a reason for conferring that honor upon it. Accordingly we shall find that in the use of some of our finest Writers, as well as in the hands of the antient Poets and Orators, it has a peculiar elegance, and imparts a beauty which the period would want without it.
>
> >  Hoc nemus, hunc inquit frondoso verdice collem,
> > (Quis Deus incertum est) habitat Deus. – Vir. Æn. 8 [33]
>
> In this instance (the first that occurred) it is gracefull. I have not time to seek for more, nor room to insert them....[34]

Does 'the first that occurred' mean the first that occurred to Cowper's memory, or, to the best of his knowledge, the earliest occurrence of parentheses in poetry? (The latter reading seems more plausible.) At any rate, we can be confident that a man who writes with this degree of attentiveness in 1782 is making no casual use of parentheses in the poem of 1790.

Lunulae are – iconically – lip-like. As metaphors for lips they are also metonymically linked to silence. As in holding a finger to your lips, the parenthesis asks for quiet, for a decrease of volume, a whisper, an approximation to the silence of the picture.

> Oh that those lips had language!

Yet those lips stay silent and closed, while the poet attributes to them a speech addressed to him, her son:

> Voice only fails, else, how distinct they say –
> Grieve not, my child, chase all thy fears away!

Voice fails, and the lips remain closed. But the eyes are not closed, nor is it said that they have failed:

> The meek intelligence of those dear eyes
> ... here shines on me still the same.

The eyes look out from the portrait as dearly and shiningly as if they were real, though of course there is some play with the sense of *shine*, to appear, to be manifest. Open eyes, of both sitter and viewer, are the measure of a portrait. Lips ought not to be shown apart, open-mouthed, according to Lessing, because then the viewer's eyes will be frustrated in the expectation of words: voice will be perceived to fail. But there is no reason why eyes should not be open, hardly an occasion, save in death, when they might be shut. Reciprocally, as the eyes of the viewer are presumed to be open for the admiration of the painting, so we may wonder whether the viewer's mouth ought not, like that of the subject, to stay closed. In Lessing's terms, would not the viewer be wise to keep silence, lest in speaking to the portrait he frustrate himself in the expectation of a response? Without the initial vocal outburst, could the poet so directly have announced: 'Voice only fails'? (This is, surely, not an objection commonly made of a portrait, but only of some thing or person with whom one is trying to speak, and from whom one is trying to elicit a response.)

Yet the eyes are not celebrated openly, neither for being open, nor for matching the openness of the poet's eyes. The eyes are subject to a serious interruptor:

> The meek intelligence of those dear eyes
> (Blest be the Art that can immortalize,
> The Art that baffled Time's tyrannic claim
> To quench it) here shines on me still the same.

The eyes are separated from their shining, and from the object on which they shine (the viewer, the son): separated spatially, and interrupted discursively. The interruption does not block the syntax, for the main clause is resumed two and a half lines later, but the separation is fixed, immortalized: the main clause will never be integrated again. Less and less does 'still the same' modify the shining of her eyes: more and more does *still the same* submit the poet, the viewer, to the order of the plastic arts, that which baffles Time and Change.

Yet this picture is not merely resisting the mutability of human nature and the decay of the flesh, even though, unlike Hermione, Cowper's mother is as she was when last seen, not as she would have been fifty (or sixteen) years later. It is in no straightforward sense, here, that Art baffles Time: this portrait will itself be protected from the ravages of time that destroy most paintings (notably those that have been the subjects of ekphrastic verse). This is a reflexive bafflement: 'Art that baffled Time's tyrannic claim': at the line ending we may assume that it is our flesh that is subject to that claim. The enjambment corrects the assumption: the complaint against Time is that it makes a claim to quench not flesh but Art. Thus the Art that immortalizes must itself succumb to the claims of Time. That conflict persists unresolved to the end of the poem, when Time and Art seem to divide the spoils in equal shares:

> And while the wings of Fancy still are free,
> And I can view this mimic show of thee,
> Time has but half succeeded in his theft,
> Thyself removed, thy pow'r to sooth me left.

Half the theft of Time is the removal of the mother; the second half of the theft would be accomplished when the image decays.

Yet returning to the poem's opening lines, that signally fail to open the mother's lips, we remain baffled. For what occurs in parentheses – the apostrophic 'Blest be...' – is syntactically dense and conceptually intricate, while the sentence that is divided by the parenthesis is simple to read and to understand, or would be, were it not for the immovable interruptor. In parentheses, the reader's voice goes quiet: how can one proclaim loudly one's praise of that which works its will against Time by remaining silent? It is a blessing that ought to be delivered in a whisper, for Time hears our voices, takes them as signs of life. And in reducing the reading voice to a near-silence, the parenthesis works its next act of mimetic power: if the lunulae look like lips, so our lips become closed in order both to resemble lunulae and to respect their injunction: thus it is the viewer's voice that fails. Given that the poet and his readers *can* speak, it is precisely our voices that fail, having succumbed to 'thy power to sooth.' Who, we now dare to ask (mutely) is this enchantress?

The final couplet is not as innocent as the melancholic tenor of the poem would suggest. The word 'left' is as constitutively liable to poetic ambiguity as 'still.' Dividing the phrase 'on me still the same' according to whether *still* is taken to modify what goes before, or after – 'on me still' or 'still the same' – brings out the two senses of stillness/silence and temporal continuance. More complicated syntactically are the ambiguities of *left*, dependent as they are on the choice of active or passive moods. Syntactically there is no obstacle to reading these lines

> Time has but half succeeded in his theft,
> Thyself removed, thy pow'r to sooth me left.

as follows: 'Time has only half succeeded in his theft: he removed you, and your power to sooth left of its own accord.' This may be stretching the 'meaning' but it is not stretching either the syntax or the idiom. Indeed, the reader may assume that 'removed' is passive – 'thyself being removed' – and therefore that there is verbal symmetry, a continuance of mood between 'removed' and 'left': 'thy power was left behind.' Yet there is, startlingly, no such symmetry. *Removed* is active: he removed thyself, but (actively) left (behind) thy power to sooth. Or: he removed thyself, but thy power was (passively) left behind. Or: he removed himself but thy power (actively) left by its own means. These ambiguities are no accident. What every reader must feel is the peculiar and troubling spondee of the very last foot: 'me left.' Why does this poem not close on an iamb? Why not (crudely): 'thy pow'r to sooth was left.'? It is only the contrived and counter-rhythmical omission of 'was' that opens the possibility that 'left' might be active. A further ambiguity is now insistent: thy power to sooth left (of its own accord) me. For if the poem is to end on an iambic foot, the suppression of *me* could be achieved only by treating *me* as the object not of *sooth* – but of *left*. That she chose to 'leave me' is a horrifying conclusion, and one that I have pleaded with the syntax to forbid.

This poem enacts and performs the opening 'Oh' of the poet's lips, the failure of the sitter's lips to respond, the almost immediate silencing (by parentheses) of the poet's voice, and 121 lines later (after a most seductive triplet at lines 25-27: 'kiss – bliss – yes') the poet's lips are closed: *left* being a shadow sound of *lips*.

'Zeuxis painted a Helen and had the courage to set under it those famous lines of Homer in which the enchanted Elders confess their emotions. Never were painting and poetry drawn into a more equal contest.'[35] Recall Lessing's citation of Anacreon: 'Keep your gaze away lest the self, bereft, suppose she speaks.'[36] Temptress? Enchantress? Seductress? Look, look now at that *tress* of hair, that the poet's lips had never dared to name (not even in parentheses, however curled, or curly.)

These ambiguities and anxieties are not (by me) to be ascribed to the son. They are to be attributed to the poet confronted by a portrait, an image (albeit of the mother) that is yet only an image. A voice is what an image promises: the silence of the image is the disappointment of that promise. Cowper's poem partakes of that silence, achieves by parenthesis its own disappointment. Thus is ekphrasis modified: the poem recognizes in the painting not something to be outlasted, but a mirror of its own conditions and limitations. This is a poem coming to terms with its own iconicity, reckoning with (in being laid-out) the frustrations and failings of (its own) voice.

## Notes

1. Shakespeare, *King Richard II*, I iii 153-61.
2. See Max Nänny, 'Alphabetic Letters as Icons in Literary Texts,' in Max Nänny and Olga Fischer (eds), *Form Miming Meaning: Iconicity in Language and Literature* (Amsterdam: Benjamins, 1999), pp. 173-198; see especially pp. 188-90, '"O" as an icon of the mouth.'
3. A comparable instance of 'performative iconicity': 'Lolita, light of my life, fire of my loins. My sin, my soul. Lo-lee-ta: the tip of the tongue taking a trip of three steps down the palate to tap, at three, on the teeth. Lo. Lee. Ta.'
4. G. E. Lessing, *Laocoön or The Limits of Painting and Poetry*, trans. William A. Steel (London: Dent, 1930), § II, p. 13.
5. Lessing, § XVII, p. 63.
6. Lessing, § XVII, p. 60.
7. Lessing, § XX, p. 78.
8. Lessing, § XXI, p. 79.
9. Lessing, § XXII, p. 81.
10. Shakespeare, *The Winter's Tale*, V iii 78-83.
11. On Reynolds and Morrison, see Peter Simonsen, *'Word-Preserving Arts': Material Inscription, Ekphrasis and Spatial Form in the Later Work of William Wordsworth* (Ph.D. dissertation, University of Copenhagen, 2002), pp. 415-17.
12. Cowper, 'To Sir Joshua Reynolds' (1781).
13. See John D. Baird and Charles Ryskamp (eds), *The Poems of William Cowper*, Volume III: 1785-1800 (Oxford: Clarendon Press, 1995), pp. 305-7 (notes to poem, 'On the Receipt of My Mother's Picture out of Norfolk the Gift of My Cousin Ann Bodham').
14. James King and Charles Ryskamp (eds), *Letters and Prose Writings of William Cowper*, Volume III: Letters 1787-1791 (Oxford: Clarendon Press, 1982), pp. 347-48.
15. Cowper, *Letters* III, p. 352.
16. Cowper, *Letters* III, p. 349.

[17] Cowper, *Letters* III, p. 359.

[18] Simonsen, p. 417.

[19] 'smiles' is the reading of the Baird & Ryskamp text of 1995, based on the two mss. books prepared for Cowper by John Johnson, and on the first (posthumous) printing of 1803; 'smile' is the reading introduced by Joseph Johnson in 1808, and followed by Cowper's editors throughout the nineteenth century. For this clarification I am indebted to Professor John Baird (letter of 3 April 2003).

[20] William Cobbett, *A Grammar of the English Language* (1823), cited by John Lennard, *But I Digress: The Exploitation of Parentheses in English Printed Verse* (Oxford: Clarendon Press, 1991), p. 142: 'It is necessarily an *interrupter*: it breaks in upon the regular course of the mind: it tends to divert the attention from the main object of the sentence.'

[21] James Thomson, *The Seasons*, ed. James Sambrook (Oxford: Oxford University Press, 1972), p. 43 ('Summer,' lines 224-227).

[22] Thomson, p. 118 ('Autumn,' lines 1088-1094).

[23] Thomson, p. 121 ('Autumn,' lines 1201-1205).

[24] Thomson, p. 108 ('Autumn,' lines 732-734).

[25] Alexander Pope, *The Dunciad*, Book II, lines 221, 243.

[26] *Olney Hymns*, I:CX (Book I, Hymn CX). *Olney Hymns* was published in 1779; of its 348 hymns, 67 were written by Cowper, the rest by John Newton.

[27] *Olney*, I:CXI. Further examples in I:V, II:IV and III:LXXV (by Cowper).

[28] *Olney*, I:LXXIX. This is one of only three parentheses to be found among the 67 hymns ascribed to Cowper: the others are in II:XI and III:XXIV.

[29] *Olney*, I:CXVI

[30] *Olney*, I:XLI.

[31] John D. Baird and Charles Ryskamp (eds), *The Poems of William Cowper*, Volume I: 1748-1782 (Oxford: Clarendon Press, 1980), pp. xviii-xix. This view is contested by D. Bruce Hindmarsh, *John Newton and the English Evangelical Tradition* (1996: 2nd ed., Grand Rapids, MI: Eerdmans, 2001), p. 260, note 8; his evidence is slim, and far from persuasive.

[32] Simonsen, p. 418.

[33] Evander is telling Aeneas of the legends of Latium (*Aeneid*, Book 8, lines 351-352): 'On this wooded hill, here,' he said 'with its leafy crest lives a god (though which god is uncertain).' In the Latin the parenthetical phrase precedes the main clause: this word order is virtually inadmissible in modern English: '(which god is uncertain) lives a god.' No pronouns are used and *Deus* occurs twice, as if antecedence could not operate through parentheses. Dryden entirely ignores the parenthesis (while distributing many of his own) in *Virgil's Aeneid* (Book 8, lines 461-462): 'Some God they knew, what God they cou'd not tell, Did there amidst the sacred horrour dwell.' James Kinsley (ed.), *The Poems of John Dryden* (Oxford: Clarendon Press, 1958), Volume III, p. 1274.

[34] James King and Charles Ryskamp (eds), *The Letters and Prose Writings of William Cowper*, Volume Two: 1782-1786 (Oxford: Clarendon Press, 1981), p. 47 (letter to

William Unwin, 27 April 1782). Popular editions of Cowper's letters show little respect for spelling or punctuation: no 'silent emendation' could be more damaging than thus dislunulating the last sentence: 'In this instance, the first that occurred, it is graceful.'

[35] Lessing, § XXII, p. 81.
[36] Lessing, § XX, p. 78.

\*\*\*

Much here is owed to others: to Peter Simonsen, whose work on *ekphrasis* in late Wordsworth has been of inestimable value; to Adam Thorpe (for turning my attention towards Thomson's *Seasons*); to John Baird, for sharing his unrivalled knowledge of Cowper's texts; to Stephen Powys Marks and Mary Blyth for assistance in tracing the portrait; and to Martin Sharman, the direct descendant, through six generations, of John Johnson ('Johnny of Norfolk') for generously granting permission to publish, with this article, his own photograph of the portrait of Cowper's mother. Engravings from the portrait have been printed in numerous editions of Cowper's verse. The present is the first occasion on which the portrait itself has been reproduced in colour, and should confirm the view of Cowper's bibliographer that the engravings do scant justice to the 'original strikingly beautiful portrait.' See Norma Russell, *A Bibliography of William Cowper to 1837* (Oxford: Oxford Bibliographical Society, 1963), p. 251, n. 1.

This essay calls out to be offered to Glen Cavaliero, with whom in March 1991 I had the privilege of visiting Mary Barham Johnson (1895-1996) on matters pertaining to her first cousin, John Cowper Powys. Showing us some of the treasures of her richly associated family, Miss Johnson pointed to a small portrait and said: 'And that's the poet's mother.' Cavaliero asked in disbelieving tones 'You don't mean ...?' and then I, staring at Cowper's mother, heard, in a voice not quite his own: 'Oh that those lips had language... .' In that vocalising this writing acknowledges its inception.

Plate 1
Dietrich Heins, *Ann Cowper, née Donne*, c. 1723.

# WILLIAM BLAKE AND THE PROPHETIC MARKETPLACE

Robert W. Rix

It is a familiar assertion that great art is timeless. It is often said of Blake, as it is of Shakespeare, that he is our contemporary. Coleridge, we remember, spoke of Shakespeare's history plays as embodying the permanent politics of human nature. In the context of Blake, it is especially his ardent opposition to all forms of tyranny and oppression that has had a particularly lasting appeal. Blake's anti-authoritarian strategies have often been invoked out of context to support programmes based on memorable claims such as 'The road of excess leads to the palace of wisdom' or the 'doors of perception' must be opened (Blake, 35, 39).[1] In the drug culture of the 1960s, the two were often pursued simultaneously with Blake as an unwitting apostle. The intellectual innovation of Huxley's psychology and the cultural alternatives spearheaded by Allan Ginsberg and Jim Morrison's *The Doors* found Blake's art of use to an agenda very much of their own time. More recently, John Diamond's psychotherapeutic self-help book *The Healing Power of Blake* (1998) shows us that Blake's poetry can apparently still have a direct effect on the life of modern man frustrated by the psychological disorientation of modern society.

As we shall see, it was Blake's wish that his art would inspire the course of individuals and their beliefs. Yet, the fundamental argument of this essay is that Blake is not our contemporary, and that whatever worth he has for the historian must begin with the recognition of his distance from us. Below, I shall therefore not discuss what Blake's art may tells us about our contemporary world (though much is undoubtedly relevant), but what Blake believed his art could tell his contemporaries.

Blake wanted his art to play a central role in the history of the individual, his nation and mankind. But this was as an end to history. He saw his art as apocalyptic in the most fundamental sense of the word; it was to bring a revelation of a New Heaven and a New Earth. The reality of the Millennium is confirmed on plate 14 of the early work *The Marriage of Heaven and Hell* (c. 1790): 'The ancient tradition that the world will be consumed in fire at the end of six thousand years is true ... the whole creation will be consumed, and appear infinite. and holy whereas it now appears finite & corrupt' (Blake, 39). But this is not an inevitability that will take place without the aid of human labour. Blake confers on his art the qualities necessary to fulfil the promise of the Millennium. Before the Last Judgement can take place, religious Error needs 'to be expunged,' which Blake will do by means of his self-invented relief etching technique. He will eradicate falsity and bring out truth 'by printing in the infernal method, by corrosives,' which are 'salutary and medicinal' as they are 'melting apparent surfaces away … displaying the infinite which was hid' (Blake, 39). This should be read alongside Blake's other image of the Platonic cave as an allegory of human knowledge. In the topsy-turvy logic of the *Marriage,* it is in Hell, rather than with the hypocritical and pious 'angels,' that Blake's speaker observes a 'Printing house,' where men are 'clearing away the rubbish from a caves mouth.' This prepares for a true perception of the external universe; just as it enables a true spiritual insight into the soul by 'hollowing the cave' (pl. 15; Blake, 40).

But as in all apocalyptic thinking, the new is predicated on a transformation of the old. Elsewhere in the *Marriage,* Blake uses the image of the 'plow' that drives 'over the bones of the dead' (pl. 7; Blake, 35). Ploughing is the dead soil turned to fertilise new growth and reverberates with familiar echoes of the prophetic Book of Isaiah, where it is a millennial image of renewal. But ploughing also leads us to think of Blake's engraving technique used in the *Marriage* and other of the works of 'illuminated printing.' The 'plow' becomes an allegory of tools used to cut into the copper plates. For Blake, the two references are meant to coincide; and it is the distribution of Truth that will finally realise the *Marriage's* concluding prophecy of eternal peace among men, which is a time when all warring kings with their 'brow'd councellors, thunderous warriors, curl'd veterans, among helms, and shields, and chariots, horses, elephants: banners, castles, slings and rock' are driven away and 'Empire shall be no more' (Blake, 45-46).

At a time when Europe was torn with wars, the radical printer Daniel Isaac Eaton published the anonymous pamphlet, *Extermination, or an Appeal to the People of England on the Present War with France* (1794). This concludes with 'Thomas Acid,' who gives us an 'Epistle to Mr. Secretary Placid' (i.e. the then Secretary of War, Henry Dundas). The Minister's false propaganda 'to delude the unwary' is the error being etched away for Truth to stand out.[2] In the same year, Eaton also published another anonymous pamphlet entitled *The Pernicious Effect of Printing upon Society,* which furthered the common radical belief that printing would dispel the ignorance that had enslaved man for centuries.

The satirical bite of the critic who delivers his criticism in public and the liquids biting into the printer's plate are also united in Blake's *Public Address,* which was sketched in connection with an exhibition of 1809: 'I will pour

Aqua fortis on the Name of the Wicked & turn it into an Ornament & an Example' (Blake, 579). In later years, when Blake had resigned himself to the fact that there was no market for his works, he does not abandon the fundamental principles of furthering the Millennium, which underwrites his whole production. Hence, in the poem *Milton*, the 'Printing-Press' of the revolutionary prophet-poet Los comes to play a significant symbolic role as the 'Wine-press' of the Apocalypse that he was working on around the same time (27.9; Blake,124). And, in his last epic poem, *Jerusalem* – of which Blake, in a letter of 12 April 1827, writes, 'it is not likely I shall get a Customer for it' (Blake, 784) – he still insists on using the 'wond'rous art of writing' given by God to impress a message onto the spirit of mankind: 'I print; nor vain my types shall be:/ Heaven, Earth & Hell, henceforth shall live in harmony' (3.1-10; Blake, 145).

***

For Blake, there is a continuum between religion and art. Art is the vehicle of Truth as is an expression of the divine Imagination. Thus, 'Jesus & his Apostles & Disciples were all Artists,' and the Bible an inspiration to all artists as 'the great Code of Art' (*Laocoön*; Blake, 74). The longest and most sustained avowal of this can be found in his essay on 'A Vision of the Last Judgment,' which was meant to accompany a painting on the theme of the Last Judgment for a planned exhibition of 1810. The essay stresses the potential of art for realizing Blake's hope of creating an 'inner' Jerusalem in every man. The painting with its hundreds of figures is thematically about the Last Judgment when Truth will conquer over Error. But Blake also stakes the claim that, for the receptive spectator, the 'truths' conveyed in and through the painting's images will bring about Last Judgment in the individual man in actual terms. There is an immediate correlation between Blake painting the liberation of those 'who are under perpetual terrors & vain dreams plots & secret deceit' (Blake, 558) and the spectator experiencing a religious conversion to Divine Truth.

> If the Spectator could Enter into these Images in his Imagination approaching them on the Fiery Chariot of his Contemplative Thought if he could Enter into Noahs Rainbow or into his bosom or could make a Friend & Companion of one of these Images of wonder which always intreats him to leave mortal things as he must know then would he arise from his Grave then would he meet the Lord in the Air & then he would be happy. (Blake, 560)

The passage contains a number of Biblical allusions: Psalm 104:3, Genesis 9, the Resurrection, and not least 2 Kings 2:11 (Elijah taken up by a whirlwind into heaven on a 'chariot of fire'). These are all passages in which an interaction, covenant, or union with God is achieved, and confer upon the painting's images qualities we may understand as visual parallels to what in the Austin/ Searle vocabulary of linguistics are described as *performative speech acts*.

The distinctiveness of this belief in the transformative potential of art becomes clear when we compare Blake's vision with that presented in S. T. Coleridge's visionary Romantic poem on coming into spiritual understanding, 'The Eolian Harp.' Where Coleridge through the enjoyment of art – the music of the harp – is lifted to vision on an 'intellectual breeze' to sense the 'God of all,' sensing the Being of all, he is just as soon brought back to earth by the 'mild reproof' of his 'pensive Sara.' Having trespassed the boundary between his own finite humanity and the infinite Divine, he returns to the human condition from which he started out, having learned to 'walk humbly with God.'[3] For Coleridge, art becomes a scouting of uncharted territory, a daring to enter into close contact with the highest truth. Yet, just as in 'The Ancient Mariner' and other poems in which the divine order of the universe is approached, it is a moral lesson. In contrast to Coleridge's speakers, who return to moralize on their brush with a cosmic order, there are issued no return tickets for a ride on Blake's 'fiery chariot.' Blake's art is not meant to soothe or bring consolation, but to create fundamental disruption that will lead to millennial renewal.

Blake's writing on his *Last Judgment* painting should not be seen only as an essay on mystical experience, however. It is also an advertisement for a painting that was meant to be exhibited and sold. That the exhibition the year before (1809) had failed compels him to charge the eighteenth-century system of patronage:

> Nations Flourish under Wise Rulers & are depressed under foolish Rulers … works of Art can only be produced in Perfection where the Man is either in Affluence or is Above the Care of it … this is a Last Judgment when Men of Real Art Govern & Pretenders Fall (Blake, 561)

This has a definite political edge, which warrants further attention.

***

For Blake, it is the strength of a nation's artists that will determine the strength of the nation and, hence, its greatness. Blake is outspoken in making art a concern of great national importance. In his national epic *Jerusalem*, he writes

'Poetry Fetter'd, Fetters the Human Race! Nations are Destroy'd, or Flourish, in proportion as their Poetry Painting and Music, are Destroy'd or Flourish' (pl. 3; Blake, 146). In his critical writing, he saw the market for art as effectively controlled by arbiters of taste who supported only what he abhors as 'contemptible Counter Arts,' destructive of Divine Truth (Blake, 580). This critique is most clearly articulated in the annotations to his copy of *Works* (1798) by Joshua Reynolds, the President of the Royal Academy of Arts, where he had entered in October 1779, at the age of 21, after having submitted a drawing. He was probably given an ivory ticket, which entitled him to draw in the Academy galleries and attend lectures and exhibitions for six years.[4]

The Royal Academy, established only ten years before Blake's admission, epitomised for him the corrupt system of patronage by which some artists were given commissions for work as political favours rather than on the merits of their achievements. Blake's annotations charge 'S.' Joshua & his Gang of Cunning Hired Knaves,' who he claims have been 'Hired to Depress Art' (Blake, 635-36). The accusation of 'hiring' is familiar rhetoric in the writings of eighteenth-century reformists and radicals and aims at the whole intricate system of patronage by which King and government would give offices and places to so-called 'hirelings' who would promise them support in return. The Royal Academy is 'Composed of the Flower of the English Nobility & Gentry,' he writes, and will only 'give advice to those who are contending for royal liberality' (i.e. patronage by charter). To this Blake comments: 'Liberality! We want not Liberality[.] We want a Fair Price & Proportionate Value & a General Demand for Art[.] Let not that Nation where Less than nobility is the Reward Pretend that Art is Encouraged by that Nation' (Blake, 637). Blake is an advocate for a relatively new consumer market for art, where the public rather than royal charters and patronage determines production. Blake holds that it is the strength of a nation's art that gives moral shape to that nation, and patronage is a part of the conspiracy engineered to uphold despotism: 'The Arts & Sciences are the Destruction of Tyrannies or Bad Governments.... Why should A Good Government endeavour to Depress What is its Chief & only Support' (Blake, 636). In his *Public Address* (1809), Blake makes clear his determination as an artist of True Religion to destroy false art produced by 'Villains' or 'Bad Men,' who are given state licence to 'both Print & Publish by all the means in their Power' (Blake, 578). When Blake vows to bring down 'the Wicked' as 'an Ornament & an Example,' he phrases this deliberately in mocking emulation of the ideology underwriting the eighteenth-century penal system. Punishments (especially the capital punishment) were used as a means first of all to deter others from similar crimes. In the same spirit, Blake writes:

> If all the Princes in Europe <like Louis XIV & Charles the first> were to Patronize such Blockheads I William Blake a Mental Prince should decollate & Hang their Souls as Guilty of Mental High Treason. (Blake, 580)

Blake militates against the 'wretched state of the Arts in this Country & in Europe,' which originated 'in the Wretched State of Political Science ... <Established> by such contemptible Politicians as Louis XIV' (Blake, 580).

The possibility of circumventing the usual channels of distribution was announced with much pomp in a Prospectus, 'To the Public,' of 10 October 1793. This is Blake's celebration of his own self-invented 'method of Printing which combines the Painter and the Poet.' He believes this to be 'a phenomenon worthy of public attention, provided that it exceeds in elegance all former methods' (Blake, 692). Blake's aim to surpass what is otherwise available on the market in terms of sales value, and, at the same time, take full control of his own production and distribution, shows his awkward attempt to position himself both within and outside commercial print culture and the book trade.

Without the patronage of the tyrannical institutions that his spiritual art was designed to overturn, the emerging consumer market was a new possibility to disseminate the Truth that would positively transform his Nation. It goes without saying that the prophet deserves a suitable reward for his labours. For Blake, Divine Art was a livelihood, and this was a possibility as the late eighteenth century continued a popular tradition of prophecy. The French Revolution reinvigorated this tradition into a rage and created a flurry of millennial visions that were consumed in what can justifiably be called 'a prophetic marketplace.' A conservative Robert Southey described how many prophecies would end up among 'those innumerable pamphlets published by inferior booksellers,' which would circulate 'among sectarians and fanatics, [but] never rise into the hands of those who are called the public, and escape the notice of all literary journals.'[5] The paradox was that although Blake's prophetic works such as *America: A Prophecy*, *Europe: A Prophecy* and *Visions of the Daughters of Albion* of the early 1790s were created on the back of a popular trend, his claims of uniqueness drowned in the proliferation of visionaries with a religious mission.

Among the most successful traders were Richard Brothers and Joanna Southcott, who have been discussed in several independent studies.[6] It is perhaps more interesting to shift attention to the tribulations of those unfortunate prophets (like Blake) who did not find popular support and struggled to communicate their visionary truths. In the first half of the 1790s, the market for prophecy was saturated and not always with works of quality.

An interesting parallel to Blake is found in the now completely unknown Henry Hardy, also a writer of prophetic works. The year before Blake issued his list of works for sale, Hardy published *A Vision from the Lord God Almighty ... that must bring about that Great and Glorious Day of Peace* (1792). The well-known London publisher James Ridgeway, who primarily concentrated on political works for the opposition, printed the pamphlet. Like his famous contemporary Richard Brothers, Hardy had been a naval officer and also declared himself the messenger of God. And, like Brothers, he entertained regicidal visions, politically dangerous at a time when the government sought to safeguard Britain against revolution. Thus it was perhaps inevitable that the *Morning Chronicle*, on 11 February 1794, would report that the Attorney-General William Garrow had led a prosecution against the 'lunatic' Hardy, who 'had styled himself the messenger of God, and declared he had a commission from heaven to exterminate all Kings, whom he called tyrants, from the face of the earth.'

The frontispiece of Hardy's pamphlet specifies that it was 'printed for the author,' which meant that the expenses of printing were paid for by the author himself. When this was the case, it was almost always because it had not been possible to find a publisher who had faith in the commercial potential of the work to undertake the financial liabilities of publication. At least, Ridgeway would to some extent have had to agree with Hardy's political conclusions, as publishers were held legally responsible for the sedition they printed.

Hardy's pamphlet describes a vision he had in 1787, in which he was told by God that Britain must repent and give up its 'trade for slaves and souls of men,' for 'however black a man may be, Christ can baptize him with fire, and place him in heaven among the foremost.'[7] This resonates with Blake's argument in 'The Little Black Boy,' in which the African child is received into Heaven and redeemed by the love of Christ. The abolitionist appeal had a direct political context, as a bill for the immediate abolition of slavery was discussed in Parliament in 1792, only to be rejected, as Pitt's alarmist government increasingly tarred all attempts at reform with the brush of revolution and civil unrest.

Hardy, who had no access to traditional channels of political power, is, however, intent on publishing his truth to the nation. Yet, it is not the fear of repression that thwarts his efforts:

> ... as I have not in my power to give every man a pamphlet, and as my present small sum of money (which I have to maintain me with) will not enable me to

reprint and give the World a second edition of my pamphlet, entitled the *Mountain Engraved*, I have taken this more cheap method, as both rich and poor may get this at a less expense.[7]

It appears from this complaint that financial necessity forced Hardy to reduce his vision from the apparently more elaborate format of his previous pamphlet, *Mountain Engraved*, to a cheaper mode of publishing.[8] We also understand the author's urgency in publishing his prophecy for the good of his fellow citizens threatened by the shadows of an imminent war. Hardy is driven by the belief that he was 'raised up by the Lord God Almighty to restore peace among Christians.'

Hardy's case is a good illustration of the predicament that Blake – who was also visually oriented and a believer in the power of his art to redeem the nation – would have encountered. Considerations of market limitations explain his decision to take control of all phases of book production. By his new method of printing, Blake achieved what Hardy yearned for: the production and distribution of his books in the form they required. Moreover, this was 'at less than one fourth of the expense' compared with the cost of standard eighteenth-century production methods. It should be said that, arguably, Blake's printing programme for his 'illuminated printing' had the effect of distancing him from the artisan and lower orders, whom the government believed posed the greatest threat of revolution. His works were priced so dearly that they appealed only to more affluent, left-liberal buyers, to whom we owe the survival of the majority of the copies of the early poems now in existence. In later years, Blake even reverted to the older economy of production, by which well-to-do patrons would commission works.

\*\*\*

In the Exhibition Catalogue of 1809, Blake reformulates Admiral Nelson: 'The times require that every one should speak out boldly; England expects that every man should do his duty, in Arts, as well as in Arms, or in the Senate' (Blake, 549). But Blake was to endure 'hardness' as a 'Soldier of Jesus Christ' (cf. 2 Tim. 2.3), and his duty to 'True Religion & Science' was curtailed both in terms of what could be said and in terms of finding an audience that would heed his message. Yet he must not give up, because 'The Art & Sciences are the Destruction of Tyrannies or Bad Governments' (ann. to Reynolds; Blake, 636). 'Science' in all of the above citations is used in its eighteenth-century sense of *knowledge*, and it is the prophet's mission to impart true *knowledge* against the deception, lies and errors propagated by priests and kings.

Around the mid-1790s, Blake's poetry went through a transition, which by some has been seen as a desertion of political engagement. Blake, to a significant degree, abandoned direct political references and increasingly substituted these references with a mythological diction of his own invention. However, this was not a move to a conservative and Royalist position, as was the case with his contemporaries Southey, Coleridge and Wordsworth. Blake's early biographer Alexander Gilchrist, who based his *Life of William Blake* (1863) on interviews with people who had known Blake, describes the artist as 'a vehement republican and sympathizer with the Revolution, hater and contemner of kings and king-craft,' who 'down to his latest days' always avowed himself a 'liberty boy,' a faithful 'Son of Liberty.'[9] In his seminal *Fearful Symmetry*, Northrop Frye has argued that Blake 'never abandoned his belief in the potential imminence of an apocalypse, he does not, like Wordsworth and Coleridge, alter the essentially revolutionary pattern of his thinking.'[10]

Even in the early and most directly political poetry, Blake never thinks that a mere change of constitutional or legal principles will automatically lead to a more benevolent government. In fact, it is a persistent and central theme from the early to the late writings that any change of society must be predicated on a radical change of man's mental disposition.

In Blake's early 'political' poems, all representation of freedom and oppression is intrinsically linked with a discussion of whether a nation is guided by true or false *religion*. In *America* (1793), the overturning of tyranny takes place as the spirit of the revolutionary fervour will 'scatter religion abroad/ To the four winds as a torn book, & none shall gather the leaves/ But they shall rot on desart sands, & consume in bottomless deeps' (8.5-7; Blake, 54). What enables revolution is a destruction of 'Christianity' as this has been usurped by priests and rulers to form a system by which they have empowered themselves. The strongest figure of revolution in these terms is Jesus himself, who is represented as an opponent of both civil and religious authority in *The Marriage of Heaven and Hell* (c. 1790) (pl.23; Blake, 43).

In the early panegyric *The French Revolution* (dated 1791), Blake's revolutionary hero Fayette (i.e. the Marquis de Lafayette, 1757-1834) is seen as the agent who activates the religious iconoclasm expressed in the writings of Rousseau and Voltaire and converts it into revolutionary practice. Blake's argument resonates with Thomas Paine's claim in *Rights of Man* (1791-92) that revolutionary action was a 'consequence of the mental revolution previously existing in France.' For example, Voltaire's 'forte lay in exposing and ridiculing the superstitions which priestcraft, united with statecraft, had interwoven with governments.'¹¹ If Blake in his poem also praises Voltaire's clear-sightedness, Revolution requires another step beyond the annihilation of priestly superstition. For 'the soldier, [to] throw down sword and musket/ And run and embrace the meek peasant' and the 'nobles shall hear and shall weep, and put off/ The red robe of terror, the crown of oppression,' a conversion to True Religion is required. In the case of Blake this is not a sectarian argument, but a mystical experience of spiritual apocalypse by which man begins to take in the infinite divinity of a benign universe. The truly liberated man will 'raise his darken'd limbs out of the caves of night, his eyes and his heart/ Expand: where is space! where O Sun is thy dwelling! where thy tent, O faint slumb'rous Moon' (lll. 213-23; Blake 295-96).

On the basis of this understanding, we need to revise the all too often foregone conclusion that a focus on the inner life automatically eclipses a sense of social involvement. Blake shares common ground with the men and women who zealously undertook a mission of religious revival for the better social good, not least because they doubted those of their contemporaries who thought of politics only in material terms.

It is a well-known fact that Blake was associated, albeit only briefly, with the Swedenborgian New Jerusalem Church in Great East Cheap, London from 1789. Among the leading members were a number of international Masons with revolutionary and republican designs.¹² They mixed with London artisans with dissenter backgrounds, some of whom, such as Blake's friend and fellow-engraver William Sharp, were also members of the London Corresponding Society. In this highly politically charged milieu, Emanuel Swedenborg was seen as an innovator in politics as much as in religion. The prophet's claim to put an end to spiritual enslavement to which the Christian Churches had subjected man easily translated into an argument for overturning the governments for which they were props. An example was the republicans' attack on the Catholic Church in France.

Carl Frederick Nordenskjöld was a Swedish Mason who, in the mid-1780s, carried a number of Swedenborg's manuscripts to the Swedenborgians in London for publication, as Swedenborgian publications were banned in Sweden. He returned home after a three-year stay to produce Swedish translations of both Swedenborg's Latin and Paine's seditious English. In his own phrase (appropriately mixing religion and politics), the aim of his publishing programme was to make Sweden 'God's Republic.'¹³

His brother August Nordenskjöld attended the first General Conference of the New Jerusalem Church, where Blake was also present. Shortly after joining the Church, he issued a pamphlet entitled *Address to the True Members of the New Jerusalem Church* (1790)[14] – a readership that may very well have included Blake. In this he argues for an effective dissemination of Swedenborg's writings in order to destroy 'the Monopoly of the Word among the Clergy' and thereby bring about 'Spiritual Liberty.' This was to go hand-in-hand with the dissemination of gold. Having experimented with alchemy, he proposes to produce enough of the noble metal to flood the market and thereby destroy the 'Monopoly of Gold, Silver, &c. in the commercial World.' The two forms of alchemy, material and spiritual, will create a synergetic effect that will destroy the full spectrum of despotic monopolies of power and bring about the Millennium.

***

Throughout the eighteenth century, more mainstream religious confessors would call attention to the dual role of religion in providing spiritual guidance to the individual believer and steering the nation towards grandeur. Evangelicals (who had adopted eschatological modes of thinking) often saw slavery, child labour, prostitution and other social ills debated at the time as crimes against God. Many of these subjects were taken up in Blake's *Songs of Innocence and of Experience*. For some, philanthropic initiatives would further the Millennium of goodness and justice; for others, reform was seen as the only way to avert the divine wrath of God that would fall upon the nation as punishment. Granville Sharp, one of the leading abolitionists at the time, published a number of dissertations with titles such as *The Law of Retribution; or, a serious warning to Great Britain and her colonies, founded on unquestionable examples of God's temporal vengeance against tyrants, slave-holders and oppressors* (?1776).

In terms of democratic politics, however, Blake would have seen the likes of Evangelicals such as William Wilberforce and Hannah More as enemies. It was among the Evangelicals one found some to the staunchest opponents of constitutional reform. Evangelicalism also promoted the kind of moralistic rectitude that would later translate into what we associate with middle-class Victorian respectability, which Blake, with his emphatic championing of free and uninhibited sexuality, persistently militates against. But Evangelicalism was championed as an antidote to Deism and empty religious observance without inner conviction or passion. In this, it drew on sources such as William Law, the translator and advocate of Blake's spiritual mentor, Jakob Boehme. Other sources were the Methodists John Wesley and George Whitefield, whom Blake, in his poem *Milton* (dated 1804), identifies as 'Prophets' sent to 'the Street of the Great City [London]' at a time when 'No Faith is in all the Earth: the Book of God is trodden under Foot' (22[24].59-

61; Blake 118). But the task of reviving the nation is not just left in the hands of others. With a sense of urgency, Blake calls out to the nation: 'Mark well my words! they are of your eternal salvation' – a sentence repeated no less than seven times in *Milton*.

It should not be forgotten that the majority of what are considered Blake's greatest works were produced or at least begun at a time when Britain was at war with France. Jerome Christensen has reminded us that 'What has been traditionally labelled first-generation Romantic poetry' was 'written under the threat of imminent invasion, during the state's emergency suspension of dailiness, amidst the din of official exhortations to unity, and in the face of brutal and systematic repression.'[15] For a radical poet such as Blake, the enemy was domestic, and the campaign was against the forces that promoted a war of cruelty and death. The aim of Blake's art is to determine a future course for the nation at a time of deep moral and spiritual crisis.

Wordsworth would call on the national poet Milton in his sonnet 'London, 1802,' composed immediately after his return from revolutionary France ('MILTON! thou shouldst be living at this hour:/ England hath need of thee').[16] Begun only a few years later, Blake's *Milton* is the story of the Renaissance poet descending into Blake's left foot to live again. Blake's physical body and, metaphorically, his corpus of poetry become vehicles for correcting Milton's mistakes and, in this respect, complete his work. Despite Milton's ultimate failure, his greatness resides in his attempt to revise Christian Truth for the good of the brotherhood of man. This is why Blake believes his revision of the national poet Milton will be for the benefit of man's 'eternal salvation.'

When Blake came to write his national epic *Jerusalem* (dated 1804), he included an address 'To the Deists' that scorns Deism as 'the Worship of the God of this World by the means of what you call Natural Religion.' It is significant that Blake connects his denunciation of Deism to a discussion of politics. For 'All the Destruction … in Christian Europe,' Blake writes, has 'arisen from Deism, which is Natural Religion' and 'Satan, Named by the Divine Name' (pl. 52; Blake, 201). The indignant address needs to be read in its historical context. The lines are written on the backdrop of the Napoleonic wars, and Blake's argument is that by rejecting the light of Christ, the deists, 'in Holiness of Natural Religion,' let Satan set up 'Kings in wrath.' These include 'Arthur Alfred the Norman Conqueror Richard John/ Edward Henry Elizabeth James Charles William George/ And all the Kings & Nobles of the Earth & all their Glories' (73.36-38; Blake 228). Tyranny is the illegitimate child begotten on a nation that is not governed by spiritual strength and conviction. For Blake, the fervour of a nation's religion is the touchstone for the strength of that nation. All human and divine powers are placed within the mind of individuals, so all social change for better or worse also has its origin here.

Scholarship is increasingly paying attention to the extent to which the Romantics saw the role of religion as a dynamic potential for reworking the political and social order. Robert Ryan, for instance, has demonstrated that the Romantics 'adopted as a goal the spiritual and moral rehabilitation of their society, a renovation that presupposed an alteration in the national religious consciousness.' Religion was not ultimately a question of 'internal consolation of belief' but of its 'civil effects, its influence on behaviour in society, its role as a blessing or a bane in human relationships.'[17] This, I will contend, applies in equal measure to an atheist such as Shelley, a sceptic such as Byron, a High-Churchman such as Coleridge or a prophetic enthusiast such as Blake. Although their evaluations of Christianity were worlds apart, they all agreed that it was what determined the social and political health of the nation.

***

Blake shares common ground with the men and women who zealously undertook a mission of religious revival in the name of social improvement, not least because they doubted those of their contemporaries who thought of politics only in material terms. In his *Public Address* of 1809, Blake writes that 'Princes appear to me to be Fools' as well as 'Houses of Commons & Houses of Lords appear to me to be fools[.] they seem to me to be something beside Human Life' (Blake, 580). This is not a 'total rejection of any form of political activity,' as, for instance, Paul A. Cantor mistakenly interprets it in consensus with many other critics.[18] Because, for Blake, the true change of society is to come not from congregated assemblies, but from a religious change within. If men are not 'Wise,' he admonishes, even 'the Freest Government is compelld to be a Tyranny' (Blake, 580).

Blake's politico-religious ideology echoes statements made by other prophetic propagators as the time, such as James Bicheno, whose *Sign of the Times: or the Overthrow of the Papal Tyranny in France, the Prelude of Destruction to Popery and Despotism* (1793) achieved wide circulation. In a later pamphlet, *Word in a Season* (1795), he writes 'the great mass of mankind should be enlightened by the wisdom of the gospel,' as we are here told that 'all governments should be formed on the broad principle of justice and benevolence,' for 'were men thus enlightened, and governments thus constituted, universal peace and happiness would follow.'[19] Blake could also have found basis for such readings of psychology in Milton, who, in his analysis of *The Tenure of Kings and Magistrates* (1650), wrote that it is from 'being slaves within doors' that a nation comes 'to favour and uphold the Tyrant of a Nation.'[20] Blake's rendering of practically the same observation is famously phrased in his poem 'London' as the 'mind-forg'd manacles.'

By way of conclusion, I will stress the need to revise the often foregone conclusion that a focus on the inner life automatically eclipses a sense of social involvement. Many political radicals of the late eighteenth century held the 'Norman yoke' as the root of tyranny and wanted to return to the liberties enjoyed under Anglo-Saxon law. For Blake, the Millennium where kings will be humbled and men live in peace and equality is not, however, achieved by exchanging one legal document for another. The Millennium was to be realized through the efforts of human intellectual and spiritual labour. It was the promise of man coming into an ultimate understanding of himself and his world. Truth cannot be set down in constitutional terms but must be explored through the practice of true Christian art of which 'The Old & New Testaments are the Great Code' (Blake, *Laocoön*, 274).

## Notes

[1] All Blake citations are from *The Complete Poetry and Prose of William Blake*, ed. David V. Erdman, rev. ed. (New York: Doubleday, 1988) and will be marked in parenthesis in the text. Plate number and verse lines are indicated when applicable.

[2] *Extermination, or an Appeal to the People of England on the Present War with France* (London: D. I. Eaton, 1794), pp. 28-30.

[3] *S. T. Coleridge*, ed. H. J. Jackson (Oxford: Oxford University Press, 1985), pp. 27-29.

[4] G. E. Bentley, Jr., *Blake Records* (Oxford: Clarendon Press, 1969), pp. 15-16.

[5] Robert Southey, *Letters from England: by Don Manuel Alvarez Espriella. Translated from the Spanish*, ed. Jack Simmons (1807; London: Cresset Press, 1951), p. 416.

[6] For example Clarke Garrett, *Respectable Folly: Millenarians and the French Revolution in France and England* (Baltimore and London: Johns Hopkins University Press, 1975), pp. 177-220; J. D. M. Derrett, *Prophecy in the Cotswolds 1803-1947: Joanna Southcott and Spiritual Reform* (Shipston-on-Stour: P.I. Drinkwater, 1994); John Barrell, *Imagining the King's Death: Figurative Treason, Fantasies of Regicide 1793-1796* (Oxford: Oxford University Press, 2000), pp. 504-47.

[7] Henry Hardy, *A Vision from the Lord God Almighty, the Great and Mighty of the Whole Earth: A Vision that must bring about that Great and Glorious Day of Peace, when Nation shall no more lift up Sword against Nation, or learn War any more* (London: printed for the author by James Ridgeway, 1792), p. 14.

[8] The pamphlet is not listed in the *English Short Title Catalogue* and must therefore be presumed lost.

9   Alexander Gilchrist, *Life of William Blake with selections from his poems and other writings*, rev. ed., 2 vols. (London: Macmillan, 1880), 1:81.
10  Northrop Frye, *Fearful Symmetry* (Princeton N.J.: Princeton University Press, 1974), p. 205.
11  *Complete Writings of Thomas Paine*, ed. Philip S. Foner, 2 vols. (New York: Citadel Press, 1969), 1:298-99.
12  Robert W. Rix, 'William Blake and Radical Swedenborgianism,' *Esoterica* 5 (2003), pp. 73-94.
13  Ronny Ambjörnsson, *Det okända landet: Tre Studier om Svenska Utopister* (Stockholm: Gidlunds, 1981), pp. 104-5.
14  The broadside is reprinted in an appendix to Marsha Keith Schuchard, 'The Secret Masonic History of Blake's Swedenborg Society,' *Blake: An Illustrated Quarterly* 26 (1992), pp. 40-51.
15  Jerome Christensen, 'The Detection of the Romantic Conspiracy in Britain,' *The South Atlantic Quarterly Review* 95 (1996), pp. 603-27 (603).
16  *The Poetical Works of William Wordsworth*, E. de Selincourt and Helen Darbishire (eds) (Oxford: Clarendon Press, 1954), p. 116.
17  Robert Ryan, *The Romantic Reformation: Religious Politics in English Literature, 1789-1824* (Cambridge: Cambridge University Press, 1997), pp. 4, 8-9. The argument correlates with that found in John Clubbe and Ernest Lovell's *English Romanticism: The Grounds of Belief* (London: Macmillan, 1983) and Richard E. Brantley's *Locke, Wesley, and the Method of English Romanticism* (Gainsville: University of California, 1984).
18  Paul A. Cantor, *Creature and Creator: Myth-Making and English Romanticism* (Cambridge: Cambridge University Press, 1984), p. 61.
19  James Bicheno, *Word in a Season; or, A Call to the Inhabitants of Great Britain, to stand Prepared for the Consequences of the Present War* (London, n.p. 1795), pp. 50-52.
20  John Milton, *Complete Prose Works*, Douglas Bush et al. (eds), 6 vols. (New Haven: Yale University Press, 1962), 3:190.

# HUME, SCOTT, AND THE 'RISE OF FICTION'

Ian Duncan

*Jane Austen and Nothing*

Writing in the flush of his own success as a new historical novelist, Walter Scott hailed Jane Austen's *Emma* (1816) as the model of a distinctively modern kind of novel committed to the representation of what Scott calls 'the common walks of life,' 'the paths of common life' – the daily habitus of 'the middling classes of society' that constitute a national reading public. The author of *Emma* narrates 'such common occurrences as may have fallen under the observation of most folks'; her characters 'conduct themselves upon the motives and principles which the readers may recognize as ruling their own and that of most of their acquaintances.'[1] In Scott's carefully indirect formulations, 'common life,' the world in which readers walk and which the novel represents to them, is a medium at once transparent and opaque. Its surface texture of events 'may have fallen' under our observation – but we do not actually observe them until the novel narrates them for us. We overlook the 'motives and principles' that regulate everday life, since we are immersed in everyday life – until the novel holds them up for our recognition.[2]

Austen herself describes the world of her novel in two separate but analogically linked set pieces, in which the heroine goes on a walk and looks at a view. Late in the novel, Emma visits Mr Knightley's manor at Donwell. She and her party wander about the grounds:

> [T]hey insensibly followed one another to the delicious shade of a broad avenue of limes, which stretching beyond the garden at an equal distance from the river, seemed the finish of the pleasure grounds. – It led to nothing; nothing but a view at the end of a low stone wall with high pillars, which seemed intended, in their erection, to give the appearance of an approach to the house, which never had been there. Disputable, however, as might be the taste of such a termination, it was itself a charming walk, and the view which closed it extremely pretty. ... It was a sweet view – sweet to the eye and the mind. English verdure, English culture, English comfort, seen under a sun bright, without being oppressive.[3]

The insensible, indirect rambling that characterizes Emma's path across the landscape is set in implicit contrast to a French, formal, absolutist style of gardening and the kinds of approach it governs. The walk's resonantly negative termination – 'It led to nothing; nothing but a view,' 'the appearance of an approach . . . which never had been there' – nevertheless yields something. It yields a general, abstract quality of national setting: 'English verdure, English culture, English comfort.' Englishness, modifying the suggestive series of abstractions (verdure, culture, comfort), turns out to be the view's sweet and formless content: its curiously rich and potent quality of 'nothing.'

Readers, if they are paying attention, will remember an earlier episode in which the heroine, 'seeing nothing,' looks at a view. Emma and Harriet go shopping in the local village:

> [W]hile [Harriet] was still hanging over muslins and changing her mind, Emma went to the door for amusement. – Much could not be hoped for from the traffic of even the busiest part of Highbury; – Mr Perry walking hastily by, Mr William Cox letting himself in at the office door, Mr Cole's carriage horses returning from exercise, or a stray letter-boy on an obstinate mule, were the liveliest objects she could presume to expect; and when her eyes fell only on the butcher with his tray, a tidy old woman travelling homewards from shop with her full basket, two curs quarreling over a dirty bone, and a string of dawdling children round the baker's little bow-window eying the gingerbread, she knew she had no reason to complain, and was amused enough; quite enough still to stand at the door. A mind lively and at ease, can do with seeing nothing, and can see nothing that does not answer. (241)

Once again, 'nothing' yields the vision of a substantial reality, which consists this time of quite a lot of descriptive detail representing local, particular activities and material objects. The narrative context, a shopping expedition, specifies the unnamed category, commerce, that governs this spectacle – so ordinary as to go overlooked or unremarked – of everyday 'traffic.' The nothing Emma sees includes the circulation of persons, commodities, and correspondence, and the union of all degrees of local society in a prosperous consumption of the fruits of an imperial economy, from the 'tidy old woman' with her full basket to the children eyeing the gingerbread. So comfortable is Highbury that the signs of poverty and struggle, far from needing to be kept out of sight, can confidently be ascribed to the quarreling curs.

The view of everyday life in the village and the view of 'English culture' at Donwell inform and sustain each other, under the shared rubric of 'nothing,' to supply Austen's representation of the world – or rather the world-system – to which her characters and their local setting belong. The conjunction of the two articulates, to be sure, the ideological theme of a national society constituted upon a harmonious conjunction between a modern economy based on imperial trade and a traditional social hierarchy based on inherited property. 'Nothing' refers not only to the everyday domain of commerce: it also refers, obliquely or metaphorically, to that reality's governing abstraction, embedded in naturalized forms and qualities, 'English' verdure, culture, comfort. 'Nothing' names, in short, an invisible cause, the force or power that regulates these conjunctions and circulations. Emma, by virtue of her caste and intelligence, is able to perceive this invisible cause, 'seeing nothing,' by constituting commerce as a view, in a motion that faithfully reiterates the reflexive form of exchange: seeing (in Austen's marvellous phrase) 'nothing that does not answer.' While Harriet is submerged in the blind life of traffic, Emma rises above it for an aesthetic appreciation allied with the ethical constancy of a mind that can regulate its own enjoyment.

At the same time, however, it is by no means clear that we can define this viewpoint as 'Emma's' – as (according to the conventions of free indirect discourse) the experience of a particular, localized subjectivity. Both passages subsume Emma's spectatorial consciousness into a generalized viewpoint shared between narrator and reader, and in doing so they provoke certain questions about the quality of this abstraction. Does Emma know what she is seeing? Does she share (as we do) the narrator's terms for this knowledge? Can this abstraction be described, on her part, as reflection – an intensified activity of consciousness – or as its reverse, a kind of absorption or reverie, in which consciousness takes a holiday?

\*\*\*

*David Hume and Common Life*
Both the positive term 'nothing' and the problematic of reflection emerge from Humean empiricism, the most rigorous and subtle attempt to describe a reality evacuated of metaphysical forms in modern British philosophy. 'Nothing' denotes the absence of divine agency and transcendental structures of meaning from the world, such as a metaphysical causality – and thus the abyss behind appearances opened up by the sceptical work of reason. And 'nothing' also designates the phenomenological substance that covers that abyss: the imaginary fabric of 'customary conjunctions' or habitual associations that makes up our positive knowledge of the world. '[All] our reasonings concerning causes and effects are deriv'd from nothing but custom,' Hume insists.[4] Custom alone – repetition and habituation – produces the effects of continuity and consistency that weave together an

intelligible, familiar world and our identities in it. In the great set piece that concludes the first book of the *Treatise on Human Nature*, Hume makes it clear that this secondary domain of the phenomenal world holds sway by virtue of its being a *social* domain. Hume's philosopher recovers from the alienation brought on by his sceptical understanding by turning again to 'the common affairs of life':

> I dine, I play a game of backgammon, I converse, and am merry with my friends; and when after two or three hours' amusement, I wou'd return to these [philosophical] speculations, they appear so cold, and strain'd, and ridiculous, that I cannot find in my heart to enter into them any farther.
>
> Here then I find myself absolutely and necessarily determin'd to live, and talk, and act like other people in the common affairs of life. ...(316)

Intercourse with others, 'the commerce and society of men' (317), constitutes the texture of common life. The world is recharged with the sentimental positivity of social exchange.

Hume's illustrious disciple Adam Smith devoted his career to theorizing the different domains and disciplines that make up the 'sphere of common life,' such as moral psychology, rhetoric, jurisprudence, and political economy. Smith discovers *exchange* as the structural principle of social life. Economic exchange (commerce), linguistic exchange (conversation), and sentimental exchange (sympathy) provide the mechanisms of mediation and continuity that sustain the empirical world. In *The Theory of Moral Sentiments* he describes a kind of white noise of affective gratification through which common life keeps itself going:

> It is decent to be humble amidst great prosperity; but we can scarce express too much satisfaction in all the little occurrences of common life, in the company with which we spent the evening last night, in the entertainment that was set before us, in what was said and what was done, in all the little incidents of the present conversation, and in all those frivolous nothings which fill up the void of human life. Nothing is more graceful than habitual cheerfulness, which is always founded upon a peculiar relish for all the little pleasures which common occurrences afford. We readily sympathize with it: it inspires us with the same joy, and makes every trifle turn up to us in the same agreeable aspect in which it presents itself to the person endowed with this happy disposition.[5]

Such language describes a reality that is customary and continuous, reproduced by microscopic transactions of exchange, so smoothly as to go unremarked; a subconscious sympathetic medium that 'makes every trifle turn up to us,' or reflexively constitutes the texture of everyday life as present and self-evident.

Smith's language also calls attention to the absence of a metaphysical ground, and its replacement by something else, a phenomenal *background*. The transactions of 'commerce and society' are 'frivolous nothings' that 'fill up the void of human life': we glimpse the abyss of scepticism behind Smith's bourgeois mimicry of a gentlemanly *sprezzatura*. Why nothings, why a void? Because Humean scepticism posits this continuous, habitual world of ordinary relations as a *fiction*. 'The memory, senses, and understanding,' writes Hume in the *Treatise*, are 'all of them founded on the imagination' (313). The imagination is the faculty that fills in the gaps between discrete sense-impressions and writes phenomena into an intelligible text of experience. It is not so much, in itself, a cognitive faculty, as the faculty that provides the conditions for cognition, as it structures an empirical reality purged of metaphysical categories. The imagination produces the necessary illusions of spatial and temporal continuity, and – by extension – subjective as well as objective identity in space and time. The identity of an object over time is a 'fiction of the imagination' (251); 'the identity, which we ascribe to the mind of man, is only a fictitious one, and of a like kind with that which we ascribe to [material] bodies' (306-307).

As I have already intimated, this imaginary production of reality is *customary*, habitual and social, rather than solipsistic; its great work of fiction, common life, is an ongoing, collective project, consensually shared and reproduced. Hume reflects on this condition in the famous passage from the *Treatise of Human Nature* cited earlier, in which the author recapitulates his philosophical argument in a confessional drama of crisis and recovery. Sceptical reason alienates the thinker from common life, throwing him into a 'philosophical melancholy'; his cure takes the form of a sentimental rather than rational reconnection with 'the commerce and society of men.' Hume insists on the dialectical structure of this reconnection. If 'nature' drives the philosopher to seek refuge in social cheer, nature will also eventually, just as surely, drive him to resume his intellectual labour – since the motive for philosophical inquiry, the desire to think through the customary fabric of everyday life, is no less pleasure-oriented. Both scepticism and distraction (what we might call an ideological mode of consciousness) are 'authentic' – or rather, authenticity belongs not to one state of mind or to the other, but to the alternation between them both. There is no release from what Hume characterizes as an organic, psychosomatic rhythm of tension and relaxation. Hume's is a 'negative' dialectic, in that it produces neither a simple return to philosophical innocence nor some sort of higher cognitive synthesis, a horizon of illumination that transcends the common and the customary. The sentimental investment in common life, in the authority of the customary, is framed, rather, by the intermittent knowledge of its fictiveness. Hume rehearses a doubled consciousness that oscillates between alienated reflection and absorption in the imaginary surfaces of life.[6] It is the mode of consciousness, in short, appropriate to the reader of a novel.

***

*The Rise of the Novel and the Rise of Fiction*
Recent critical discussions of the 'rise of the novel' in modern British culture, reviewing the influential thesis of Ian Watt, have endorsed the historiographic status of the mid-eighteenth century – the epoch of Richardson and Fielding as well as Hume – as a kind of watershed. It marks a developmental horizon at which the genre realizes its potential, 'comes into its own,' of which the rhetorical signs are an access of 'self-consciousness' and an overt affirmation of 'fictionality.'[7] Lennard Davis, refuting the traditional genealogy that makes 'romance' the novel's ancestral form, separates the origins of the novel altogether from the category of fiction. He sets in place, instead, the matrix of what he calls a 'novel/news discourse' in early modern culture: the novel disguises itself with the trappings of fact so as to evade the censure that attends the category of fiction, which is associated with a falsification of religious or (increasingly) scientific orders of truth. This commits the early novel, in Davis's words, to 'an inherent doubleness and reflexivity,' as the 'factual fiction's' denial of its fictionality generates an uncertainty among readers as to the truth-status of what they are reading. By the middle decades of the eighteenth century, however, certain novelists (notably Fielding) grow confident enough to affirm the fictional status of their work, while nevertheless retaining the 'doubleness and reflexivity' that have become attached to the genre.[8] Catherine Gallagher argues, with greater precision, that what she calls 'the novel's most important trait: its overt fictionality' does not precede 'but is rather coterminous with the rise of the novel'; she adduces legal and economic developments in the status of the author and the rise of a discourse of sympathy to explain why this might be so.[9] Meanwhile, according to John Bender, the claim upon a 'guarantee of factuality' in the natural sciences 'increasingly required the presence of its opposite, a manifest yet verisimilar fictionality in the novel.'[10] Bender refers to Michael McKeon for an account of the formation of that aesthetic of 'manifest yet verisimilar fictionality' in the mid-eighteenth century debate between Richardson and Fielding.[11] These critical narratives, very different

from although not necessarily exclusive of one another, concur in finding a strong, overdetermined recourse by British novelists to a rhetoric of fiction in the middle decades of the eighteenth century – not in order to abandon or evade the representation of 'real life,' but on the contrary to take firmer hold of it.

In a recent book on the theory of fiction, Wolfgang Iser also identifies the second half of the eighteenth century as the era when a distinctively secular rhetoric of 'the fictive' began to define itself in European culture. Iser characterizes the fictive in terms that should by now sound familiar: it is 'an operational mode of consciousness,' 'an act of boundary-crossing' that 'simultaneously disrupts and doubles the referential world.'[12] These terms express the subjective effects cultivated by the modern novel, as well as Hume's characterization of a philosophical relation to common life. Indeed, Iser locates the conceptual emergence of the fictive in British empiricist philosophy, and he grants Hume a pivotal role in this emergence, thanks to Hume's categorical separation of fiction from its pre-modern cultural associations with falsehood and inauthenticity.[13]

Iser's recognition of Hume's contribution (although, in my view, it does not go far enough) may serve as a point at which to summarize my argument so far. In affirming the epistemological primacy of the imagination, endowing it with a socially productive and normative function, Hume establishes the philosophical matrix for the ascendancy of fictional realism in British literature. Humean empiricism generates a 'novelistic' model of the imagination that poses a fertile alternative to the Kantian-Coleridgean 'lyric' model, associated (in modern academic criticism) with English Romantic poetry, which casts the imagination as trace of an alienated transcendental cognition.[14] Hume's philosophical legitimation of the fictive as an 'authentic' representation of common life, since common life is a consensually reproduced fiction, coincides chronologically with the affirmation of fictionality in a cluster of major English novels (from *Tom Jones* to *The Female Quixote* and *Tristram Shandy*). Fiction, traditionally stigmatized as inauthentic for its divergence from truth or fact, becomes the mode of representation best fitted to render the 'nothing' that is the empirical domain of common life: first, because that 'nothing' has gone unremarked by the historical record; and second, because this domain is itself already fictive, an intersubjective representation sanctioned by custom.

Nevertheless, these philosophical and novelistic realizations of the fictive do not yet fully converge in the middle decades of the eighteenth century. There remains a gap between Hume's theory and the practice of the English novelists. As Iser notes, Hume continues to repeat the 'negative' associations of fiction, in his thoroughly conventional pronouncements on poetic genres – even as Hume's general epistemology gives fiction a critical force as the mental medium of common life.[15] Conversely, novelists continue to appeal to a non-fictional discourse, the discourse of 'history,' as a protective shield for their work. History, in fact, is the category that occupies the gap between the philosophical theory of fiction and its novelistic realization in the second half of the eighteenth century. History and the novel share – and dispute – a common border.[16] Historians draw upon novelistic techniques as they expand the scope of their writing to accommodate a more complete range of human experience, including the discourses of common life.[17] At the same time a rivalry intensifies between the genres, as they compete for prestige and market share. As novelists call their works 'histories' in a bid for cultural legitimacy, they subject historiographic conventions to a destabilizing pressure, which threatens to reduce history itself to the status of just another (however officially sanctioned) kind of fiction.[18] The threat drives historians, in turn, to claim scientific norms of evidence in the attempt to set their work apart from mere invention. Hume himself, of course, when it came to applying his own philosophical principles to narrative writing in his later career, turned to history and not the novel – in acceptance of the customary, hierarchical difference between them – as the authoritative representation of common life: as, in Zimmerman's phrase, 'the inclusive fiction that constitutes our social world and enables our understanding of it.'[19]

In the later eighteenth century history divorces itself from membership in the general category of 'literature' (formerly inclusive of all forms of written discourse, and now increasingly associated with poetry and the novel), and begins to claim the methodology and status of a scholarly discipline.[20] The scientific and disciplinary hardening of history – its separation out of the literary field – assists the dialectical definition of the rejected term, fiction, which thus comes to characterize the 'literary' itself. That dialectical definition is precipitated, certainly, by the epoch-breaking shock of the French Revolution, the event that recasts history in the mode of crisis – both as collective lived experience and as rationalizing account of that experience – and brings in its wake a catastrophic perturbation of all narrative categories. Scott's novels, published in the aftermath of the Revolutionary and Napoleonic wars, at once enact and thematize the formal emergence of fiction in British literary history. They specify fiction as the rhetorical principle that distinguishes the novel from other narrative genres, such as memoir and history, and that marks out an autonomous cultural position and function for it. Fiction, in short, moves from theory to substance, as it becomes the dominant principle and identifying term of a literary genre.

Bender notes that perhaps the first usage of 'fiction' as a synonym for novel or romance occurs in the title of John Dunlop's *History of Fiction*, published in 1814: the same year as *Waverley*.[21] And while the formal identification of the novel with fictionality occurs elsewhere in the second decade of the nineteenth century – in Austen's novels, for example, with which this essay began – Scott's combination of romance and history gives it an unprecedented analytic thoroughness.

***

*Scott, History and Fiction*
Scott invests the novel with fictionality, paradoxically, through the very recourse to history. The invention of the historical novel – the achievement with which Scott is most often associated – has not always, despite some recent revisionary scrutiny, been clearly understood. Both history *and* fiction (given its historicist title, 'romance') achieve definition through their dialectical combination; Scott's novels narrate, paradigmatically, the production of these categories through one another. Typical accounts of Scott describe him as infusing the form of the novel with a dignifying, authenticating charge of historical reality. More sophisticated versions of this argument have cast history in formal terms, rather than simply as content – although there are still plenty of instances of the kind of argument that sees the novel as merely a vessel into which the author pours historical-realist content.[22] Certainly Scott summons history to the novel in unprecedentedly rigorous, disciplinary and indeed scientific terms: not just bringing a greater density of historical information to the novel, or even sophisticated techniques of the historiographic shaping of collective experience (although both cases are true), but invoking history *as* a discipline: a salutary empirical corrective to the hero's expensive, dangerous, premature romanticism.

I wish to emphasize, instead, the strategy by which Scott's invocation of history precipitates a reflexively distinct work of fiction, and so defines the place and function of the novel in modern culture. The historicist address of Scott's work distinguishes it from the formalist claim on aesthetic value with which, according to a number of recent critics, 'literature' emerges as an autonomous category in the Romantic period.[23] Scott produces the category of fiction by, precisely, historicizing it: narrating its 'rise' as a historical mode of engagement with social reality.[24] The narrative of *Waverley* co-ordinates the hero's progress from adolescent illusion through sentimental and moral crisis to mature settlement with the nation's violent transition from its historical past (Catholic, feudal, tribal) to the horizon of the present, modern civil society. This development is co-ordinated, in turn, with the novel's internal allegory of its own emergence as a literary form, from archaic modes of romance and allegory, to become the fit genre of modern life. This developmental complex rehearses the Humean dialectic between reason and imagination, sceptical alienation and socializing absorption, that governs the 'enlightened' relation to common life. Like Hume's philosopher, young Waverley must move from 'romance,' a naïve investment in illusion, through a harsh disenchantment by the force of experience, to a reconnection with common life – set at the horizon of civil society and our own act of reading, at the end of the story. The comic conclusion of Scott's novel establishes a sceptical, melancholy, and aesthetic distance in relation to historical reality that nevertheless (and hence the melancholy) accepts the authority of that reality, parsed as the authority of custom.

As some recent cultural theorists have insisted, the sceptical demystification of social law by Enlightenment critics such as Hume tended to enhance the law's power, to make it more immoveable, not less. The critical dissolution of the mystical foundations of social law, and the revelation of the arbitrariness of custom, installed instead the sanction of collective consent, manifest over time, rooted in historical contingency.[25] Zizek quotes Pascal: 'Custom is the whole of equity for the sole reason that it is accepted. Anyone who tries to bring it back to its first principle destroys it.'[26] In other words, the person who appeals to fundamental principles is an adversary of the modern political and social order; he is, in the key term that Hume mobilizes in his historical writing and Scott takes up in his novels, a *fanatic*, the name for a cast of mind antithetical to civil society – a cast of mind, to put it bluntly, that refuses to accept reality in the form of a fiction, and rejects fiction, concomittantly, as the mode of representation of a liberal society.[27]

In his historical and political writings Hume justifies the Hanoverian succession very much in these terms. The current dynasty's claim on the British throne is a fictitious title that has acquired the weight and force of reality because it has been in place, it has been a fact, for half a century – it is by now accepted, even though reason might reveal the legal or genealogical basis of the claim to be a fiction. The Jacobite counter-insurgency of 1745 might have had 'truth' on its side, in foundational terms, but it represented a fanatical attempt to destroy civil society. This is the political argument, and the view of modern national history (both British and Scottish), that Scott takes over in *Waverley* and its successors. In tracing the intellectual legacy of the so-called conjectural history of Adam Smith, Adam Ferguson and John Millar, scholars have underestimated the extent both to which Scott's politics agree with what David Miller calls Hume's 'conservative scepticism,'[28] and to which Hume's history shapes Scott's, just as Hume provides the theory of fiction that governs Scott's practice.

To bring all this into focus I turn, briefly and finally, to another novel by Scott – one that has claims to be his best, and is certainly his most Humean. *Redgauntlet,* suggestively subtitled 'A Tale of the Eighteenth Century,' appeared ten years after *Waverley* (in 1824); it performs an overt revisitation and reconsideration of Scott's first novel and of the general project of national historical romance. Where the historical topic of *Waverley* was the 1745 rebellion, *Redgauntlet* involves its heroes (there are now two of them) in a second return of Prince Charles Edward Stuart to Britain for a final Jacobite rising, in 1765. However, in striking contrast to *Waverley* and its successors, this historical event – the 'history' that is supposed to guarantee the historical novel – is actually a fiction, Scott's invention. No such secret return took place.[29] The last pages of the novel relate the rising's failure, as it falls apart before it gets off the ground. The event's fictive status is predicated on this collapse, in a kind of circular logic. Scott is free to make up his fiction on condition of its lack of consequences – his counterfactual invention depends on the failure of the Jacobite cause to change the course of history, and indeed it endorses that failure. What is overtly a fiction sets history in place all the more firmly. Scott's emphasis thus differs from the overtly utopian or dystopian deployments of counterfactual history by his contemporaries (such as Mary Shelley in *Valperga*)[30] or, for that matter, by postmodern novelists who combine the historical novel with science fiction (e.g., Philip K. Dick in *The Man in the High Castle*).

Scott's novel plays out its logic brilliantly. The Jacobite insurrection falters when it becomes apparent that the ideological categories that are meant to mobilize it can no longer hold; neither the Prince nor his followers can sustain a coherent feudal or absolutist discourse of allegiance and of the relation between private and public life. Their language is irremediably infected with modern concepts and distinctions. The decisive blow falls when the government reveals that it already knows about the conspiracy – and at the same time refuses to recognize the conspirators as historical agents. The Hanoverian General Colin Campbell strolls calmly into their midst, unarmed and in private dress:

> 'Come, do not be fools, gentlemen; there was perhaps no great harm meant or intended by your gathering together in this obscure corner, for a bear-baiting, or a cock-fighting, or whatever other amusement you may have intended; but it was a little imprudent, considering how you stand with government, and it has occasioned some anxiety. ... I have come here, of course, sufficiently supported both with cavalry and infantry, to do whatever might be necessary;

but my commands are – and I am sure they agree with my inclination – to make no arrests, nay, to make no further inquiries of any kind, if this good assembly will consider their own interest so far as to give up their immediate purpose, and return quietly home to their own houses.'[31]

In what must be the most devastating performative utterance in all of historical fiction, Campbell cuts off the Jacobites from history and sentences them decisively, ignominiously, to common life – identified as the sphere of private 'amusement' that we ourselves, as readers of the novel, currently occupy. Well might the chief conspirator throw up his hands and cry, in a suggestively Humean phrase, 'the cause is lost for ever!'[32] The very fictionality of common life – its production by chains of contingency and an accreted force of customary acceptance, rather than by original right or metaphysical truth – endows it with the invincible, melancholic weight of historical necessity.

## Notes

[1] Ioan Williams (ed.), *Sir Walter Scott on Novelists and Fiction* (New York: Barnes & Noble, 1970), pp. 230-31. Scott's article first appeared in the *Quarterly Review*, Vol. 14 (1815-16).

[2] Miranda J. Burgess discusses Scott's review of *Emma* in the light of both authors' investment in a national public sustained by novel-reading: 'Domesticating Gothic: Jane Austen, Ann Radcliffe, and National Romance,' in Thomas Pfau and Robert F. Gleckner (eds), *Lessons of Romanticism: A Critical Companion* (Durham: Duke University Press, 1998), pp. 392-95.

[3] Jane Austen, *Emma*, ed. Ronald Blythe (Harmondsworth: Penguin, 1966), p. 355. Future references to this edition will be given in the text.

[4] David Hume, *A Treatise of Human Nature*, ed. Ernest C. Mossner (Harmondsworth: Penguin, 1969), p. 234. Future references to this edition will be given in the text.

[5] Adam Smith, *The Theory of Moral Sentiments*, ed. D. D. Raphael & A. L. Macfie (Oxford: Clarendon Press, 1976), pp. 41-42.

[6] On Hume's dialectic see Donald W. Livingston, *Hume's Philosophy of Common Life* (Chicago: University of Chicago Press, 1984), pp. 30-31; David Miller, *Philosophy and Ideology in Hume's Political Thought* (Oxford: Clarendon Press, 1981), pp. 36-39; Leo Damrosch, *Fictions of Reality in the Age of Hume and Johnson* (Madison: University of Wisconsin Press, 1989), pp. 17-23.

[7] See J. Paul Hunter, *Before Novels: The Cultural Contexts of Eighteenth-Century English Fiction* (New York: Norton, 1990), p. 27.

[8] Lennard Davis, *Factual Fictions: The Origins of the English Novel* (New York: Columbia University Press, 1983), pp. 36, 70, 210-11.

[9] Catherine Gallagher, *Nobody's Story: The Vanishing Acts of Women Writers in the Marketplace, 1670-1820* (Berkeley: University of California Press, 1994), pp. 155-74 (p. 164).

[10] John Bender, 'Enlightenment Fiction and the Scientific Hypothesis,' *Representations*, Vol. 61 (Winter 1998), pp. 6-28 (p. 6).

[11] Michael McKeon, *The Origins of the English Novel, 1600-1740* (Baltimore: Johns Hopkins University Press, 1987), pp. 39-64, 118-28.

[12] Wolfgang Iser, *The Fictive and the Imaginary: Charting Literary Anthropology* (Baltimore: Johns Hopkins University Press, 1993), pp. xiv-xv.

[13] Ibid., pp. xvi, 87, 111.

[14] See Cairns Craig, 'Coleridge, Hume, and the Chains of the Romantic Imagination,' in Leith Davis, Ian Duncan, and Janet Sorensen (eds), *Scotland and the Borders of Romanticism* (Cambridge: Cambridge University Press, forthcoming). The most suggestive discussion of Hume's influence on 'literary' genres is by Susan Manning, *Fragments of Union: Making Connections in Scottish and American Writing* (Houndsmill: Palgrave, 2002), pp. 27, 34-64.

[15] Iser, p. 111; Jeremy Bentham, instead, develops the first fully affirmative theorization of 'the fictive,' pp. 112-30.

[16] See Everett Zimmerman, *The Boundaries of Fiction: History and the Eighteenth-Century British Novel* (Ithaca: Cornell University Press, 1996), pp. 43-44.

[17] See Mark Salber Phillips's comprehensive discussion, *Society and Sentiment: Genres of Historical Writing in Britain, 1740-1820* (Princeton: Princeton University Press, 2000).

[18] Zimmerman, p. 237.

[19] Ibid., p. 239. On Hume's turn to history see David Wootton, 'David Hume, "the historian",' in David Fate Norton (ed.), *The Cambridge Companion to Hume* (Cambridge: Cambridge University Press, 1993), pp. 281-84.

[20] See Lionel Gossman, *Between History and Literature* (Cambridge, Mass.: Harvard University Press, 1990), pp. 227-30.

[21] Bender, p. 21.

[22] Such, despite its sophisticated attention to Romantic anxieties about the contamination of historical truth by fiction, remains the emphasis of Anne Rigney's *Imperfect Histories: The Elusive Past and the Legacy of Romantic Historicism* (Ithaca: Cornell University Press, 2001). The most subtle account of Scott's recourse to history as undertaking a discursive promotion of prose fiction remains Ina Ferris's *The Achievement of Literary Authority: Gender, History and the Waverley Novels* (Ithaca: Cornell University Press, 1981).

[23] Clifford Siskin identifies the novel rather than poetry as the Romantic discourse where this takes place: *The Work of Writing: Literature and Social Change in Britain, 1700-1830* (Baltimore: Johns Hopkins University Press, 1998), pp. 172-90.

[24] In the discussion that follows, I review my own analysis of *Waverley* in *Modern Romance and Transformations of the Novel: The Gothic, Scott, Dickens* (Cambridge: Cambridge University Press, 1992), pp. 79-105.

25 For example, Slavoj Zizek, *The Sublime Object of Ideology* (London: Verso, 1989), pp. 36-40; Giorgio Agamben, *Homo Sacer: Sovereign Power and Bare Life*, trans. Daniel Heller-Roazen (Stanford: Stanford University Press, 1998).

26 Zizek, p. 37.

27 On Scott and liberalism see David Kaufmann, *The Business of Common Life: Novels and Classical Economics between Revolution and Reform* (Baltimore: Johns Hopkins University Press, 1995), pp. 93-137; Jerome Christensen, *Romanticism at the End of History* (Baltimore: Johns Hopkins University Press, 2000), pp. 153-75.

28 Miller, pp. 204-5.

29 The present discussion complements my account of *Redgauntlet* in 'Authenticity Effects: The Work of Fiction in Romantic Scotland,' *South Atlantic Quarterly* Vol. 102:1 (Winter 2003), pp. 93-116. On the fictional status of 'history' in *Redgauntlet* see also James Kerr, *Fiction Against History: Scott as Story-Teller* (Cambridge: Cambridge University Press, 1989), pp. 102-23; H. B. DeGroot, 'Fiction and History: The Case of *Redgauntlet*,' in J. H. Alexander and D. Hewitt (eds), *Scott in Carnival: Selected Papers from the Fourth International Scott Conference* (Aberdeen: Aberdeen University Press, 1993), pp. 358-69; Homer O. Brown, *Institutions of the English Novel: From Defoe to Scott* (Philadelphia: University of Pennsylvania Press, 1997), pp. 145-70.

30 See Tilottama Rajan's 'Introduction' to her edition of *Valperga* (Peterborough, ON: Broadview, 1998), pp. 9-38; and Deidre Lynch, 'Mary Shelley, Historical Novelist: The "Author of *Frankenstein*" and "The Author of *Waverley*",' in Esther Schor (ed.), *The Cambridge Companion to Mary Shelley* (Cambridge: Cambridge University Press, forthcoming).

31 Walter Scott, *Redgauntlet: A Tale of the Eighteenth Century*, G. A. M. Wood and D. Hewitt (eds), (Edinburgh: Edinburgh University Press, 1997), pp. 372-73.

32 Ibid., p. 373. On representation and politics in *Redgauntlet* see, especially, Robert P. Irvine, *Enlightenment and Romance: Gender and Agency in Smollett and Scott* (Bern: Peter Lang, 2000), pp. 214-15; Yoon Sun Lee, 'Giants in the North: *Douglas*, the Scottish Enlightenment, and Scott's *Redgauntlet*,' *Studies in Romanticism* Vol. 40:1, (Spring 2001), pp. 109-21.

# POETRY AND IGNORANCE

Andrew Bennett

'So we are sent back to the originary infantile situation,' declares Jean Laplanche, in a richly suggestive essay on the otherness that inhabits the transference in psychoanalysis: 'The sexual enigma is presented to the child by adults in an *address*, and this address is enigmatic in so far as the other (the one who sends it) does not entirely know what he is saying: he is other to himself.'[1] Indeed, Laplanche links the relationship between the analyst and the analysand to the more general condition of communication in which the defining condition of 'cultural production,' of the scene of communication and culture more generally, is that it is 'situated from the first *beyond all pragmatics*, beyond any adequation of means to a determinate effect.' For Laplanche, the cultural necessarily involves 'an address to an other who is out of reach, to others "scattered in the future", as the poet says'.[2] For Laplanche, indeed, the very condition of the poet – the one who writes for an audience of the future, who writes for an anonymous and unknown, unpredictable and unprogrammable audience – is in fact the condition more generally of the subject of communication, of 'culture.' A Laplanchean poetics, therefore, would involve a double disturbance of knowledge, a double institution of the enigma within writing: for Laplanche, the author neither knows for whom he writes nor in the end *what* he writes, since he is both other to himself and other to the other for whom he writes. In *Romantic Poets and the Culture of Posterity*, I have tried to suggest that this condition of ignorance in relation to audience or addressee might be conceived as a specifically Romantic predicament, or, more precisely, as a predicament at the centre of a certain conception of Romantic poetics. Romanticism might be conceived, in other words, precisely in terms of the representation of audience as unknown and unknowable, might be interpreted as constitutively positing its acts of communication as directed towards an unknown and unknowable future, as directed towards posterity.[3] But in this paper, I would like to suggest that Romantic poetics may also be conceived in terms of a particular emphasis on the poet's ignorance of what it is that he is writing *about* – that there is a particular emphasis in Romantic poetry and poetics on the fact that the poet's 'address is enigmatic' to the extent that the poet himself 'does not entirely know what he is saying,' since he is 'other to himself.' In fact, I would suggest that the two opacities, the two levels of ignorance – of addressee and speaker – are intimately linked in as much as the speaker is other to him- or her-self just *because* his or her interlocutor is fundamentally and irremediably other. What Romanticism brings into focus – what indeed it institutionalizes at the core of what it begins to know as and to term 'literature' – is that one can neither know to whom one addresses a poem nor, in part because of this ignorance, the entirety of what one is saying.

***

'What creates the intense pleasure of not knowing?' asks John Keats in a marginal annotation in his copy of *Paradise Lost*. Keats thinks he knows the answer to this question: 'A sense of independence, of power, from the fancy's creating a world of its own by the sense of probabilities.'[4] Perhaps we know Keats's poetry too well, so that we forget that not knowing is one of its keenest pleasures, that ignorance is celebrated – in his sonnet 'To Homer', for example, where the poet's 'giant ignorance' is likened to Homer's 'triple sighted' blindness. In a rather more troubled engagement with poetic ignorance, Shelley argues in the *Defence of Poetry* that ignorance both is and fundamentally is not intrinsic to poetry, to the work of the poet. In this essay, Shelley responds to Peacock's declaration in 'The Four Ages of Poetry' that modern poets are 'wallowing in the rubbish of departed ignorance'[5] by declaring both that poetry is the 'centre and circumference of knowledge,' and that it is 'not subject to the control of the active powers of the mind' and has 'no necessary connection with consciousness or will':[6] poets, Shelley says, are themselves 'the most sincerely astonished at [art's] manifestations,' 'hierophants' as they are of an '*un*apprehended inspiration,' their words expressing 'what they understand *not*.'[7] Shelley is responding, not least, to Socrates' declaration in *Ion* that the poet is a 'light and winged and sacred thing' who is 'unable to indite until he has been inspired and put out of his senses, and his mind is no longer in him.'[8] More generally, though, the problem of knowing and its relationship with not knowing is embedded within the Romantic canon. In Keats's odes, for example, not knowing, mistaking, misunderstanding, neglecting, disregarding, ignoring are crucial concerns. 'Ode to Psyche' probes the question of whether the poet sees or dreams: 'Surely I dreamt to-day, or did I see/ The wingèd Psyche with awakened eyes?'. 'Ode to a Nightingale,' which also closes with such a question – 'Fled is that music – Do I wake or sleep?' – is a poem fully concerned with not knowing, with ignorance and forgetting. In this poem, the poet wishes to 'Fade far away, dissolve, and quite forget' what the bird 'among the leaves [has] never known' – he is concerned to take on the form of the unknowing nightingale, a desire which seems to be achieved in the sensory deprivation of stanza five when he 'cannot see what flowers are at my feet,/ Nor what soft incense hangs upon the boughs.' In 'Ode on a Grecian Urn' the rapt contemplation of the urn is itself *structured* by ignorance – ignorance of the ancient symbolism inscribed on the urn. The multiplying questions in stanzas one and four ('What leaf-fringed legend...? What men or gods...? What maidens loth...?'; and 'Who are these coming...? To what green altar...? What little town...?', and so on) offer few answers – as befits a poem which ends in a statement of inhuman knowledge, of knowing which also loudly declares the poet's and our own ignorance, declares the limits of our knowledge, a statement that has baffled readers and critics ever since. We know it, only too well: '"Beauty is truth, truth beauty, – that is all/ Ye know on earth, and all ye need to know".'

We also know that Keats's letters are full of the appreciation and evocation of ignorance – such as his declaration that what goes into forming a 'Man of Achievement' is 'negative capability,' a capacity for 'being in uncertainties, Mysteries, doubts, without any irritable reaching after fact & reason.'[9] But there seems to be in Keats – as there is in Shelley and Plato – a particular concern with the part that ignorance plays in composition itself, with the idea, for example, that Shakespeare's sonnets are 'full of fine things said unintentionally – in the intensity of working out conceits.'[10] In the Summer of 1820 Richard Woodhouse recorded some more extensive comments by Keats on his own inspirational compositional ignorance:

> He has said, that he has often not been aware of the beauty of some thought or expression until after he has composed & written it down – It has then struck him with astonishment – & seemed rather the production of another person than his own – He has wondered how he came to hit upon it [...] – Perhaps every one in the habit of writing verse or prose, may have had a somewhat similar feeling, that of the extreme appositeness & happiness (the curiosa felicitas) of an idea, of the excellence of which he was unaware until he [...] came to read it over. It seems scarcely his own; & he feels that he could never imitate it or hit upon it again: & he cannot conceive how it came to him – Such Keats said was his Sensation of astonishment & pleasure when he had produced the lines 'His white melodious &c' – It seemed to come by chance or magic – to be as it were something given to him. –[11]

Keats's comments suggest that the poem is not only 'other' to the reader but other indeed to the author him- or her-self. The author is only aware of the 'beauty of some thought or expression' after he has written it down. The expression strikes him with 'astonishment,' and as work not his own: he 'cannot conceive how he came upon it,' he cannot conceive, that is to say, how he conceived it, this chance or magic that comes upon him – just as, in 'Hyperion,' Apollo declares to Mnemosyne, the goddess of memory and of poetry, as his 'white melodious throat' 'throbs' with syllables, that her 'name is on my tongue, I know not how' (book 3, line 83). Rather than taking ignorance as a 'theme' in Romantic poetry, I want to focus on this idea of compositional ignorance as a mode of writing, and to consider its relationship with authorial intention and the notion of authorial identity, since some of the central critical and theoretical concerns that cluster around Romantic theories of poetry but which also have wider ramifications for culture, for the cultural, generally – issues of authorship, interpretation, reading, composition, inspiration and the nature of the literary institution, for example, as well as, at a further remove, aesthetic ideology, ethics, politics, personal identity, and indeed psychoanalytical, new historicist or other schools of contemporary criticism – are brought into focus by thinking about the question of poetic or compositional ignorance, by thinking about this question concerning the very possibility of poetic thinking.

***

In his search for a topic for his epic poem in Book One of *The Prelude* Wordsworth lists the various narratives that his poem might retell, narratives of history, of politics, of mythology. But he rejects them all and comes to the possibility that his poem might articulate 'some tale from my own head.' Again, though, he rejects this alternative since it would 'lack/ Foundation,' and he turns to philosophy, as a more properly 'foundational' discourse:

> Then, last wish –
> My last and favorite aspiration – then
> I yearn towards some philosophic song
> Of truth that cherishes our daily life,
> With meditations passionate from deep
> Recesses in man's heart, immortal verse
> Thoughtfully fitted to the Orphean lyre;
> But from this awful burthen I full soon
> Take refuge, and beguile myself with trust
> That mellower years will bring a riper mind
> And clearer insight. Thus from day to day
> I live a mockery of the brotherhood
> Of vice and virtue, with no skill to part
> Vague longing that is bred by want of power,
> From paramount impulse not to be withstood;

> A timorous capacity, from prudence;
> From circumspection, infinite delay.
> Humility and modest awe themselves
> Betray me, serving often for a cloak
> To a more subtle selfishness, that now
> Doth lock my functions up in blank reserve,
> Now dupes me by an over-anxious eye
> That with a false activity beats off
> Simplicity and self-presented truth.
> Ah, better far than this to stray about
> Voluptuously through fields and rural walks
> And ask no record of the hours given up
> To vacant musing, unreproved neglect
> Of all things, and deliberate holiday.
> Far better never to have heard the name
> Of zeal and just ambition than to live
> Thus baffled by a mind that every hour
> Turns recreant to her task, takes heart again,
> Then feels immediately some hollow thought
> Hang like an interdict upon her hopes.
> This is my lot; for either still I find
> Some imperfection in the chosen theme,
> Or see of absolute accomplishment
> Much wanting – so much wanting – in myself
> That I recoil and droop, and seek repose
> In indolence from vain perplexity,
> Unprofitably travelling towards the grave,
> Like a false steward who hath much received
> And renders nothing back.[12]

This marks the end of the false-start of Wordsworth's epic, the end of his search for a topic, and it is followed by the conventional epic beginning, 'Was it for this...,' which introduces the narrative of the poet's own life. But the passage is nevertheless exemplary of a certain conception of the nature of poetic knowledge and poetic thinking. In particular, it contrasts poetry with philosophy, suggesting indeed that poetic indolence is generated by means of a reaction against literature's other, by a reaction against 'philosophy' – as generated against the discipline of knowledge in the abstract sense of truth or wisdom. The 'Induction' to Wordsworth's poem – the opening 271 lines – is much troubled by the paradox of a writer writing about writer's block, of a writer writing about his inability to discover a topic. Indeed, it may be argued that it is through this realisation of the atopicality of poetry – a realisation that is engineered or provoked by the thought of philosophy – that Wordsworth discovers his subject, through the realisation that poetry, unlike philosophy, has nothing to say, no knowledge to impart, the realisation that the only proper topic of poetry can be the neglectful, voluptuous, vacant, vain and indolent topic of how the poet becomes a poet, of poetry about poetry.

In a letter to Thomas Poole of July 1800, Coleridge comments on precisely such an interdiction of thinking in Wordsworth's compositional practice. In a remark that might be taken as a gloss on this passage from *The Prelude*, Coleridge comments that his friend 'is well, unless he uses any effort of mind – then he feels a pain in his left side, which threatens to interdict all species of composition to him.'[13] The line 'Hang like an interdict upon her hopes' is itself something of an interdiction on thought, a speech act that may be said to come between the mind's own thoughts. Wordsworth presents a mind (a curiously feminized mind) that baffles itself, a mind baffled by 'some hollow thought' that hangs 'like an interdict upon her hopes.' Not only does the line comment on its own status as language, as poetry, through the rhetorical self-reflexion of and on the simile, but it also manages to baffle thought by the curiously abstract way in which the thought is concretized. It puts into question the opposition of philosophy to literature or at least puts into question one of the ways in which that opposition may be conceived – as the opposition of the abstracting, idealizing, transcendentalizing thought of *philosophy* to the contingent, visceral, rhetorical, linguistic performance of *poetry*. We are asked to imagine, that is to say, a 'hollow thought,' a thought with the physical quality of absence. This itself is something of a hollow thought, a thought with nothing inside, a thinking that baffles the mind – or, more properly put, we might say that Wordsworth evokes here a mind, a state of mind, an intellect or *nous*, that baffles thinking. In an involution of thinking – of the thought of thinking – that matches the self-reflexive involutions encountered in Keats's poem on *his* own mind, 'Ode to Psyche,' Wordsworth describes the work of a mind that baffles the subject by being itself baffled by thought. The thought that baffles the mind is itself somewhat baffling (we encounter the difficulty of thinking about a 'hollow thought'), a befuddlement that is only exacerbated by the simile. The thought, Wordsworth suggests, is like a particular kind of speech act, an 'interdict,' that kind of speech act which comes between in order to prohibit or forbid. In this case, the interdiction involves a prohibition on speech, on language: it is an act of speech that stops speech. The work of writing, of language, in other words, is what prevents the work of writing, of language.

As Coleridge's comments on the interdiction of composition consequent upon 'any effort of mind' suggest, and as this passage acknowledges, Wordsworth's poetry is in many ways determined by, organized around, a certain bafflement of thinking. Thinking in Wordsworth tends to form a site of linguistic and conceptual disturbance around which poems gather. *The Prelude* itself is full of strange, thoughtful moments of thought, of thinking, but we might equally recall some famous moments from *Lyrical Ballads* to illustrate the point. There is, for example, the Wordsworthian narrator's turn to the reader to insist that he or she should *think* in 'Goody Blake and Harry Gill' ('Now think, ye farmers all, I pray/ Of Goody Blake and Harry Gill'), or in 'Simon Lee' ('had you in your mind/ Such stores as silent thought can bring,/ O gentle Reader! You would find/ A tale in every thing');[14] there is the presentation of thinking as bearable or unbearable in 'Anecdote for Fathers,' where the narrator can 'bear/ To think, and think, and think again' – by contrast with Gordon in 'Ellen Irwin,' who 'cannot bear the thoughts/ That through his brain are travelling'; there is a more fully elaborated but strangely unresolved thinking about thinking in 'Lines Written in Early Spring,' a poem about the way that 'pleasant thoughts/ Bring sad thoughts to the mind,' and in which the narrator's heart 'grieves' 'to think/ What man has made of man,' in which he is moved to declare that he 'cannot measure' the thoughts of the birds around him (a strange thought, this) thinking that 'I must think, do all I can,/ That there was pleasure there,' troubled as he is that he 'these thoughts may not prevent'; there is the curious opacity of just what it was that the Idiot Boy can have been thinking in his travels over night around which the poem of that name revolves; there is an equally opaque thinking of the old man travelling, a man who 'does not move with pain, but moves/ With thought'; there is the veritable thesaurus of different kinds of thought that someone might entertain in 'Tintern Abbey,' with its evocation of 'half-extinguished thoughts,' of 'thoughtless youth,' of 'elevated thoughts,' of 'a motion and a spirit, that impels/ All thinking things, all objects of all thought,' and of the speaker's 'purest thoughts,' 'lofty thoughts,' 'healing thoughts,' and so on;[15] and there is, finally, the most difficult, the most uncanny thought, the thought of death, a thought which 'slides' into the lover's head in 'Strange Fits of Passion.' 'The mind often does not think, when it thinks that it is thinking,' Wordsworth is reported to have said in a comment that complicates our thinking of Wordsworth's thoughts about thinking.[16] And certainly his thought of death as 'A place of thought' in the Immortality ode (a thought that is later deleted after a baffled comment by Coleridge), gives a sense of the difficulties of, the complications in, Wordsworth's thinking of thinking.[17] In *The Prelude* itself, poetry appears to include a certain resistance to thinking, a particular kind of (non-)thinking which in its beguiling subtleties, its blank reserves, its vacant musings, its baffling recreance, disturbs the hard-won discriminations of philosophy: poetry is a 'mockery' of morality and epistemological certainty, beyond good and evil and beyond the thinking of the philosophers that Nietzsche in the preface to the book of that name names 'dogmatists.'[18] It is not by chance therefore that Coleridge ends his poem written after hearing Wordsworth recite *The Prelude* in 1807 with just such a thought or a thought of thought in suspense, when he describes himself as 'Scarce conscious,' with 'my being blended in one thought/ (Thought was it? or aspiration? or resolve?)/ Absorbed, yet hanging still upon the sound... .'[19]

In this context, the Wordsworthian or more generally the Romantic thinking of poetry may be conceived in terms of the interdict, in terms of speech-acts that come between and prohibit or suspend a certain conception of language, language as the bearer of knowledge, science, fact, truth – of thought. Poetry in this context may be aligned with what Richard Poirier in *Poetry and Pragmatism* calls a 'saving uncertainty and vagueness,'[20] or with insignificance, as Paul Fry has commented in *A Defense of Poetry*, when he defines poetry as a response to the 'blank opacity with which the world discloses its being.'[21] Both Poirier and Fry make compelling cases for a resistance to the idea of poetry as significant or meaningful, to the idea of poetry as promoting what Leo Bersani calls a 'culture of redemption' which finally makes the human subject significant.[22] And it is this resistance to the human, in particular to humanism's *conception*, its thinking, to the human linked with consciousness or thought, indeed with truth or knowledge, that Wordsworth may be understood to be articulating in *The Prelude*, with its reserves of blankness and vacany, its oppositions of the anthropomorphized mind to the absence or hollowness of thought. Against a perhaps more obvious reading of the final lines of the poem's introductory passage, lines which would load 'imperfection,' 'wanting,' 'indolence,' 'vain perplexity,' 'unprofitably,' 'grave' and 'false steward' with a sense of sheer condemnation, I want to suggest that it is precisely perplexity and imperfection that the poetry may be said to celebrate. Poetry, by this account, encapsulates, provokes, stimulates or performs – beyond a certain point – a certain thoughtlessness or thoughtful unthinking, a certain ignorance.

***

One of the problems raised by such a thinking of poetry or by such a thinking of thinking in poetry is its challenge to a certain sense of authorial intention. The compositional problem with which Wordsworth is engaging as he starts to write *The Prelude* may be conceived rather differently as being bound up with an apparently more 'modern' – or even post-Romantic – concern, with the question of authorial intentionality. E. D. Hirsch, whose work on intentionality has now spanned four decades, is the most consistent and most well-known advocate for intentionalism in literary criticism, for the intentionality of the literary act. His two books, *Validity in Interpretation* and *The Aims of Interpretation* from 1967 and 1976 respectively have been followed by two essays, 'Meaning and Significance Reinterpreted' from 1984 and 'Transhistorical Intentions and the Persistence of Allegory' from 1994. Both of the essays are concerned with a problem which was touched upon but not, to Hirsch's mind at least, satisfactorily resolved in the earlier books – the problem with which we began, of future reading, of the reading of posterity. As Hirsch argues, certain kinds of writing – including writing that since the Romantic period we have tended to call 'literature' – 'typically intends to convey meaning beyond its immediate occasion into a future context which is very different from that of its production.'[23] In his *Intentionalist Interpretation: A Philosophical Explanation and Defense* (1999), William Irwin has recently elaborated this idea by addressing the question of the conventional notion that literary texts are supposed to be 'universal' or 'timeless.' On the face of it, this might seem to work against the intentionalist position that the meaning of a text is synonymous with what the author intended by it, since when we talk about the 'timelessness' of a Shakespeare sonnet, for example, what we mean is that such a text can be interpreted *differently* at *different* times. If this was not the case, rather than being 'timeless' the sonnet would be time-bound and its interest ultimately limited or finite. For Irwin, this is where criticism comes in. 'Criticism,' Irwin remarks, 'is an essential operation in keeping literary texts fresh, alive, and read with each passing generation and era': criticism therefore has the 'vital task' of 'demonstrating the relevance of the text to our own time – showing that what Shakespeare wrote was indeed timeless.'[24] But Irwin goes on to argue that this 'need not be at odds with the meaning the author intends':

> As Hirsch says of Shakespeare's Sonnet 55...'The author's intention in this poem (and this is characteristic of literature, law, and religion) includes an intention to communicate effectively into the future'. This underscores the point that authors of literary texts may have intentions of various types.... An author's intention may be specific or vague, firmly grounded in the present or open to future applications, productive of logical reasoning or of aesthetic experience. The possibilities are nearly endless.... Whatever the author intended to communicate is, as we have argued, the meaning of the text'.[25]

Hirsch is right, I think, to say that Shakespeare's sonnet appears to include 'an intention to communicate effectively into the future.' But it is significant that in both his 1984 and his 1994 essays he chooses to focus on this particular poem, one that takes as its subject-matter the idea of communicating effectively into the future. In this sonnet, it is precisely the nature of such a future which is at stake:

> Not marble, nor the gilded monuments
> Of princes shall outlive this pow'rful rhyme,
> But you shall shine more bright in these contents
> Than unswept stone besmearched with sluttish time.
> When wasteful war shall statues overturn,
> And broils root out the work of masonry,
> Nor Mars his sword, nor war's quick fire shall burn
> The living record of your memory.
> 'Gainst death, and all oblivious enmity
> Shall you pace forth, your praise shall still find room,
> Even in the eyes of all posterity
> That wear this world out to the ending doom.
> So, till the judgement that yourself arise,
> You live in this, and dwell in lovers' eyes.[26]

I want to suggest that the success of the poem's 'communication' with the future is a function of the fact that the intention to last, to live on, *conflicts with* the intention to communicate, with the intention to 'communicate effectively,' and indeed that poetry may be conceived precisely in terms of the production of *and* the resistance to, the suspension of, 'communication.' But what happens to Irwin's declaration that 'Whatever the author intended to communicate is...the meaning of the text' – what happens to this claim if what the author intends to communicate is the *resistance* to communication? While we might accept that texts of law or religion have it as their purpose, their 'intention,' to 'communicate effectively' with the future as well as the present, it may be that what makes a poem a poem, and what indeed makes it last, is its disturbance of 'effective communication.' In the end, I want to suggest, this links with our concern with ignorance, the author's and the reader's. But before I get to this point, it might be helpful to read from a certain perspective Shakespeare's sonnet.

The force of Shakespeare's 'powerful rhyme' is constituted, at least in part, by an aporia, by the figure of non-interpretability – of unreadability, to use Paul de Man's term – by the figure of the resistance to communication.

Shakespeare's poem, I think, is exemplary just in as much as it presents an opacity, a blockage or barrier to interpretation in relation to its presentation of temporality, in its striving to 'communicate effectively into the future.' The argument of the poem is that 'you' – the young man who appears to be the addressee of the first 126 of the sonnets – will 'live in this,' will live on in this poem beyond the young man's and presumably the author's own death but also, more importantly, beyond the life-span of 'marble' and 'gilded monuments' since, as material artifacts, these are necessarily subject to decay and destruction, necessarily subject to 'sluttish time.' And yet, in a familiar irony, the addressee, the 'you,' of the poem does not 'live' in the poem, even metaphorically, *except* in this address, in this 'you,' since the poem is not concerned to describe the young man or to list his qualities but rather to describe his survival in words, to figure him in language, substituting his life, his survival, for the poem's, indeed for the poem's argument *about* his survival. What lasts is not the young man but the poem, this 'powerful rhyme' and its powerful arguments concerning the survival not so much of young men but of poems. It is only to the extent that the poem lives on that the young man will, and then only by association, only tangentially, incidentally – only indeed as the subject of a deictic gesture of reference. This, as I say, is a familiar irony, as is the fact that, at the same time, memorializing the young man means, in effect, killing him, figuring his death, representing his being dead: 'you live in this,' declares the speaker but only, implicitly, to the extent that 'you' are text, *only* in this – only in this 'this' (or this 'you', this word 'you'). As the double deixis reveals in its gesture of concealment of this fact, the young man lives only to the extent that he is *not* present, only to the extent that he is constitutionally, fundamentally absent, only to the extent that this 'this' and this 'you' is language. But such a reading of the sonnet, such an interpretation of Shakespeare's intention, works against that other reading, works against our understanding that the poem is about the intention to effect the young man's survival, the sense that the performative address, the apostrophic 'you,' allows the young man to live, to live on, to live now. On a very basic level, then, Shakespeare's sonnet 'communicates' (at least) two contradictory senses, senses that work against each other and resist the imputation of effective communication. Hirsch's point is that Shakespeare's intention in the sonnet 'includes an intention to communicate effectively in the future' and that he intended that 'his future meaning should *not* be restricted to his own moment.'[27] What I want to suggest, as I say, is that the poem communicates effectively precisely to the extent that it *fails* to comunicate effectively: for the poem to succeed, for the poem both to 'communicate' and to 'live' or to survive, to go on being read, the reader must remain in a state of uncertainty, of communicative suspense, must remain in a state of what we are calling ignorance. Beyond the numerous questions of verbal and rhetorical detail that vex Shakespeare's commentators on this sonnet, there are a number of overarching questions: is the young man represented as alive or dead? what is it exactly in this regard that the poem is attempting to communicate? These of course are questions which may be subsumed within another urgent, unanswerable question: what, finally, does the author intend? Does he intend to celebrate the young man's survival, or his death and the poem's superior, more powerful, more enduring life? Paradoxically, of course, it is precisely this resistance to interpretation, to communication, that enables us, that forces us to go on reading the poem, that makes it 'timeless' in Hirsch's sense of that term (which means, as it usually does in this context, something like 'timely,' of and in time, operating over time and through time): the uncertainty of what Shakespeare intends is what makes the poem 'timeless.'

Hirsch himself concedes some of this in his 1984 essay, 'Meaning and Significance Reinterpreted.' As we have seen, for Hirsch, Shakespeare's intention 'includes an intention to communicate effectively in the future.' By allowing for this future communication, Hirsch also allows for the possibility that such communication includes elements unforeseen by the author himself, he allows that the author may be communicating something that he did not intend, he allows for what he calls the 'provisionality' of the intention. But Hirsch still argues for the coherence and 'self-identity' of authorially intended meaning, for the author's 'self-same meaning' even while admitting that 'minor conceptual adjustments' will be produced by historical changes in understanding. By contrast, I want to suggest that what we mean by poetry – what we mean by the word because this is what the Romantics have perhaps unwittingly programmed us to mean by the word – involves a certain programmed unprogrammability, a resistance to the understanding, coherence, self-identity, that for Hirsch makes meaning. It is precisely this incalculability, this unprogrammability that Derrida points to when he announces in *Glas* – in a statement which can be taken to be axiomatic of all reading, of all acts of interpretation – that 'you can take interest in what I am doing here only insofar as you would be right to believe that – *somewhere* – I do not know what I am doing.'[28] According to the strong intentionalist case – that of Hirsch and Irwin – my reading of the poem is valid only in so much as it coincides, somewhere, with the intention of the poem's author, allowing for that intention to include a certain 'tolerance,' certain minor semantic or hermeneutic perturbations over the centuries. But I want to suggest that such coincidence is written out of this poem. Or, to put it more accurately, the poem also resists such coincidence. If I have properly analyzed Shakespeare's intention, if I have accurately interpreted the text as including the intention at once to communicate effectively and to resist communicating effectively, then he will have failed in his intention, or at least in part of it, in his intention to resist effective communication. If my reading is right it is wrong, in other words, but this can only mean that communication has failed, which means, in another sense, succeeded.

In his recent edition of the sonnets, Colin Burrow allows himself a certain levity in wittily under-stating that the sonnets are 'not easy poems.' But if they 'thwart readers' desires to know,' he goes on, they 'do so artfully and with a systematic elusiveness.'[29] While we might agree that the poems thwart readers' desires to know, we might at the same time question the terms of this thwarting, its artfulness and systematization. What Burrow's formulation fails to allow, to allow for, is a Keatsian sense of fine things being said unintentionally, or a Laplanchean sense that the one who sends a message is other to himself and 'does not entirely know what he is saying,' or a Derridean sense that we might take an interest in a text just insofar as we are right to believe precisely that 'somewhere' the author does not know what he is doing. This is not of course simply to argue against authorial intention in acts of interpretation. My intention (I promise) is not to argue for or against Hirschian or other models of authorial intention as such, but to suggest that the very project that Hirsch is involved in, the ascription of 'meaning' to a poem, itself begs the question of authorial ignorance. There is much, too much, we do not know about Shakespeare and about his poetry. What I want to suggest, however, is that in reading Sonnet 55 we are dealing not only with our ignorance of Shakespeare's intentions but with an ignorance deep within acts of speech themselves, as it is deep within the transference and deep within the literary 'speech-act,' the poem, as conceived by Romanticism. Shakespeare's sonnet is constituted in and by an exemplary ignorance, an ignorance that amounts to a certain unprogrammability: the poem's future of reading, the poem's future reading, is the unknown, unknowable axis of its meaning.

***

Literary language, according to Gilles Deleuze, 'seems to be seized by a delirium which forces [language] out of its usual furrows.'[30] I want to finish with a brief coda that will help to illustrate this thought and connect it to ignorance by returning to two generations of Romantic poets, to Keats and Wordsworth. Both poets present us with famously strange moments of poetic communication that also involve ignorance, not knowing. It is well known that in Book Five of *The Prelude* Wordsworth recounts a dream told to him by his friend in which his friend meets an Arab holding a stone and a shell. The stone represents geometry or mathematics, while the shell represents poetry. The poet[31] holds the shell to his ear and hears

> ...that instant in an unknown tongue,
> Which yet I understood, articulate sounds,
> A loud prophetic blast of harmony,
> An ode in passion uttered... (Book 5, lines 94-7)

The 'articulate sounds' of the ode are, impossibly, both understood and in an 'unknown tongue': the passage presents poetry as both the subject of understanding and the subject of ignorance. It is poetry because it is both. There is no coincidence, I think, in the fact that a similar but here highly eroticized effect is encountered in Keats's 'La Belle Dame sans Merci,' where the speaker declares that the gorgeous, deathly woman he encounters speaks to him in a language which is at the same time 'strange' *and* translatable:

> And sure in language strange she said –
> 'I love thee true'. (lines 27-8)

The language is strange, foreign, other, and yet understood. And the translation is framed by an uncertain knowing, a knowing uncertainty. 'Sure' denotes both the poet's certainty that this is what the woman said and the woman's sense of security in speaking a strange language. But at the same time the word includes the possibility of *uncertainty*, 'sure' as suggesting that the poet has doubts: *surely* she said that, *surely* I have understood....[32]

This is poetry, then, and reading: a certain uncertainty, the state of being 'sure,' *surely*, that one reads aright this language strange, this unknown tongue, this poetry. It is an effect in effect of ignorance, of not knowing (quite) what one is reading, because of the determination of poetry by a certain ignorance, because of our certainty that poets are people like us, that poets – somewhere – do not know what they are doing.

## Notes

[1] Jean Laplanche, 'Transference: Its Provocation by the Analyst,' in *Essays on Otherness* (London: Routledge, 1999), p. 229.

[2] Ibid., p. 224.

³ See my *Romantic Poets and the Culture of Posterity* (Cambridge University Press, 1999) for an elaboration of the idea that while this predicament is not confined to the Romantic poet, it is nevertheless a distinctively Romantic thinking of poetry, a distinctively Romantic poetics.
⁴ John Keats, *Collected Poems*, ed. John Barnard, 3rd edn. (London: Penguin, 1988), p. 521. Quotations from Keats's poems are from this edition.
⁵ Thomas Love Peacock, 'The Four Ages of Poetry,' in David Bromwich (ed.), *Romantic Critical Essays* (Cambridge University Press, 1987), p. 208.
⁶ Percy Bysshe Shelley, *Poems and Prose*, ed. Timothy Webb (London: Dent, 1995), pp. 273, 277.
⁷ Ibid., p. 279 (italics added).
⁸ Plato, *Ion*, trans. W. R. M. Lamb (London: William Heinemann, 1952), p. 423 (534B). 'Mind' in Plato is 'nous' – 'intellect,' 'mind,' 'nous'.
⁹ *The Letters of John Keats, 1814-1821*, 2 vols., ed. Hyder Edward Rollins (Cambridge, Mass.: Harvard University Press, 1958), I. 193.
¹⁰ Ibid., I. 188.
¹¹ *The Keats Circle*, 2nd edn., 2 vols., ed. Hyder Edward Rollins (Cambridge, Mass.: Harvard University Press, 1965), I. 129 (cancelled readings and contractions omitted).
¹² William Wordsworth, *The Prelude, 1799, 1805, 1850*, ed. Jonathan Wordsworth, M. H. Abrams, and Stephen Gill (New York: Norton, 1979): 1805, book 1, lines 228-71.
¹³ *Collected Letters of Samuel Taylor Coleridge*, ed. Earl Leslie Griggs, vol. 1 (Oxford University Press, 1956), p. 608.
¹⁴ Wordsworth and Coleridge, *Lyrical Ballads*, eds R. L. Brett and A. R. Jones (London: Methuen, 1968).
¹⁵ See John A. Hodgson, *Wordsworth's Philosophical Poetry, 1797-1814* (Lincoln: University of Nebraska Press, 1980), pp. 29-40, on the permutations of thinking and thought in 'Tintern Abbey.'
¹⁶ Alexander B. Grosart, ed., *The Prose Works of William Wordsworth*, vol. 3 (London: Edward Moxon, 1876), p. 460.
¹⁷ See 'Ode: Intimations of Immortality' (1807), line 121, and Coleridge, *Biographia Literaria*, ch. 22. Compare Frances Ferguson, *Wordsworth: Language as Counter-Spirit* (New Haven: Yale University Press, 1977), pp. 123-25, on the way that in the 'Immortality Ode' thought itself 'becomes an almost unimaginable subject for contemplation' (p. 126).
¹⁸ Friedrich Nietzsche, *Beyond Good and Evil: Prelude to a Philosophy of the Future*, trans. Helen Zimmer, 4th edn. (London: George Allen, 1923), pp. 1-2.
¹⁹ Samuel Taylor Coleridge, 'To William Wordsworth,' in *The Complete Poems*, ed. William Keach (London: Penguin, 1997), p. 342.
²⁰ Richard Poirier, *Poetry and Pragmatism* (London: Faber and Faber, 1992), p. 4.
²¹ Paul H. Fry, *A Defense of Poetry: Reflections on the Occasion of Writing* (Stanford: University of Stanford Press, 1995), p. 7. Compare Jacques Derrida on the idea

that 'poetry and literature have as a common feature that they suspend the "thetic" naivety of the transcendent reading' in 'This Strange Institution Called Literature: An Interview with Jacques Derrida,' in *Acts of Literature*, ed. Derek Attridge (London: Routledge, 1992), p. 45.

22. Leo Bersani, *The Culture of Redemption* (Cambridge, Mass.: Harvard University Press, 1990).
23. E. D. Hirsch, Jr., 'Transhistorical Intentions and the Persistence of Allegory,' *New Literary History* 25 (1994), p. 552.
24. William Irwin, *Intentionalist Interpretation: A Philosophical Explanation and Defense* (Westport, Connecticut: Greenwood Press, 1999), pp. 116-17.
25. Ibid., p. 117; quoting Hirsch 'Meaning and Significance Reinterpreted,' *Critical Inquiry* 11 (1984), p. 205.
26. William Shakespeare, *Complete Sonnets and Poems*, ed. Colin Burrow (Oxford University Press, 2002), p. 491.
27. Hirsch, 'Meaning and Significance,' pp. 205-6.
28. Quoted in Peggy Kamuf, *Signature Pieces: On the Institution of Authorship* (Ithaca: Cornell University Press, 1988), p. 125.
29. Burrow, ed., *Complete Sonnets and Poems*, p. 138.
30. Gilles Deleuze, 'Literature and Life,' *Critical Inquiry* 3 (1997), p. 9.
31. In 1850, the subject of the dream, the dreamer, is explicitly figured as the poet himself.
32. See my *Keats, Narrative and Audience: The Posthumous Life of Writing* (Cambridge University Press, 1994), pp. 114-15.

# HOME THOUGHTS FROM ABROAD: WORDSWORTH'S 'MUSINGS NEAR AQUAPENDENTE'

Peter J. Manning

This essay begins in lines from Wordsworth's little considered last published separate volume, *Poems, Chiefly of Early and Late Years*:

> Utter thanks, my Soul!
> Tempered with awe, and sweetened by compassion
> For them who in the shades of sorrow dwell,
> That I – so near the term of human life
> Appointed by man's common heritage,
> Frail as the frailest, one withal (if that
> Deserve a thought) but little known to fame –
> Am free to rove where Nature's loveliest looks,
> Art's noblest relics, history's rich bequests,
> Failed to reanimate and but feebly cheered
> The whole world's Darling. . . .(88-98)[1]

It does not seem too crude to paraphrase this passage as 'Scott is dead, but thank God I'm alive,' a sentiment that struck me as so brutally self-regarding that I could not get it out of my head. I attempt to understand the lines by working through their contexts and their functions, moving between biography, literary history, and criticism. Stephen Gill observes that in 'Musings Near Aquapendente' 'Wordsworth's strongest poetic strategies operate once again in what is his last of many poems of friendship and his last substantial elegy,'[2] but the oddity of the poem leads to questions about the uses of friendship, the nature of Wordsworthian strength, and the intrinsically comparative nature of literary reputation.

'Musings Near Aquapendente,' subtitled 'April, 1837,' purports to be a spontaneous rumination on Wordsworth's visit to the waterfall and the town named for it. 'Musings' recalls the deliberately low key 'Lines' of 'Lines written a few miles above Tintern Abbey,' a poem which also includes a date in its title as a signal of fidelity to experience. Unlike 'Tintern Abbey,' composed within days of Wordsworth's return visit to the Wye, 'Musings Near Aquapendente' was not written until 1841, when Wordsworth had long since returned to England (See *PW* 3:490).[3] The delayed composition is typical, but the date underscores that Wordsworth represented his friendship with Scott only at Scott's death in 1832 and afterwards.

Scott and Wordsworth learned of each other in the Fall of 1800.[4] In September 1803 William and Dorothy, touring Scotland, paid Scott a surprise visit. Scott recited the unfinished *Lay of The Last Minstrel*, leading Wordsworth to declare that 'the clear picturesque descriptions, and the easy glowing energy of so much of the verse, greatly delighted me' (Johnson, 213). On returning to Grasmere Wordsworth sent Scott, at his request, a sonnet he had composed during their visit, signing his letter: 'Your sincere Friend, for such I will call myself, though slow to use a word of such solemn meaning to anyone.'[5] Gill nicely contrasts this affection with the coolness he had shown to De Quincey just three months before: 'My friendship it is not in my power to give: this is a gift which no man can make, it is not in our own power: a sound and healthy friendship is the growth of time and circumstance' (Gill, *Life* 216; *EY* 400). In January 1805 Wordsworth sent Scott 'Yarrow Unvisited,' commenting that he wrote the stanzas 'not without a view of pleasing you.'

By March 1805 Wordsworth had received from Scott the published *Lay of the Last Minstrel*, and wrote to say that 'High as our expectations were, I have the pleasure to say that the Poem has surpassed them much. We think you have completely attained your object; the Book is throughout interesting and entertaining, and the picture of manners as lively as possible' (*EY* 553). The hint that 'your object' might be different from Wordsworth's own became explicit when he received Scott's next narrative poem in 1808: 'Thank you for Marmion which I have read with lively pleasure – I think your end has been attained; that it is not in every respect the end which I should wish you to propose to yourself, you will be well aware from what you know of my notions of composition, both as to matter and manner.' Such candor might seem ungenerous, especially when Wordsworth continues that he has 'heard that in the world' *Marmion* is not 'as well liked as the Lay,' and concludes that he has been misquoted:

> in the notes you have quoted two lines of mine from memory [from 'Yarrow Unvisited'], and your memory admirable as it is, has here failed you. The passage stands with you
> The Swans in (or on) *sweet* St. Mary's lake –
> The proper reading is –
> The *Swan* on *still* St Mary's lake
> I mention this in order that the erratum may be corrected in a future edition.[6]

Wordsworth devotes as much space to observing a single-line misquotation in a note as he does to Scott's 377-page poem, fails even to acknowledge Scott's gracious quoting 'my friend Mr. Wordsworth's lines,' and while complaining that Scott has been inattentive to his verse and demanding a correction, cannot even trouble to quote Scott correctly – 'in (or on)'; Scott wrote 'on.'

The gap between the two men *as poets* had been apparent from the beginning. John Lockhart, drawing on Wordsworth's conversation, reconstructs his first impressions of Scott:

> [O]n the whole he attached much less importance to his literary labours or reputation than to his bodily sports, exercises, and social amusements; and yet he spoke of his profession as if he had already given up almost all hope of rising by it; and some allusion being made to its profits, observed that 'he was sure he could, if he chose, get more money than he should ever wish to have from the booksellers.'[7]

To Wordsworth, in his thirties with his reputation to establish, Scott's man-of-the-world ease and unabashed focus on the financial aspects of his poetry must have been particularly surprising.

The distance between Wordsworth's concern for his art and Scott's professionalism did not estrange the two men. In August 1805 Scott came to the Lakes and climbed Helvellyn with Wordsworth. In April 1807 the Wordsworths met Scott in London and he returned with them in May to Coleorton, the home of Sir George Beaumont, where they had wintered. In July the Wordsworths visited Bolton Abbey, and by the end of the year Wordsworth began *The White Doe of Rylstone*, based on a legend in Thomas Whitaker's *History and Antiquities of the Deanery of Craven* (1805). The Border setting of this episode from the great Rising in the North of 1569 would have suggested that Wordsworth, disappointed by the returns of *Poems, In Two Volumes* the year before, was influenced by the popularity of Scott's narratives, even had Whitaker not himself made the connection: 'Had the milk-white doe performed her mysterious pilgrimage from Ettrick Forest to the precincts of Dryburgh or Melrose, the elegant and ingenious editor of the "Border Minstrelsy" would have wrought it into a beautiful story.'[8] Scott proffered Wordsworth some information about the protagonists of *The White Doe*, which Wordsworth firmly rejected: 'Thank you for the interesting particulars about the Nortons: I shall like much to see them for their own sakes; but so far from being serviceable to my Poem they would stand in the way of it; as I have followed (as I was in duty bound to do) the traditionary and common historic records — Therefore I shall say in this case, a plague upon this industrious Antiquarianism that has put my fine story to confusion –' (*MY* 237).

After such a demarcation, it does not surprise that for the next fifteen years the exchanges between Scott and Wordsworth were largely confined to occasional meetings in London, though Scott claimed in 1807 to have made Francis Jeffrey 'admire the song of Lord Clifford's Minstrel, which I like exceedingly myself,'[9] and Wordsworth permitted him to include *Tintern Abbey* in his 1810 collection, *English Minstrelsy* (Johnson, 308). Scott anonymously reviewed himself and Wordsworth in 'The Living Poets of Great Britain,' in the *Edinburgh Annual Register for 1808*. There he declared that 'A better heart, a purer and more manly source of honourable and virtuous sentiment beats not . . . within Britain,' but he characterized Wordsworth as 'hitherto an unsuccessful competitor for poetical fame,' and ascribed his lack of popularity to his seclusion, pointedly comparing him to 'a person accustomed to navigate a small boat upon a narrow lake, to whom, if he possess an active imagination, the indentures of the shore, which hardly strike the passing stranger, acquire the importance of creeks, bays, and promontories.'[10] In so doing his assessment converges with that expressed by Francis Jeffrey in his review of *Poems, In Two Volumes* in the *Edinburgh Review*.

In Scott's review the relationship between Wordsworth and Scott shifts from the biographical to the public, and the citation of Jeffrey seals the shift in my discussion. Scott is surprisingly absent from Wordsworth's poetry through 1815, but their conjunction is sharp in the November 1814 issue of the *Edinburgh Review*, the issue that notoriously begins with Francis Jeffrey's unsigned review of *The Excursion*: 'This will never do.' Jeffrey accuses the poem of 'bear[ing] no doubt the stamp of the author's heart and fancy; but unfortunately not half so visibly as that of his peculiar system.' Jeffrey deepens Wordsworth's 'peculiarity' into the symptoms of an incurable disease, a stubborn refusal to adapt, caused by '[l]ong habits of seclusion, and an excessive ambition of originality.' Dismissing Wordsworth as 'fantastic, obscure, and affected,' he repeatedly excoriates his 'wretched and provoking *perversity* [my italics] of taste and judgment.'[11]

In the same issue of the *Edinburgh Review* Jeffrey also noticed Scott's *Waverley*.[12] Juxtaposing the opening sentence of this favorable review with the condemnation of Wordsworth focuses Jeffrey's assumptions. 'It is wonderful,' Jeffrey begins, 'what genius and adherence to nature will do.' Genius, the term that in contemporary critical discourse usually licenses transgression, Jeffrey firmly subordinates to nature: 'The secret of this success

. . . is merely that the author is a person of genius; and that he has, notwithstanding, had virtue enough to be true to nature throughout, and to content himself, even in the marvellous parts of his story, with copying from actual existences, rather than from the phantasms of his own imagination.'

Throughout Jeffrey praises Scott for a 'faithful and animated picture of the manners and state of society that prevailed in this northern part of the island, in the earlier part of the century,' insisting on 'the perfect accuracy of the picture' Scott has drawn. The emphasis on ocular fidelity connects with the second article in the volume, which Jeffrey as editor presumably deliberately placed immediately following the review of *The Excursion*, a discussion of the claims of the Cassegrainian Telescope that renders explicit the standards of exact observation and empirical truth that underlie the endorsement of Scott. Jeffrey particularly lauds the 'extraordinary felicity . . . with which all the inferior agents in the story are represented.' Even those who lack first-hand knowledge of 'the traits of Scottish national character in the lower ranks,' he argues, will appreciate the justice of the portrayal: 'It requires only a general knowledge of human nature, to feel that they must be faithful copies from known originals.'

The contrast between healthy, extroverted Scott and pathologized, introverted Wordsworth became commonplace.[13] In the review of *The Excursion* that Wordsworth read as it appeared in *The Examiner* from August to October 1814, Hazlitt observed of Wordsworth that '[a]ll other interests are absorbed in the deeper interest of his own thoughts' and continued that his 'poems in general are the history of a refined and contemplative mind, conversant only with itself and nature.' Solitude in nature becomes morbid in Hazlitt's succeeding generalization: 'All country-people hate each other.'[14] In the lecture 'On the Living Poets' with which Hazlitt concluded his *Lectures on the English Poets* in 1818 he remarked that Scott 'never obtrudes himself on your notice to prevent your seeing the subject. What passes in the poem, passes much as it would have done in reality. The author has little or nothing to with it.' Wordsworth Hazlitt characterizes as 'the reverse of Walter Scott in his defects and excellencies,' throwing this faint praise into relief: 'His poetry is not external, but internal . . . he furnishes it from his own mind, and is his own subject. . . . His egotism is in some respects a madness.'[15] Hazlitt printed a reduction of his *Examiner* review in *The Round Table* in 1817, and returned to Wordsworth and Scott in *The Spirit of the Age* in 1825. He there argues that Scott's novels had rightly eclipsed his metrical romances: Scott, he contends, 'does not soar above and look down upon his subject, imparting his own lofty views and feelings to his descriptions of nature' (Maclean, 225-26). Wordsworth then appears as Scott's antithesis:

'We do not think our author has any very cordial sympathy with Shakespear. How should he? Shakespear was the least of an egotist of any body in the world.' The chapter concludes with warning Wordsworth of the danger 'of becoming the God of his own idolatry!' (Maclean, 258, 261).

The distinctions the reviewers drew were dramatized when Scott visited the Lakes in August 1825, for festivities honoring him and George Canning, the Foreign Secretary. In letters to his wife, Scott's daughter, Lockhart narrated the first encounter between the two men in ten years:

> Wordsworth is old and pompous, and fine, and absurdly arrogant beyond conception – evidently thinks Canning and Scott together not worth his thumb. . . .[W]e with Wordsworth and his daughter went to Keswick, – he spouting his own verses very grandly all the way. . . .[D]uring all these rides, etc. the Unknown was continually quoting Wordsworth's Poetry and Wordsworth*ditto*, but that the great Laker never uttered one syllable by which it might have been intimated to a stranger that your Papa had ever written a line either of verse or prose since he was born. (Grierson, 9:207n.2, 211n.1)

By their next meeting bankruptcy had fallen on Scott, followed by overwork, illness, and a stroke.[16] News of a seizure drew from Wordsworth a direct avowal: 'Dear Sir Walter! I love that Man, though I can scarcely be said to have lived with him at all; but I have known him for nearly 30 years.'[17] Scott's doctors advised him to winter in Italy, and in August 1831 he wrote urging Wordsworth to fulfill his longstanding promise to visit, 'adding that if I did not come soon to see him it might be too late' (*LY*, 421). Wordsworth was not in much better health; he and Dora arrived on September 19, just five days before Scott's departure. He found Scott 'a good deal changed' (*LY*, 441); the gravely ill host took his visitors to Newark Castle, and two days later wrote a few stanzas in Dora's album, misspelling his own name, and telling her that 'I should not have done anything of this kind but for your Father's sake: they are probably the last verses I shall ever write' (*PW* 3:526).

Wordsworth was shaken, and his emotion turned him to his own poetry. The tour that had begun with the visit to Scott produced the 'Poems Composed During a Tour in Scotland, and on the English Border, in the Autumn of 1831' that make up the first section of *Yarrow Revisited*. The specter of Scott, as Gill astutely notes, also drove Wordsworth to put 'in order past poetry, so that, should he be afflicted like Scott, fair-copy manuscripts would be ready for the press' (Gill, *Life* 372). In June 1832 he published a further, four-volume, *Collected Works*.

Before Scott left for Italy Wordsworth had sent him 'Yarrow Revisited,' closing the series that had begun when he sent him 'Yarrow Unvisited' in 1805, and a sonnet, 'On the Departure of Sir Walter Scott from Abbotsford, for Naples.' 'Yarrow Revisited' is familiar, but the sonnet is less well known:

> A trouble, not of clouds, or weeping rain,
> Nor of the setting sun's pathetic light
> Engendered, hangs o'er Eildon's triple height:
> Spirits of Power, assembled there, complain
> For kindred Power departing from their sight:
> While Tweed, best pleased in chanting a blithe strain,
> Saddens his voice again, and yet again.
> Lift up your hearts, ye Mourners! For the might
> Of the whole world's good wishes with him goes:
> Blessings and prayers in nobler retinue
> Than sceptred King or laurelled Conqueror knows,
> Follow this wondrous Potentate. Be true,
> Ye winds of ocean, and the midland sea,
> Wafting your Charge to soft Parthenope![18]

As 'Mourners' (l. 8) suggests, the poem is a proleptic elegy for Scott. The poem adheres to the scene Wordsworth saw as the two men came back from Newark Castle:

> On our return in the afternoon we had to cross the Tweed directly opposite Abbotsford. The wheels of our carriage grated upon the pebbles in the bed of the stream, that there flows somewhat rapidly; a rich but sad light of rather a purple than a golden hue was spread over the Eildon hills at that moment; and, thinking it probable that it might be the last time Sir Walter would cross the stream, I was not a little moved, and expressed some of my feelings in the sonnet. (*PW* 3:526)

The light is also that which Wordsworth had specified in the 'Essay Upon Epitaphs' appended to *The Excursion*:

> The character of a deceased Friend or beloved Kinsman is not seen, no – nor ought to be seen, otherwise than as a Tree through a tender haze or a luminous mist, that spiritualizes and beautifies it. . . .

Placing Scott at the center of the sonnet, Wordsworth casts the action as

'Spirits of Power, assembled there, complain[ing]/ For kindred Power departing from their sight' (ll. 4-5) rather than as the exercise of his own imaginative powers: the Wordsworthian 'I' is missing from the poem.[19] This elimination correlates with the imagining of Scott as already deceased: the double disappearance enables an act of generosity that forgets all Wordsworth's condescension to Scott's poetic practice and envy of his success.[20] The unremarkable conventionality of the language carries the impersonality Wordsworth had praised in that essay: 'The first requisite, then, in an Epitaph is, that it should speak, in a tone which shall sink into the heart, the general language of humanity as connected with the subject of Death.'[21]

Though not strictly an epitaph, because neither inscribed on a gravestone nor exploiting the fiction that it is, the impersonality marks the poem as a representative gesture, speaking 'the whole world's good wishes' rather than Wordsworth *in propria persona*. This public quality makes it appropriate that in early December 1831 Wordsworth sent the poem to Alaric Watts for publication in the *Literary Souvenir*. It was published on p. 1 of the *Literary Souvenir* for 1833 not long after Scott's death on September 21, 1832 (*LY* 462 and n.5): Wordsworth thus appeared almost immediately as Scott's elegist, and so shaped the narrative of their relationship. The poem's power to fix Wordsworth as Scott's deeply grieving friend was magnified when Lockhart used it in the *Memoirs* – to which I will return – to close his chapter on Scott's last night at Abbotsford before the futile trip to Italy, where it occupies a page by itself (Lockhart, 7:311).

Scott figures also in the 'Extempore Effusion Upon The Death Of James Hogg.' Reading in November 1835 of the death of James Hogg, Wordsworth was moved within the half hour to compose the elegy that opens by twinning Hogg with Scott:

> When first, descending from the moorlands,
> I saw the Stream of Yarrow glide
> Along a bare and open valley,
> The Ettrick Shepherd was my guide.
>
> When last along its banks I wandered,
> Through groves that had begun to shed
> Their golden leaves upon the pathways,
> My steps the border minstrel led.

> The mighty Minstrel breathes no longer,
> Mid mouldering ruins low he lies;
> And death upon the braes of Yarrow,
> Has closed the Shepherd-poet's eyes.[22]

The losses – the *Effusion* also memorializes the deaths of Coleridge, Lamb, Crabbe, and (from 1836) Felicia Hemans – provoke an urgent question:

> Yet I, whose lids from infant slumbers
> Were earlier raised, remain to hear
> A timid voice, that asks in whispers,
> 'Who next will drop and disappear?'

If these deaths lead Wordsworth to look toward his own death, they also intensify the need to define his place before his voice too is silenced, as the uncharacteristically immediate composition corroborates. The death of Hogg, not a personal friend, was the occasion for Wordsworth publicly to fix an era. Despite his repeated declaration that 'I do not like to publish . . . in a newspaper, nor in any periodical,' Wordsworth sent the 'Effusion' to the paper in which he had read of Hogg's death, the *Newcastle Journal*.[23] The verses appeared under a heading that effectively converted the mourning the poem narrates into a celebration of the poet:

> The following exquisite Verses, which need no comment at our hands, have been transmitted to us by one of the most distinguished of England's Bards – one of her best and most loyal subjects – the poet Wordsworth. We feel highly flattered by the compliment thus paid to us by our kind-hearted and excellent friend. (*Last Poems*, 305)

By the time *Yarrow Revisited* appeared in April 1835 Scott had been dead for almost three years. The hopes expressed for Scott's recovery had been deceived, but placed in Wordsworth's most successful publication in many years the poem set for good the image of an enduring friendship between Wordsworth and the loved author whom, as Wordsworth had earlier acknowledged, 'I can scarcely be said to have lived with . . . at all.'

Before turning at last to 'Musings Near Aquapendente' I need to consider one more name in the contemporary comparison of Wordsworth to Scott: Byron. Hazlitt begins his essay on Byron in *The Spirit of The Age* by marking Scott and Byron as 'afford[ing] a complete contrast to each other, in their poetry, in their prose, in their politics, in their tempers, no two men can be more unlike' (Maclean, 235). The contrast between Byronic self-centredness and spleen, and Scott's self-effacing 'truth and nature,' between a poet who 'chiefly thinks how he shall display his own power' (Maclean, 235) and one with whom 'the veil of egotism is rent' (Maclean, 236), resonates when two chapters on Hazlitt specifies Wordsworth's 'solitary musing' (Maclean, 255) and contemns his egotism (Maclean, 258). Such triangulation of the three dominant authors was inevitable, and commonplace, but consider its effect on Wordsworth through the years. Hazlitt writes:

> Lord Byron we have called, according to the old proverb, 'the spoiled child of fortune.' Mr. Wordsworth might plead, in mitigation of some peculiarities, that he is 'the spoiled child of disappointment.' We are convinced, if he had been early a popular poet, he would have borne his honors meekly, and would have been a person of great *bonhomie* and frankness of disposition. But the sense of injustice and of undeserved ridicule sours the temper and narrows the views. To have produced works of genius, and to find them neglected or treated with scorn, is one of the heaviest trials of human patience.
> (Maclean, 260)

These contrasts between his own popularity and writers whom he linked as exemplifying the merely fashionable acquired a new force in the 1830s. In 1830 Thomas Moore published the *Letters and Journals of Lord Byron* in two splendid quarto volumes, dedicating them to Scott. The controversy the biography ignited only added to its success. Murray then republished the work as the first six volumes of the great seventeen-volume edition of 1834: *The Works of Lord Byron: With His Letters and Journals, and His Life, by Thomas Moore*. The year after Scott's death the 48-volume 'Magnum Opus' edition of his work concluded, drawing into one uniform set the novels, poems, and assorted prose together with fresh and appealing notes by the author himself.[24] Then in 1837 came Lockhart's seven-volume *Memoirs of the life of Sir Walter Scott, Bart.*, a moving, detailed, and highly influential study of Scott, his circumstances, and the development of his career.

Wordsworth's turn to Scott in 'Musings Near Aquapendente' has Lockhart as its stimulus: Wordsworth and Henry Crabb Robinson were reading the biography in Italy in 1837.[25] Though his distaste softened as he read the later volumes Crabb Robinson repeats Wordsworth's disdain for Scott's concern with popular success: 'I found the book, what Wordsworth declared it to be, a degradation of the literary character of our countryman. Walter Scott was a trader in poetry, the size of his poem being adapted to that of the building it was written to pay for' (*HCR*, 2:534).

Here then a tangle of motives underlying the treatment of Scott in 'Musings Near Aquapendente.' If Wordsworth thought Lockhart's frankness degraded 'the literary character of our countryman,' his views of Scott's poetry did not vary from his condescension to *The Lay of the Last Minstrel* in 1805 to his conversation in 1844: 'He does not consider that it any way goes below the surface of things . . . it is altogether superficial' (Hayden, 381-82), or, more tersely, as in Aubrey de Vere's reminiscence of his speaking of Scott's poetry 'with contempt' (Peacock, 340). If the lines on Scott were intended to counter Lockhart's portrait of his father-in-law, Wordsworth's assessment of the poetry, and its subordination to commercial interests, was even more severe. Praising Scott in 'Musings,' Wordsworth associated himself with a far more popular author, given new dignity by his struggle against adversity, by reasserting the story of their friendship already narrated in 'Yarrow Revisited.'

'Musings Near Aquapendente' is the first poem in 'Memorials of a Tour in Italy, 1837.' The sequence is preceded by a dedication to Henry Crabb Robinson, Wordsworth's companion and guide on the tour. It opens the sequence in the register of friendship, but the verso observes of the Italian Lakes: 'Neither of these lakes, nor of Venice, is there any notice in these Poems, chiefly because I have touched upon them elsewhere. See, in particular, "Descriptive Sketches," "Memorials of a Tour on the Continent in 1820," and a Sonnet upon the extinction of the Venetian Republic' (96). This note, like the printing of *Poems, Chiefly of Early and Late Years* with a supplementary title-page that inserts the new collection as volume seven of *The Poetical Works of William Wordsworth*, reminds the reader of the accumulating oeuvre of the poet and reveals the rhetorical pose inherent in Wordsworth's subsequent self-description as 'one withal . . . but little known to fame.'

The purposes underlying that pose become clearer if we consider that if the European tour poems recall another poet it is Byron rather than Scott. 'Nature's loveliest looks/ Art's noblest relics, history's rich bequests' sounds like a synopsis of cantos III and IV of *Childe Harold's Pilgrimage*. This is no accidental connection: I propose that the tour poems are a deliberate anti-*Childe Harold*, that in them the poet who had been steadily criticized for his seclusion in the Lakes set out to show that he could be as cosmopolitan as Byron. Incorporating at the start of the poem lines that he had written for *Michael* in 1800 ('Onward thence . . . border bards') Wordsworth stubbornly displayed himself as still the poet of the Lakes, for whom Italy serves to renew his ties to 'my own Fairfield . . . old companionship . . . Seat Sandal' (47-52), while now exploring 'Pisa's Campo Santo' in the best Byronic manner.

Juxtapose the following lines, for example, with Byron's descriptions of the Colosseum or of St. Peter's dome in the Fourth Canto of *Childe Harold's Pilgrimage*:

> – Oh what a spectacle at every turn
> The Place unfolds, from pavement skinned with moss,
> Or grass-grown spaces, where the heaviest foot
> Provokes no echoes, but must softly tread;
> Where solitude with Silence paired stops short
> Of Desolation, and to Ruin's scythe
> Decay submits not. (192-98)

In the Byronic manner, but with a crucial difference: where Byron was libertine, Wordsworth is pious; where Byron was Titanic, Wordsworth is modest:

> If one – while tossed, as was my lot to be,
> In a frail bark urged by two slender oars
> Over waves rough and deep, that, when they broke,
> Dashed their white foam against the palace walls
> Of Genoa the superb – should there be led
> To meditate upon his own appointed tasks,
> However humble in themselves, with thoughts
> Raised and sustained by memory of Him
> Who oftentimes within those narrow bounds
> Rocked on the surge, there tried his spirit's strength
> And grasp of purpose, long ere sailed his ship
> To lay a new world open. (119-30)

Behind these lines lies a famous episode from Moore's *Life of Byron*:

Toward the latter end of June, as we have seen in one of the preceding letters [27 June 1816], Lord Byron, accompanied by his friend Shelley, made a tour in his boat round the Lake. . . . In the squall off Meillerie, which he mentions, their danger was considerable. In the expectation, every moment, of being obliged to swim for his life, Lord Byron had already thrown off his coat, and, as Shelley was no swimmer, insisted upon endeavouring, by some means, to save him. This offer, however, Shelley positively refused; and seating himself quietly upon a locker, and grasping the rings at each end firmly in his hands, declared his determination to go down in that position.

To Byron's account Moore subjoins Shelley's:

> I felt, in this near prospect of death (says Mr. Shelley), a mixture of sensations. Among which terror entered, though but subordinately. My feelings would have been less painful, had I been alone; but I knew that my companion would have attempted to save me, and I was overcome with humiliation, when I thought that his life might have been risked to preserve mine. When we arrived at St. Gingoux, the inhabitants, who stood on the shore, unaccustomed to see a vessel as frail as ours, and fearing to venture at all on such a sea, exchanged looks of wonder and congratulation with our boatmen, who, as well as ourselves, were pleased to set foot on shore.[26]

That this episode stands behind Wordsworth's lines becomes indisputable in the Fenwick note on the passage:

> We took boat near the light-house at the point of the right horn of the bay, which makes a sort of natural port for Genoa, but the wind was high & the waves long and rough, so that I did not feel quite recompensed by the view of the city, splendid as it was, for the danger apparently incurred. The boatman (I had only one) encouraged me, saying we were quite safe, but I was not a little glad when we gained the shore, tho' Shelley and Byron – one of them at least who seemed to have courted agitation from every quarter – would have probably rejoiced in such a situation, more than once I believe were they both in extreme danger even on the Lake of Geneva. Every man however has his fears of some kind or other; &, no doubt, they had theirs – of all men whom I have ever known Coleridge had the most of passive courage in bodily peril, but no one was so easily cowed when moral firmness was required in miscellaneous conversation or in the daily intercourse of social life.[27]

The Fenwick notes, which appeared for the first time in the 1857 edition, constitute 'Wordsworth's last great act of imaginative self-assessment,' as Stephen Gill rightly concludes.[28] In this instance they confirm that what purports to be merely a biographical incident from 1837 is Wordsworth's multi-layered re-situating of himself in literary history: Byron's practical courage and Shelley's speculative calm – and in the Notes, Coleridge's lack of moral firmness – yield to Wordsworth's account of his own (ostensibly) humble meditations, and if the capital letter in 'Him' colors the scene with echoes of Christ walking upon the waters, so much more strongly is the comparison enforced between piety and radical 'agitation.'

The treatment of Scott unfolds within the same self-validating pattern. Wordsworth follows his imaginative transport from Italy back to the Lake District by asking: 'who that travels far/ To feed his mind with watchful eyes could share/ Or wish to share it (54-56)?' If this query exposes his gesture to charges of provincialism, Wordsworth rebuts them by invoking Scott:

> – One there surely was,
> 'The Wizard of the North,' with anxious hope
> Brought to this genial climate, when disease
> Preyed upon body and mind – yet not the less
> Had his sunk eye kindled at those dear words
> That spake of bards and minstrels; and his spirit
> Had flown with mine to old Helvellyn's brow,
> Where once together, in his day of strength,
> We stood rejoicing, as if earth were free
> From sorrow, like the sky above our heads. (56-65)

The maneuver of legitimating his poem by incorporating Scott's approval is reinforced by the Fenwick note: 'His, Sir W. Scott's, eye *did* in fact kindle at them for the lines "places forsaken now" & the two that follow were adopted from a Poem of mine which nearly 40 years ago was in part read to him and he never forgot them' (Curtis, 69). Instead of the polarity of healthy, extroverted Scott and pathologized, introverted Wordsworth developed by Jeffrey and Hazlitt, instead of his own condescension to Scott's art, Wordsworth gives us himself and Scott standing together atop the mountain associated with Wordsworth, the mountain where Haydon placed Wordsworth in his famous portrait of the same year as the publication of *Poems, Chiefly of Early and Late Years*.[29]

'Musings' continues:

> Still, in more than ear-deep seats,
> Survives for me, and cannot but survive
> The tone of voice which wedded borrowed words
> To sadness not their own, when, with faint smile
> Forced by intent to take from speech its edge,
> He said, 'When I am there, although 'tis fair.
> 'Twill be another Yarrow.' (71-77)

At the conclusion of 'Tintern Abbey' Wordsworth composes his ideal vision of himself by forecasting how his sister is to remember him. A similar act of ventriloquism obtains here, only instead of his younger sister, it is a celebrated poet who immortalizes Wordsworth's poetry: 'These words were quoted to me from "Yarrow Unvisited," by Sir Walter Scott when I visited him at Abbotsford, a day or two before his departure for Italy,' runs the note in *Poems, Chiefly of Early and Late Years* (147). Absent is vexation at Scott's misquotation of 'Yarrow Unvisited' in *The Lay of the Last Minstrel*; absent is any hint that such misquotation 'betray[ed] his own uncritical principles of composition,' as Wordsworth had declared in 1827 (see n. 6). If the quotation attests Scott's tactful minimizing of his doubts that Italy would restore him, and his generosity to Wordsworth, a generosity repaid in Wordsworth's brief revival of Scott's voice, its deployment here also suggests Wordsworth's covert self-endorsement.

'Musings' concludes with an anticipation of Wordsworth's visit to Rome, trenching ever more directly on the territory of Canto IV of *Childe Harold's Pilgrimage*, but Wordsworth's Rome is not that of the butchered gladiator, of Nemesis and the revenges of history, or of the sculpture gallery, but of 'Christian Traditions!' (291). The vision of Sts. Peter and Paul in the 'Mamertine prison' (305) rises to an affirmation of the need of 'religious faith' (337) in a secular 'chilled age' (325), a reiteration of the arguments of the maligned *Excursion*. 'Let us now/ Rise, and to-morrow greet magnificent Rome' (371-72).

This conclusion echoes Milton's 'Lycidas,' and just as Milton's poem is less a personal lament for Edward King than Milton's meditation on his poetic vocation, so is 'Musings Near Aquapendente' less a straightforward poem of friendship than an *apologia* for Wordsworth's career. More persuasive than Wordsworth's pretenses of indifference and humility are the lines that introduce the episode in Genoa harbor: 'Who would keep/ Power must resolve to cleave to it through life,/ Else it deserts him, surely as he lives' (115-17). What Hazlitt stigmatized as egotism takes the form of Wordsworth's seizing the opportunity to shape literary history in his own terms.

By the 1840s the inner 'fluxes and refluxes of the mind' had been filled with the representations of him by others. Wordsworth's 'musings' are no longer the product of solitude, as his critics had insisted, but a theater filled by the rival actors and authors of the previous decades in a performance that he scripted and directed. The outer became the inner, to be rebroadcast publicly by the new poem. Wordsworth's private censure of Scott's poetry may be understood as the envy of a fastidious craftsman for the greater success, in remuneration and reputation, of a less demanding writer. Yet the private pique drove the seventy-year-old poet to renewed creation, and such striking images as that of the survival, 'in more than ear-deep seats,' of Scott's transmission of his own words. The phrase recalls the 'Thoughts that do often lie too deep for tears' at the conclusion of the 'Intimations Ode,' the poem that continued to close every one of Wordsworth's collections.[30] Its intensified inwardness points to the place of 'Musings Near Aquapendente,' which is less a record of the tour in Italy than of Wordsworth's stocktaking of English literary fame: the imaginative return to England at the start of the poem is a significant gesture. The Wordsworth of 1841, nine years past Scott's death, and four years removed from an Italy colored by annoyance at Lockhart's biography of Scott, more secure of his reputation than in previous years, still worried about his standing.

Wordsworth while alive could not have a Moore or Scott to establish his reputation, and he was determined to control his depiction. Wordsworth had always been his own biographical subject; now he wrote as if he were already past, in every way except for the anxious energy expended on his public self-construction. 'Musings' again summons Chiabrera, whose Epitaphs he had translated and who figures prominently in the 'Essays on Epitaphs' associated with *The Excursion*. At Savona, city of his birth, Wordsworth sought but failed to find any of his epitaphs: 'not a stone,/ Mural or level with the trodden floor,/ In Church or Chapel' (236-38). 'Yet,' Wordsworth writes,

> in his page the records of that *worth*
> Survive, uninjured; – glory then to *words*,
> Honour to word-preserving Arts (248-50)[31]

For those who look, Wordsworth's page blazons his own name. 'Imaginative self-assessment,' as Gill terms it, was for Wordsworth inseparable from his differential assessment of others: in 'Musings Near Aquapendente' he is at once his own elegiac subject and the chronicler of his times, re-presenting his earlier works and ensuring his place for posterity.

## Notes

[1] Quotations from the text of *Poems, Chiefly of Early and Late Years* (London: Edward Moxon, 1842), which has no line numbers. The numbers in brackets are those from *The Poetical Works of William Wordsworth*, ed. E. de Selincourt and Helen Darbishire, 2nd edn. 5 vols. (1954), 3:202-12. References to this edition hereafter cited parenthetically in the text as *PW*.

[2] Stephen Gill, 'Wordsworth, Scott, and Musings Near Aquapendente,' *Centennial*

*Review* 36 (1992), pp. 221-30 (p. 222).
3. The late composition may partly explain why the poem lacks the reflections on Italian nationalism that mark the succeeding poems in the sequence. On this aspect of the 'Memorials,' see John Wyatt, *Wordsworth's Poems of Travel, 1819-42* (Basingstoke: Macmillan, 1999), pp. 131-35.
4. This review of the relationship of Scott and Wordsworth is compiled chiefly from Edgar Johnson, *Sir Walter Scott: The Great Unknown*, 2 vols. (New York: Macmillan, 1970), hereafter cited parenthetically in the text as Johnson, and Stephen Gill, *William Wordsworth: A Life* (Oxford: Clarendon, 1989).
5. *The Letters of William and Dorothy Wordsworth*, I: *The Early Years 1787-1805*, ed. Ernest de Selincourt, 2nd. edn. rev. Chester L. Shaver (Oxford: Clarendon, 1967), pp. 413-14. Hereafter cited parenthetically in the text as *EY*.
6. *The Letters of William and Dorothy Wordsworth*, II: *The Middle Years 1806-1811*, ed. Ernest de Selincourt, 2nd. edn. rev. Mary Moorman (Oxford: Clarendon, 1969), p. 264. Hereafter cited parenthetically in the text as *MY*. More than twenty years later Wordsworth was still irked by the misquotation: 'W. Scott quoted, as from me, "The swan on Sweet St. Mary's Lake Floats double, swan and shadow," instead of *still*; thus obscuring my idea, and betraying his own uncritical principles of composition.' Christopher Wordsworth, Jr., from the Summer of 1827, as quoted in Markham L. Peacock, Jr., *The Critical Opinions of William Wordsworth* (1950; rpt. New York, Octagon, 1969), p. 339. Hereafter cited in the text parenthetically as Peacock.
7. John Lockhart, *Memoirs of the Life of Sir Walter Scott, Bart.*, 7 vols. (Cadell: Edinburgh, 1837), 1:405. Hereafter referred to parenthetically in the text as Lockhart.
8. Quoted in Alice Pattee Comparetti, *The White Doe of Rylstone by William Wordsworth: A Critical Edition*, Cornell Studies in English XIX (Ithaca: Cornell University Press, 1940), p. 44. Though quoting liberally from Whitaker, and even alluding to Scott's *Minstrelsy of the Scottish Border* (162), Wordsworth does not cite this compliment, or prompt. In its quarto format of narrative poem followed by notes *The White Doe*, when published at last in 1815, looks a great deal like *The Lay of the Last Minstrel* and *Marmion*, a connection Wordsworth was still at pains to deny decades later in the notes dictated to Isabella Fenwick: 'The subject being taken from feudal times has led to its being compared to some of Walter Scott's poems that belong to the same age and state of society. The comparison is inconsiderate' (*PW* 3: 543).
9. H. J. C. Grierson, ed., *The Letters of Sir Walter Scott*, 12 vols. (London: Constable, 1932), 1:390. Hereafter cited parenthetically in the text as Grierson.
10. Quoted in Robert Woof, ed. *William Wordsworth: The Critical Heritage*, I (London: Routledge, 2001), pp. 297-98. Hereafter cited as Woof.
11. All quotations from *Edinburgh Review* 24 (November 1814), 1-30, as reprinted in Woof, pp. 381-404.
12. All quotations from *Edinburgh Review* 24 (November 1814), pp. 208-43, as reprinted in John O. Hayden, ed., *Scott: The Critical Heritage* (New York: Barnes & Noble, 1970), pp. 79-84. Hereafter cited parenthetically in the text as Hayden.

13. On the contrast between the 'basically sane and healthy Scott' and the weakness and subjectivity of the other Romantics, see J. H. Alexander, 'The Treatment of Scott in Reviews of the English Romantics,' *Yearbook of English Studies* 11 (1981), pp. 67-86.
14. All quotations from *The Examiner* (21, 28 August and 2 October 1814, pp. 541-42, 555-58, 636-38), as reprinted in Duncan Wu, ed., *The Selected Writings of William Hazlitt*, 9 vols. (London: Pickering and Chatto, 1998), 2:321-40.
15. William Hazlitt, *Lectures on the English Poets and The Spirit of the Age*, ed. Catherine Macdonald Maclean (London: Dent, n.d), pp. 143-68. Hereafter cited parenthetically in the text as Maclean.
16. I pass over their convergence in London in 1828. Haydon's comparison of the two men at that time works a penetrating variation on the stock opposition: 'Scott enters a room and sits at table with the coolness and self-possession of conscious fame: Wordsworth with a mortified elevation of head, as if fearful he was not estimated as he desired. Scott is always cool and very amusing; Wordsworth often egotistical and overwhelming. Scott seems to appear less than he really is, while Wordsworth struggles to be thought at the moment greater than he is suspected to be. I think that Scott's success would have made Wordsworth insufferable, while Wordsworth's failure would not have rendered Scott a whit less delightful' (*Autobiography*, quoted in Johnson 1052).
17. *The Letters of William and Dorothy Wordsworth, V, The Later Years, Part II, 1829-1834*, ed. Ernest de Selincourt, 2nd edn. rev. Alan G. Hill (Oxford: Clarendon, 1979), p. 328. Hereafter cited parenthetically in the text as *LY*.
18. Text from *Yarrow Revisited* (London: Longman and Moxon, 1835), p. 9.
19. On this feature, see Jill Rubinstein, 'Wordsworth and "Localised Romance": The Scottish Poems of 1831,' *Studies in English Literature* 16 (1976), pp. 579-90.
20. On the envy see, for example, the letter to Samuel Rogers announcing *The Excursion*: 'I shall be content if the publication pays its expenses, for Mr. Scott and your friend Lord B. flourishing at the rate they do, how can an honest *Poet* [Wordsworth's differentiating italics] hope to thrive?' (*The Letters of William and Dorothy Wordsworth, The Middle Years, Part II, 1812-1820*, ed. Ernest de Selincourt, 2nd edn. rev. Mary Moorman and Alan G. Hill (Oxford: Clarendon, 1970), p. 148).
21. Wordsworth, 'Essay on Epitaphs,' *The Excursion* (London: Longman, 1814), pp. 440-41.
22. Text from *Last Poems, 1821-1850*, ed. Jared Curtis (Ithaca: Cornell University Press, 1999), p. 305. Hereafter cited parenthetically in the text as *Last Poems*.
23. The representative utterance is from a letter of February 4, 1841, to Moxon (*The Letters of William and Dorothy Wordsworth, VII, The Later Years, Part IV, 1840-1853*, ed. Ernest de Selincourt, 2nd edn. rev. Alan G. Hill (Oxford: Clarendon, 1988), p. 176). The poem was then published in *The Atheneum*, guaranteeing still wider diffusion.
24. See Jane Millgate, *Scott's Last Edition* (Edinburgh: Edinburgh University Press, 1987).

[25] See *Henry Crabb Robinson on Books and Their Writers*, 3 vols. (London: Dent, 1938) 2:524. Hereafter cited parenthetically in the text as *HCR*.

[26] Thomas Moore, *Letters and Journals of Lord Byron*, 2 vols. (London: John Murray, 1830), 2:31-32.

[27] Quoted from *The Fenwick Notes of William Wordsworth*, ed. Jared Curtis (London: Bristol Classical Press, 1993), pp. 69-70. Hereafter cited parenthetically in the text as Curtis.

[28] Stephen Gill, 'Copyright and the publishing of Wordsworth, 1850-1900,' *Literature in the Marketplace*, eds. John O. Jordan and Robert L. Patten (Cambridge: Cambridge University Press, 1995), pp. 74-92.

[29] Wordsworth's success in establishing the perception of the friendship between himself and Scott can be gauged by George Cattermole's painting of Scott and Wordsworth at Newark Castle, which became widely known through the lithograph by James Duffield Harding. Its source must be Wordsworth's poems in *Yarrow Revisited* and the account of the final visit to Abbotsford that Wordsworth communicated to Lockhart for inclusion in his biography of Scott.

[30] I owe this parallel to Alan Richardson.

[31] I am happy to call attention to the as-yet unpublished dissertation of Peter Simonsen, 'Word-Preserving Arts,' defended at the University of Copenhagen in February 2003, for which I was honored to serve as a reader.

# SELF GENERATIONS: ON WORDSWORTH'S FRONTISPIECE PORTRAITS

Peter Simonsen

> Round about were hung
> The glorious features of the bards who sung
> In other ages – cold and sacred busts
> Smiled at each other. Happy he who trusts
> To clear Futurity his darling fame!
> John Keats, 'Sleep and Poetry' (1817)[1]

> I had rather leave a good portrait of myself behind me than have a fine epitaph. The face, for the most part, tells what we have thought and felt – the rest is nothing. I have a higher idea of Donne from a rude, half-effaced outline of him prefixed to his poems than from any thing he ever wrote.
> William Hazlitt, 'On the Knowledge of Character' (1821)[2]

One of the most significant and innovative aspects of William Wordsworth's later work is his use of authorial frontispiece portraiture. Wordsworth authorised the first such portrait in 1836 and in 1845 he published another quite different portrait. The frontispiece portrait epitomizes Wordsworth's persistent concern with the messages conveyed by a book's layout and is indeed one of the most important bibliographical features of the codex book. As such it constitutes what Gérard Genette describes as a 'threshold of interpretation' from which we may reach 'a more pertinent reading of [a text] (more pertinent, of course, in the eyes of the author and his allies).'[3] The frontispieces point beyond the anti-pictorialist iconoclasm that is a central feature of the poet of the Great Decade (1798-1808), who famously proclaimed the eye to be 'The most despotic of our senses.'[4] They, in fact, make evident a tendency in Wordsworth's work which invests the visible and material with positive value and runs counter to the poet's at times outspoken distrust of the eye and of visual representations. Borrowing W. J. T. Mitchell's phrase, a 'pictorial turn' can be discerned in the later Wordsworth.[5] To understand this turn is both to understand what is central about this often depreciated and misunderstood part of his work, and to reach a better and more adequate recognition of the rich complexity of his work considered as a whole.

In his essay, 'On Sitting for One's Picture,' William Hazlitt points to portraiture's potential to generate a new self: 'The fact is, that the having one's picture painted is like the creation of another self; and that is an idea, of the repetition or reduplication of which no man is ever tired, to the thousandth reflection.'[6] This potential was deeply attractive to certain Romantic authors, who integrated it into their general artistic projects. As Thomas Hood writes in 'Fancy Portraits' (1826), 'As soon as a gentleman has proved, in print, that he really has a head, – a score of artists begin to brush at it.... Sir Walter is eternally sitting like Theseus to some painter or other; – and the late Lord Byron threw out more heads before he died than Hydra.'[7] Had Hood written a decade or two later, Wordsworth might have been mentioned, because with the exception of Scott, Wordsworth had more portraits taken during his lifetime than any other poet in the Romantic period.[8] As Judith Pascoe has suggested, these portraits implicate 'Wordsworth's stagings of self in ... the all-encompassing theatricality of romantic era culture.'[9]

Wordsworth's likeness had circulated since February 1819 when the *New Monthly Magazine* published Henry Meyer's engraving of Richard Carruthers' 1817 portrait of him, striking what had become, since the Renaissance, the characteristic pose of pensive poetic melancholy: the right hand held to the forehead where according to the popular quasi-sciences of physiognomy and phrenology, inspiration and imagination were placed.[10] While Henry Crabb Robinson found the Carruthers portrait to exhibit 'a languor approaching to disease,' Wordsworth appears to have liked it.[11] So did the wife of the publisher Alaric Watts, who reports that 'Of the various portraits which have been published of him, one painted by Mr. Carruthers, and engraved for Galignani's edition of his poems, issued in Paris in 1828, reminds me more of the poet, as I remember him, than any other.'[12] However, because the engraving of Carruthers was reproduced as the frontispiece portrait for Galignani's 'pirated' edition, Wordsworth's move to issue a different authorised portrait may have been motivated to counteract its dissemination. Thus in 1836 the collected works were published with an engraving by W. H. Watt from H. W. Pickersgill's well-known 1832 portrait of the poet reclined on a rock with pen and paper in hand (plate 2).

Quickly after its first publication Wordsworth expressed a vehement desire to replace Pickersgill's portrait. Thus a new frontispiece was engraved by William Finden from Sir Francis Chantrey's neoclassical 1820 bust and published in 1845, to the poet's full satisfaction (plate 3). However, Wordsworth's posterity has preferred Benjamin Robert Haydon's well-known *Wordsworth on Helvellyn* (1842) as its image of the Poet. As Elizabeth Barrett Browning wrote in 1842, 'A vision free/ And noble, Haydon, hath thine art released – / No portrait this with academic air!/ This is the poet and his poetry.'[13] In 'Recollections of Wordsworth' (1869), Robert P. Graves said that Haydon's portrait 'alone deserves to be the historic portrait of Wordsworth. Nothing can be truer to the original than the droop of the head weighed down by the thoughts and feelings over which the active imagination is pleasurably brooding.'[14] Indeed, Matthew Arnold's 1879 selection from Wordsworth's poetry, which largely produced the twentieth century's impression of the poet, used an engraving from Haydon's portrait as frontispiece.

Wordsworth regarded portraiture with scepticism even though his sitting for a large number of them in his later years raised it in his estimate. In 1846, for instance, he wrote to the painter William Boxall, whose first portrait had been of Wordsworth (1831), wishing that Boxall had 'found for [his] Pencil more interesting employment than mere Portraits, – but I am afraid,' says Wordsworth, 'that little else is suitable to English demand.'[15] Yet portraits of Wordsworth proliferated and he chose to make use of them as frontispieces. 'How explain,' asks Frances Blanshard, 'that Wordsworth could endure so often the tedium of sitting for an artist? ... Was he willing to face it because he was particularly vain? The suspicion that this might be so vanishes when we consider how many of the artists for whom he sat were youngsters or amateurs.... He allowed them to practise on him, partly because he was genuinely kind, and hated to refuse beginners who hoped his face would make their fortune.'[16] This, however, is only part of the explanation of what motivated Wordsworth's generations of self in his frontispiece portraits. These particular portraits signal a complex three-fold desire for survival by offering a kind of imagistic life-after-life, for enhanced communication by presenting the author-speaker 'in person,' and for sheer profit by presenting the image of the author as a commodity valued by contemporary book buyers and collectors.

The Romantic age was an 'age of personality,' as Coleridge noted, and it not surprisingly witnessed a mania for portraits.[17] In the late eighteenth and early nineteenth century, the cost of reproducing portraits decreased due to new techniques of reproduction and coupled with an increase of the wealth of potential buyers, engraved portraits became common objects of collectors' desires. According to Robert Southey, in *Letters from England* (1807), the desire to collect engraved portraits had arisen since the publication of Samuel Granger's *Biographical History of England* (1769), which included 'a biographical account of all persons whose likeness had been engraved in England.'[18] The effect of this book was that 'you rarely or never meet an old book here with the author's head in it; all are mutilated by the collectors.'[19]

Plate 2

The first authorised frontispiece portrait of Wordsworth. Engraved in 1836 by W. H. Watt from the portrait taken by H. W. Pickersgill in 1832.

Plate 3

The second authorised frontispiece portrait of Wordsworth. Engraved in 1845 by W. Finden from the bust made by F. Chantrey in 1820.

Yet to be recognised as the true author of a book, a Romantic writer had to make his or her face available for the public. As Hood writes, 'A book without a portrait of the author, is worse than anonymous. As in a church-yard, you may look on any number of ribs and shin-bones, as so many sticks merely, without interest; but if there should chance to be a scull near hand, it claims the relics at once, – so it is with the author's head-piece in front of his pages. The portrait claims the work.'[20] A portrait of the author individualises and personalises a book and invests the words with a certain 'interest'. As Hood knows, readers' interest must be stimulated by something placed on a book's cover if the words of an author are to be released from their inscribed death.

While the practice of presenting a portrait of a text's author alongside the text itself dates back to the very first written papyrus scrolls, the individualized and particularized engraved frontispiece portrait of the single author appeared for the first time in a book printed in Milan in 1479.[21] As the arts of printing and engraving developed and enabled a more economic reproduction, frontispiece portraiture flourished with the portrait genre from the sixteenth century, reflecting the growing interest in the individual as well as the gradual emergence of the modern idea of the author as the originator and hence proprietor of a work.[22] A frontispiece portrait indicates the author of a book and functions both 'to reinforce the notion that the writing is the expression of an individuality that gives authenticity to the work' and as a marketing device to attract customers and increase the monetary value of a book.[23] For Steven Rendall, frontispiece portraits 'figure a subject that claims not only to have produced the work but also, through the immanence of an individual intention, to determine – that is, to limit – its *meaning*.'[24] Yet a frontispiece portrait surely can be said to *add* meaning as much as to limit it, to reveal as much as conceal.

Wordsworth's use of the frontispiece portrait demands special attention because with Wordsworth this bibliographical item may be said to change its significance. While Wordsworth cannot be said to have revolutionised the practice, for the autobiographical poet *par excellence*, whose highest ambition was to look into the mind of man, to publish with a frontispiece portrait is surely a significant act. After Wordsworth we cannot but read an author's frontispiece portrait as both an illustration and, in the sense Martin Meisel has recuperated, a 'realization' of the *subject* of the book.[25] If Harold Bloom was right when he said that Wordsworth 'was the inventor of modern poetry, and he found no subject but himself,' then until we have considered his use of the frontispiece portrait, we have barely begun to understand the ways in which he articulated this subject.[26]

To understand Wordsworth's frontispiece portraits and by implication what motivated their publication, we must attend to what informed his artistic project, particularly after 1807: his strong conviction that his art was created with a future audience in mind and consequently needed to be cast in a form that might last.[27] Wordsworth tended to see works of visual art as permanent and imperishable.[28] By having himself rendered as a work of visual art, Wordsworth by implication rendered 'himself' imperishable. As Nathaniel Hawthorne puts it in 'Prophetic Pictures' (1837), 'Nothing in the whole circle of human vanities takes stronger hold of the imagination than this affair of having a portrait painted…. It is the idea of duration – or earthly immortality – that gives such a mysterious interest to our portraits' which are 'to be [our] representatives with posterity.'[29] In one of the many ekphrastic poems belonging to his later period, 'Lines Suggested by a Portrait from the Pencil of F. Stone' (1835), painting is characterised as an 'Art divine,/ That both creates and fixes, in despite/ Of Death and Time, the marvels it hath wrought.'[30] This poem was published the year before Wordsworth issued his first frontispiece portrait, and along with a number of other poems on portraiture from the later period (especially the sonnet on Pickersgill's original portrait, 'To the Author's Portrait' (1832), it can be read as articulating one of the motives underlying this act.

Wordsworth's decision to publish with a frontispiece portrait may also relate to his awareness of and resistance to the dislocation between poetry and the poet caused by writing. By representing a tangible, embodied form of the author-speaker, the frontispiece portrait simulates a context of oral performance, which may reflect Wordsworth's persistent wish to present himself as a 'man speaking to men.' Having detailed Wordsworth's looks and his 'manner of reading his own poetry,' in *The Spirit of the Age* (1825), Hazlitt speculates, 'Perhaps the comment of his face and voice is necessary to convey a full idea of his poetry.'[31] A frontispiece portrait is one way of indicating the presence of the speaker in order to facilitate the reader's comprehension of the 'full idea' of a poet's work. From a communicative as well as affective point of view, a frontispiece portrait may thus be intended to present the speaker in order to enhance the truth value and emotional effect of his discourse as well as to stabilise its meaning and range of reference.

The frontispiece portrait also fashions the authorial subject as a spectacular commodity, with potentially severe consequences both for the expressive-communicative function and the 'immortality effect' promised by frontispiece portraiture. The commercial use and abuse of frontispiece portraiture in the Romantic period is articulated by Southey in his long poem on portraiture, 'Epistle to Allan Cunningham,' first published in Cunningham's annual, *The Anniversary* in 1829.[32] Southey attacks publishers 'Who fix one's name for public sale beneath/ A set of features slanderously unlike' (ll. 105-6). As Southey laments, 'Against the wrong/ Which they inflict Time hath no remedy' (ll. 107-108); therefore he 'appeal[s]/ Against the limner's and the graver's wrong;/ Their evil works survive them' (ll. 136-138). In an 1824 letter this kind of experience is referred to as 'too common to excite either surprize or anger' to someone operating in the Romantic public sphere, who must expect to be 'ill used.'[33] Southey does not oppose the practice of using visual portraiture for commercial marketing purposes, but takes it for granted; as well he might writing in a culture that feared it was witnessing the displacement of the word by the image and publishing his poem in an annual giftbook, a medium symptomatic of the valuation of a book by its covers, looks and graphic illustrations.[34] Southey merely laments the fact that his publishers apparently show little concern over the veracity of the portraits they employ to ensure that a book sells. This is experienced by Southey as a fundamentally alienating process because the making public of the private and personal – although he was in many ways deeply complicit – is carried out by agents often acting out of control of the subject in question, because motivated to maximise profits rather than gratify the subject's wishes.

Wordsworth's first venture into publishing with a frontispiece portrait was a catastrophe. The decision seems to have been motivated more by commercial than by communicative or aesthetic considerations with making a certain impression on future generations of readers. In 1832, Wordsworth planned to have an engraving made from Pickersgill's portrait to be sold as a kind of fan poster in multiple reproductions. To facilitate this, he wrote to Edward Moxon, who was then employed by Wordsworth's publisher Longman, asking him 'to receive the names of such persons as it *might* suit [to buy the engraving], to write them down in your Shop.'[35] This scheme appears never to have been realized although Wordsworth refers to it again in the 1836 letter where for the first time he announces the plan to use the engraving as frontispiece or 'vignette.'[36] As a frontispiece rather than an independent poster, Wordsworth's image could both answer the rising demand for a visual likeness of the poet and help increase the chronically low sales of his poetry.[37] In a letter to Moxon, who was now his publisher, Wordsworth writes concerning the 1836 edition, 'I have heard such strong opinions given respecting the disadvantages the Ed: will labour under in not having one illustration at least for each Vol. that I regret much ... that an arrangement was not made ... to include this.'[38] The market for unillustrated volumes of poetry by single authors was in a state of severe crisis and depression and needed the image to function.[39] In 1836 Wordsworth wanted to increase his profits by using illustration, even though he had written to

Moxon in 1833 that 'It is a disgrace to the age that Poetry wont sell without prints,' and that he is 'a little too proud to let [his] Ship sail in the wake of the Engravers and the drawing-mongers.'[40] Yet his first attempt harboured a warning to be more careful about the visual medium, and about the implications for the frontispiece's communicative and expressive function of the process of engraving needed to facilitate reproduction.

In the process of transforming the original Pickersgill into a reproducible portrait through engraving, the portrait was altered in significant ways that seem to have given Wordsworth certain intimations of mortality. In the engraving important parts of the original are cut out: arms, legs, background, the ground on which the subject sits, as well as the poet's professional identity markers, pen and paper. The bodily signs that remain in a truncated form in the picture thus assume new meaning. As Wordsworth complained in 1836, 'partly owing ... to its having preserved the inclination of the body (natural in a recumbent attitude) without an arm to explain it or account for it, the whole has an air of feebleness and decrepitude which I hope is not yet authorized by the subject.'[41] By featuring the face out of the context of the body, the engraving fashions an auraless image of the author marked by decay and age that did not match his idea of what he should look like in the public eye. If a good portrait challenges 'the transiency and irrelevancy of human existence,' and if 'the portrait artist must respond to the demands formulated by the individual's wish to endure,' as Richard Brilliant suggests, a bad portrait is doubly bad.[42] Rather than challenge death, a bad portrait can be said to articulate and exemplify 'the transiency and irrelevancy of human existence.' What in Pickersgill's original portrait signifies 'recumbent' – a neutral, descriptive term here – gets interpreted by Wordsworth as 'feebleness' and 'decrepitude' in the reproduction that was made to (mis)inform the reception of his poetry. As Robert Graves concluded, 'I can have little doubt that that frontispiece, conveying a false impression of the poet, has even conduced with many to a misinterpretation of his poetry.'[43]

Almost as soon as the 'feeble' and 'decrepit' portrait was published, Wordsworth began to plan its substitution and thus to engage in the difficulties of regenerating his public image in order to improve his last impression. In a letter to Moxon in June, 1845, Wordsworth writes that 'I think I mentioned to you that I had an utter dislike of the Print from Pickersgill prefixed to the Poems. It does me and him also great injustice. Pray what would be the lowest expense of a respectable engraving from Chantrey's Bust? That I should like infinitely better.'[44] Despite or perhaps because 'sculpture [had begun] to suffer from anachronism early in the nineteenth century,' according to Michael North, and 'had become antique in the pejorative sense, completely dependent as it was on antiquity for its models of idealization,' Chantrey's bust was the image of himself that Wordsworth wished to transmit to posterity.[45] Yet he never explicitly motivates his choice of it as frontispiece over for example Haydon's *Wordsworth on Helvellyn*, which he found the 'best likeness, that is the most characteristic, which had been done of [him].'[46]

Crabb Robinson comes as close as any to explaining why Wordsworth preferred the bust as frontispiece. In 1821, he wrote to Dorothy that 'I have heard the opinion of several who do not know [Wordsworth], and who consider it (as I do) as the *idea of a poet*.... But I think too that it is a good likeness – and there is a delicacy & grace in the muscles of the cheek which I do not recollect in the Original.'[47] Wordsworth concurred with this view writing in 1822 that the bust 'can be of little value as to the likeness, but as a work of fine Art I may be excused if I say that it seems to me fully entitled to that praise which is universally given to Mr Chantry's Labours.'[48] As an idealised, fine work of art rather than a 'mere' portrait it contributes to making the collected works, the Book itself, into a work of art rather than a mere anthology of poems by the same author. The motive is further hinted at by Crabb Robinson when in 1825 he asked Dorothy, 'why not by a first rate hand, a print of the bust? I am aware that busts do not engrave well generally: But certainly this is the least unsatisfactory of the attempts to "snatch from fleeting time" an image of your brother's countenance.'[49] That Wordsworth should want to correct the realistic image of himself as 'decrepit' with an idealised image of himself as an eternal artwork rescued and preserved from time in statuesque perfection is understandable in this light simply as a means to overcoming the bodily decay articulated by the engraving from Pickersgill. As Kenneth Gross writes, 'we recognize in the statue an image of the fate of bodies, a fate elected out of a desire to deny our vulnerable, penetrable, wasting, and dying physical persons, to provide ourselves with idealized stone mirrors.... The lure of the statue is that it becomes a shield, a wedge between myself and my death.'[50]

When John Gibson Lockhart published his *Life* of Sir Walter Scott in 1838, the idealisation evident in the bust became the subject of an exchange that casts light on the theatricality involved in Wordsworth's self-fashioning for posterity. Lockhart had quoted a letter from Scott to Chantrey's secretary, Allan Cunningham, in which Scott writes of Wordsworth, 'I do not know a man more to be venerated for uprightness of heart and loftiness of genius. Why he will sometimes choose to crawl upon all fours when God has given him so noble a countenance to lift to heaven I am as little able to account for as for his quarrelling (as you tell me) with the wrinkles which time and meditation have stamped his brow withal.'⁵¹ To this allegation Wordsworth responds,

> I have a crow to pick with 'honest Allan [Cunningham]', as he has misled Sir W. by misrepresenting me. I had not a single wrinkle on my *forehead* at the time when this bust was executed, and therefore none could be represented by the Artist (a fact I should have barely been able to speak to, but that it was noticed by a Painter while drawing a Portrait of me a little while before) but deep wrinkles I had in my cheeks and the side of my mouth even from my boyhood – and my Wife, who was present while the Bust was in progress, and remembered them, from the days of her youth, was naturally wishful to have those peculiarities preserved for the sake of likeness, in all their force. Chantrey objected, saying those lines if given with shut mouth, would sacrifice the spirit to the letter, and by attracting undue attention, would greatly injure instead of strengthen the resemblance to the living Man. My own knowledge of Art led me to the same conclusion. I supported the Sculptor's judgment in opposition to my Wife's desire: this is the plain story, and it is told merely that I may not pass down to posterity as a Man, whose personal vanity urged him to importune a first-rate Artist to tell a lie in marble, without good reason; but in reality the sacrifice of truth would have been much greater, if the principles of legitimate art had been departed from. Excuse so many words upon what may be thought, but I hope not by yourself, an insignificant subject.⁵²

The performance of 'Wordsworth' has rarely been more lucidly drawn out than in this passage, which takes us behind the scenes of the generation of the author-image he imagined would 'pass down to posterity.' Mary's desire for 'likeness' is overruled in the interest of 'resemblance' and an aesthetic rationale is provided for the idealisation, the 'lie [told] in marble,' in Chantrey's bust. By the same token, Wordsworth explains why Chantrey's bust was used as the pretext for the last frontispiece. It was chosen to generate an image of Wordsworth's authorial self as an ideal, polished and immutable work of art in opposition to the real, rugged and mutable world of nature.

To study Wordsworth's concern with generating and regenerating his public 'image' – in both a strictly material and literal sense and in a more abstract sense – by studying these frontispieces is to study the culmination of his career. Frontispiece portraiture adds to our understanding of what Pascoe calls the 'theatrical imperative'⁵³ of Romantic literary culture by staging the performative generation of authorial identity within what has been called the 'hand-held theatre' of the book.⁵⁴ The implications of the kind of self-promotion entailed by publishing with a frontispiece portrait during the Romantic period compels us to raise with renewed force the question of Wordsworthian 'sincerity' in relation to his often assumed imperviousness *vis-à-vis* the demands of the commercial market for poetry. More significantly it problematises the traditional understanding of Wordsworth as someone in full possession of an essential, stable, centered self that precedes its representation, rather than a relational, flexible, and mobile self that emerges as an effect of its representation. Whether the self precedes or is generated by its representation, the presence of radically different frontispiece portraits questions its singularity and suggests that we need to think of it as a complex, hybrid phenomenon. If the frontispiece is meant to stabilise the meaning of a certain discourse by showing us who is 'speaking,' the presence of two very different portraits, which accordingly posit and evaluate 'Wordsworth' differently, raises rather than settles the question of who is speaking in Wordsworth's poetry.

## Notes

[1] John Barnard (ed.), *John Keats: The Complete Poems* (London: Penguin, 1988), p. 92, ll. 355-59.

[2] Ronald Blythe (ed.), *William Hazlitt: Selected Writings* (Harmondsworth: Penguin Books, 1982), p. 99.

[3] Gérard Genette, *Paratexts: Thresholds of Interpretation*. Trans. Jane E. Lewin (Cambridge: Cambridge Univesity Press, 1997), p. 2. Cf. Jerome McGann's critique of Genette for not including non-linguistic features of print in his discussion of paratextuality in *The Textual Condition* (Princeton: Princeton University Press, 1991), pp. 13-16. For Wordsworth's concern with typography and layout, see Alan D. Boehm, 'The 1798 *Lyrical Ballads* and the Poetics of Late Eighteenth-Century Book Production,' in *English Literary History* 63:2 (1996), pp. 453-87, and Mark L. Reed, 'Wordsworth's Surprisingly Pictured Page: *Select Pieces*,' in *The Book Collector* 46:1 (Spring 1997), pp. 69-92.

[4] Jonathan Wordsworth, M. H. Abrams, and Stephen Gill (eds), *The Prelude 1799, 1805, 1850* (New York and London: Norton, 1979), Book XI, l. 173, p. 424. The dominant line of twentieth-century interpretations of Wordsworth (e.g. A. C. Bradley, Willard Sperry, M. H. Abrams, Geoffrey Hartman, and Harold Bloom) has taken this and similar locutions as essential Wordsworth and has thus tended to neglect any other and potentially contradictory tendencies in the poet's work.

[5] See W. J. T. Mitchell, *Picture Theory: Essays on Verbal and Visual Representation* (Chicago: The University of Chicago Press, 1994). To understand this tendency we need to consider Wordsworth's later work in terms of William Galperin's study, *The Return of the Visible in British Romanticism* (Baltimore and London: The Johns Hopkins University Press, 1993).

[6] William C. Hazlitt (ed.), *The Plain Speaker: Opinions on Books, Men, and Things* (London: George Bell and Sons, 1909), p. 148.

[7] Thomas Hood, *Whims and Oddities in Prose and Verse. A New Edition* (London: Charles Tilt, 1836), p. 188.

[8] See Frances Blanshard's seminal study, *Portraits of Wordsworth* (Ithaca: Cornell University Press, 1959). Blanshard counts eighty-seven portraits of Wordsworth and notes that these are three times as many portraits as were taken of Southey, Coleridge or Lamb, and four times as many as of Byron.

[9] Judith Pascoe, *Romantic Theatricality: Gender, Poetry, and Spectatorship* (Ithaca: Cornell University Press, 1997), p. 189. The opposite approach informs Gillen D'Arcy Wood's *The Shock of the Real: Romanticism and Visual Culture, 1760-1860* (Basingstoke: Palgrave, 2001), which problematically maintains Wordsworth as the other of Romantic visual culture.

[10] See Frances Blanshard, pp. 35-36; 56. According to Haydon, 'In phrenological development [Wordsworth] is without constructiveness while imagination is as big as an egg.' Tom Taylor (ed.), *The Autobiography and Memoirs of Benjamin Robert Haydon* 2 Vols. (London: Peter Davies, 1926), Vol. I, p. 210.

[11] Cited in Frances Blanshard, p. 56.

[12] Alaric Alfred Watts, *Alaric Watts. A Narrative of His Life* (1884), in Peter Swabb (ed.), *Lives of the Great Romantics by Their Contemporaries: Wordsworth* (London: William Pickering, 1996), pp. 463-64.

[13] Elizabeth Barrett Browning, 'Sonnet on Mr Haydon's Portrait of Mr Wordsworth.' Cited from the first published version in *Atheneum* October 29, 1842.

[14] In Peter Swabb (ed.), p. 280.

[15] Ernest de Selincourt (ed.), Alan G. Hill (rev. ed.), *The Letters of William and Dorothy Wordsworth: The Later Years, 1821-1853* 4 Vols. (Oxford: Clarendon Press, 1978-1993), Vol. IV, p. 780.

[16] Frances Blanshard, p. 30. See also p. 68.

[17] Walter Jackson Bate and James Engell (eds), *Biographia Literaria or Biographical Sketches of My Literary Life and Opinions* 2 Vols. (Princeton: Princeton University Press, 1983), Vol. I, p. 41. See also William Henry Ireland, *Chalcographimania; or the Portrait-Collector and Printseller's Chronicle* (London: R. S. Kirkby, 1814).

[18] Jack Simmons (ed.), *Letters from England by Robert Southey* (London: The Cresset Press, 1961), p. 117.

[19] Ibid.

[20] Thomas Hood, p. 194.

[21] See Kurt Weitzmann, *Ancient Book Illumination* (Cambridge, MA: Harvard University Press, 1959), p. 116, and Rudolf Hirsch, *Printing, Selling and Reading, 1450-1550* (Wiesbaden: Otto Harrassowitz, 1974), p. 49.

[22] On authorial portraiture, see David Piper, *The Image of the Poet: British Poets and Their Portraits* (Oxford: Oxford University Press, 1982). On the history of portraiture, see Lorne Campbell, *Renaissance Portraits: European Portrait-Painting in the Fourteenth, Fifteenth and Sixteenth Centuries* (New Haven: Yale University Press, 1990). On the emergence of the modern idea of the author, see Michel Foucault, 'What is an Author?' in Josué V. Harari (ed.), *Textual Strategies: Perspectives*

*in Post-Structuralist Criticism* (Ithaca: Cornell University Press, 1979), pp. 141-60, and Lawrence Lipking, 'The Birth of the Author,' in Warwick Gould and Thomas F. Staley (eds), *Writing the Lives of Writers* (New York: St. Martin's Press, 1998), pp. 36-53.

23. Roger Chartier, *The Order of Books: Readers, Authors, and Libraries in Europe Between the Fourteenth and Eighteenth Centuries*. Trans. Lydia G. Cochrane (Cambridge: Polity Press, 1994), p. 52. On the commercial aspects of frontispiece portraiture, see Cynthia J. Brown, *Poets, Patrons, and Printers: Crisis of Authority in Late Medieval France* (Ithaca and London: Cornell University Press, 1995), p. 61. et passim.

24. Steven Rendall, 'The Portrait of the Author,' in *French Forum* 13:2 (1988), p. 144.

25. Martin Meisel, *Realizations: Narrative, Pictorial, and Theatrical Arts in Nineteenth-Century England* (Princeton: Princeton University Press, 1983), p. 30.

26. Harold Bloom, *The Visionary Company: A Reading of English Romantic Poetry* (Ithaca and London: Cornell University Press, rev. ed., 1971), p. 461.

27. On the significance of posterity as the necessary audience envisioned by Wordsworth and the other canonical male Romantic poets, see Andrew Bennett, *Romantic Poets and the Culture of Posterity* (Cambridge: Cambridge University Press, 1999).

28. Martha H. Shackford, *Wordsworth's Interest in Painters and Painting* (Wellesley, MA: The Wellesley Press, 1945), p. 8. See also James A. W. Heffernan, *The Museum of Words: The Poetry and Poetics of Ekphrasis from Homer to Ashbery* (Chicago and London: The University of Chicago Press, 1993), pp. 91-107.

29. Nathaniel Hawthorne, 'The Prophetic Pictures,' from *Twice-Told Tales*, in Charvat, Pearce, Simpson et al. (eds), *The Centenary Edition of The Works of Nathaniel Hawthorne* (Columbus: Ohio State University Press, 1974), Vol. IX, p. 173.

30. Ernest de Selincourt and Helen Darbishire (eds), *The Poetical Works of William Wordsworth* 5 Vols. (Oxford: Clarendon, 1967-1972), Vol. IV, p. 122. See Matthew C. Brennan, 'Wordsworth's "Lines Suggested by a Portrait from the Pencil of F. Stone": "Visible Quest of Immortality"?' in *English Language Notes* 35:2 (December 1997), pp. 33-44.

31. William Hazlitt, *The Spirit of the Age; Or Contemporary Portraits* (London: Everyman's Library, 1967), p. 257.

32. Robert Southey, *Poetical Works* 10 Vols. (London: Longman, 1838), Vol. III, pp. 305-18.

33. Kenneth Curry (ed.), *New Letters of Robert Southey* 2 Vols. (New York and London: Columbia University Press, 1965), Vol. II, p. 266.

34. On the annuals, see Peter Manning, 'Wordsworth in *The Keepsake*,' in John O. Jordan and Robert L. Patten (eds), *Literature in the Marketplace: Nineteenth-Century British Publishing and Reading Practices* (Cambridge: Cambridge University Press, 1995), pp. 44-73.

35. Ernest de Selincourt (ed.), Alan G. Hill (rev. ed.), *The Letters ... Later Years*, Vol. II, p. 555.

36. Ibid., Vol. III, p. 262.

37 On the demand for a likeness, cf. also letter to Crabb Robinson November 25, 1835, 'ask Moxon if the engraving from my Portrait has been begun – It is often enquired after.' Ibid., Vol. III, p. 122.
38 Ibid., p. 307.
39 See Lee Erickson, *The Economy of Literary Form: English Literature and the Industrialization of Publishing, 1800-1850* (Baltimore and London: The Johns Hopkins University Press, 1996), p. 26 et passim.
40 Ernest de Selincourt (ed.), Alan G. Hill (rev. ed.), *The Letters ... Later Years*, Vol. II, p. 617.
41 Ibid., p. 319.
42 Richard Brilliant, *Portraiture* (Cambridge, MA: Harvard University Press, 1991), p. 14.
43 In Peter Swabb (ed.), p. 279.
44 Ernest de Selincourt (ed.), Alan G. Hill (rev. ed.), *The Letters ... Later Years*, Vol. IV, p. 676. The decision to change frontispiece was made already in January 1837 when Wordsworth wrote to his nephew Christopher at Cambridge, 'If we live to see another Ed: an engraving from Chantrey's Bust shall replace it.' Ibid., Vol. III, pp. 343-44.
45 Michael North, *The Final Sculpture: Public Monuments and Modern Poets* (Ithaca and London: Cornell University Press, 1985), p. 19.
46 Letter to Haydon, January 24, 1846. Ernest de Selincourt (ed.), Alan G. Hill (rev. ed.), *The Letters ... Later Years*, Vol. IV, p. 753.
47 Edith J. Morley (ed.), *The Correspondence of Crabb Robinson with the Wordsworth Circle* 2 Vols. (Oxford: Clarendon Press, 1927), Vol. I, p. 102.
48 Ernest de Selincourt (ed.), Alan G. Hill (rev. ed.), *The Letters ... Later Years*, Vol. I, p. 138.
49 Edith J. Morley (ed.), Vol. II, p. 139.
50 Kenneth Gross, *The Dream of the Moving Statue* (Ithaca: Cornell University Press, 1992), pp. 17-19.
51 Lockhart quoted in Ernest de Selincourt (ed.), Alan G. Hill (rev. ed.), *The Letters ... Later Years*, Vol. III, p. 561 n1.
52 Ibid., p. 561.
53 Judith Pascoe, p. 9.
54 D. F. McKenzie, 'Typography and Meaning: The Case of William Congreve,' in Giles Barber and Bernhard Fabian (eds), *Buch und Buchhandel in Europa im achtzehnten Jahrhundert/The Book and the Book Trade in Eighteenth-Century Europe. Fünftes Wolfenbütteler Symposium* (Hamburg: Dr. Ernst Hauswedell & Co, 1977), p. 83.

# POETIC LAMENTS OF P. B. SHELLEY: CONVENTIONS, FAMILIAR MYSTERIES, AND CRITICAL RESPONSES

Karsten Engelberg

Shelley's early death drastically changed the conditions under which the polarised discussion of his life and works was developing. The fierce controversies of the last years of his life had suddenly had their object removed, and the format of the continued debate was thrown into question. Attacks on moral, political and religious grounds certainly continued, but they lost some of their urgency.[1] The threat from a man who was still active, was much more frightening than that from a dead poet. The restraining conventions associated with death established themselves, and his death abruptly excluded any promise of future development. As a result the critical discussion for decades after struggled to establish productive approaches to Shelley. During his life, appreciations relying on argumentative prose for their format had functioned in an open-ended context. The controversies implicitly assumed continued developments, but with Shelley's death the debate suddenly lost much of its inner drive. An end had occurred, long before the dialogue had produced any of the conclusions being more or less openly sought.

But his early death also activated a conventional literary response, the lament, which renewed dialogue in two new basic formats: dialogue between mourners or dialogue with Shelley himself as one of the interlocutors. Here, then, was a type of text that could offer readers both a set of conventional responses to the death of a fellow human being and the opportunity to continue the dialogue that death seemed to have stopped. Moreover, the lyrical format personalised the dialogue and opened it up to the responses appropriate to intimate discourse with its appeals to spontaneous reactions. The lament proved to be a successful framework for responses that did not strive for the conclusions of the critical essay, but accommodated most of the contradictory assessments of Shelley without any attempt to resolve the contradictions. The laments were crucial in establishing comfortable familiarity with Shelley among the reading public.

As will be apparent, the poetic qualities of the texts often leave much to be desired, but because they represent reactions quite different from the critical assessment in argumentative prose, they constitute a set of responses whose significance to the development of Shelley's reputation must be approached not with the standards of good poetry, but with a sense of their importance in establishing familiarity with his works. Their limited poetic qualities have also meant that they have been committed to the oblivion of literary history.[2] Consequently, the texts are not widely accessible, and for that reason, most of the texts discussed are reprinted in full in this article.

In purely quantitative terms, the poetic texts remained a fairly constant element in critical responses to Shelley in the decades after his death.[3] They were, as one might expect, particularly numerous in 1822-1823, and early examples still accommodated some barbed comments along with softer, more restrained reactions. In 'Elegy on the Death of Shelly [sic]' published in *The Bard* a few months after his death,[4] we meet Shelley the brave challenger of conventional thinking. In the last moments of his life, however, he 'looks to heav'n in penitence and prayer;/And his last words are – "PITY AND FORGIVE!"' (p. 40). At the heart of his challenge, then, was Christian devotion, even if it emerged in full only at the end of his life. Here is the conclusion to the address:

> What ray could cheer that conscious bosom, torn
> By doubts more fearful as the truth draw nigh? –
> In death, could stoic fortitude, or scorn,
> The bless'd tranquillity of HOPE supply? –

The poem stops short of open triumph, but it confirms its readers in the assumption that mortal man cannot defy death. Shelley, too, accepted such common human conditions, and so became an inspiration for the hope that only faith can create.

There are early hints in this poem of the significance that readings of the Bible were to acquire in making Shelley more widely accepted among the reading public. Broadly evangelical perceptions of the Bible as a concrete guide to desirable behaviour provided a range of role models that were echoed in the poetic laments of Shelley. The texts did not consciously allude to specific passages in the Good Book, but they drew more generally on qualities associated with Biblical figures such as the prophet, the saviour and even the Messiah. These roles served also as focal points for a widely shared sense of the need for social and moral reform. The full effect of this did not show itself in the poetic laments until the middle of the nineteenth century. By that time two not specifically literary codes of thought had established themselves: evangelicalism and radicalism. These concepts must be thought of in the broadest possible terms, as becomes evident when looking at the poetic laments published in the 1840s and 1850s. At first glance, the texts seem to have no identifiable context other than the most basic chronological one. The writers range from Alexander Baillie Cochrane,[5] conservative MP and the first Baron Lamington, to John Alfred Langford, chairmaker and self-educated teacher of literature at the Birmingham and Midland Institute. On closer inspection, however, they shared a commitment to moral and social reform. Cochrane was a member of the Young England movement and spent much energy on improving conditions at his Lamington estate, and he was an ardent student of literature. Langford's career provides ample evidence of self-help. Without any formal education – other than his skills as a chairmaker – he became Honourable Secretary of the Birmingham Co-operative Society, taught evening classes, opened his own bookshop, and was a member of the Birmingham School Board, in addition to being an active Unitarian. The group also incorporated the poet Thomas Wade, presumably self-educated, and Robert Buchanan, a staunch follower of Robert Owen's socialist visions and author of *The Past, the Present, and the Future* (1840), a long epic poem written from a belief that poetry is a superior vehicle for instruction. Common to these writers – and the other, anonymous poets that will probably remain anonymous for ever – is the personal, individual commitment to moral and social reform. Their activities all reflected the broadly accepted ideals of self-help, of seriousness of purpose, of abstinence and self-denial, ideals for which the Bible, when read in a literal-minded fashion, provided amble concrete guidance, not least in perceptions of the prophet, the saviour, and the Messiah.[6]

The periodicals that published the texts represent an equally heterogeneous group, but again broadly united in the conviction of the need for moral and social reform. Thomas Cooper, the Chartist, published his *Cooper's Journal: or, Unfettered Thinker and Plain Speaker for Truth, Freedom, and Progress.* *Chambers's London Journal* had as its declared aim to satisfy, in a suitably inexpensive form, the growing public appetite for instruction, while Robert Owen and his followers spread their thoughts on and in *The New Moral World.*[7]

In short, the moral and social ideals of these writers were perhaps widely different in theoretical terms, but they shared a conviction that personal, practical commitment was of the utmost importance. In that respect, the Bible provided man with concrete guidance on acceptable behaviour. The lyrical mode offered just the right individual and specific context in which to explore such personal commitment. It could echo Biblical roles in a free and non-specific fashion, and theoretical disagreements and rational arguments could be legitimately ignored in such texts. Instead, the poetic lament created a framework of broadly shared belief in a better world, and

Shelley became an important force in man's progress towards its realization.

The first stanza of Alexander Baillie Cochrane's 'On Percy Bysshe Shelley' implies both the restraints conventionally acknowledged in laments and the openings offered by the lyrical mode.

> OH! Name it not – think it not! breathe it not now,
> For cold is his aspect, and damp is his brow;
> For his errors we'll weep, for his sins shed a tear,
> But we'll wrong not his name now he's stretched on his bier.[8]

Restraint in the face of death becomes a condition of the dialogue. Shocking statements and claims must be kept out of talk about Shelley. He is entitled to respect. But at the same time the poem opens a dialogue with its reader of a kind that resembles conversation between two mourners trying to come to terms with the shock they have experienced. The shock is registered in the failure, implicit in the opening denials, of the wish to remove any mention of the loss from the conversation. The failure testifies to the forceful nature of the experience, one that defies rational control, and it points forward to the dual-nature image of the second stanza:

> He burst on the senses, he flash'd on the sight,
> Like the meteor which burns in the darkness of night:
> Let the tear-drop fall soft on the turf which ye tread,
> Whom ye honoured when living, oh! wrong not when dead.

The destructive, light-bearing meteor embodies the forceful inevitability of its own course, the intensity of any encounter with it, and the ultimate promise of access to a new existence. And the doubleness continues into the third and final stanza, leaving the reader with an implied sense that Shelley's death is no conclusion:

> His life had no twilight, in splendour he set,
> And the beams of his glory are lingering yet;
> In death, 'mid the cold blasts of envy he stood,
> Ye know he was great, oh! believe he was good.

The appeal of the last line comes as a fitting climax to a text that attempts to engage its reader in a process of mounting enthusiasm. The poem reveals the precariousness of this process in its imploring, almost desperate tone, and the process could certainly be claimed as unsuccessful, ending in a melodramatic gesture of sentimentality. All the same, the appeal captures the ambiguous nature of the final response, the precariousness of the entire process and, not least, the transfer of the experience into the realm of belief. An act of faith seems both fitting and inevitable, and it implies a perception of Shelley that may draw on Christian and elegiac conventions.

Some of these qualities shape the response in Thomas Wade's 'Shelley':

> Holy and mighty Poet of the Spirit
> That broods and breathes along the Universe!
> In the least portion of whose starry verse
> Is the great breath the sphered heavens inherit –
> No human song is eloquent as thine;
> For, by a reasoning instinct all divine,
> Thou feel'st the soul of things; and thereof singing,
> With all the madness of a skylark, springing
> From earth to heaven, the intenseness of thy strain,
> Like the lark's music all around us ringing,
> Laps us in God's own heart, and we regain
> Our primal life etherial! Men profane
> Blaspheme thee: I have heard thee *Dreamer* styled –
> I have mused upon this wakefulness and smiled.[9]

The vocabulary of the poem is noticeable in its religious colouring; even readers who refuse to acknowledge Shelley's sincere offer of interlocution, are termed blasphemers. The dialogue proposed, however, is different in nature from the one in Cochrane's poem. The apostrophe to Shelley annihilates the reality of death and positions Shelley not as the interlocutor in a shared experience of loss, but as a prophet, even a saviour who moves beyond common human understanding. One can detect faint echoes of the story of Martha and Mary in the conversation that the poem offers: recognize the one thing needful, place yourself by his feet and you will commune with perceptions that reach far beyond the cares and conditions of this world. Common conversation, therefore, will not suffice. Attentive listening is essential, but the language of the poem can only offer an approximation of the experience being proposed. In its diverse attempt to capture the nature of the experience, the poem relies on a series of conventional comparisons. The continued existence of the deceased in the natural elements lends him both immortality and immediate presence in the physical world as well as omnipresence and limitless range. Almost paradoxical powers are granted to Shelley: 'by a reasoning instinct all divine,/Thou feel'st the soul of things.'

The suggestion carries a sense that human qualities are integrated, not divided and divisive, a sense that the limitations of human existence have been cancelled. Shelley appears as a prophet or even the Messiah who gives man access to God. And the language in which Shelley addresses his readers is not the limiting language of words. It is the far more suggestive language of music. The poem ends on a note of assurance, quite different from the desperation of the poem discussed above. It is the assurance of the converted, safe in the knowledge that the dialogue is firm, even if it is far from evenly balanced.

The central Christian paradox of immortality achieved through mortality echoes in J. W. King's sonnet 'Shelley.'

> Star of the Olympia-crowned! Thy titan deeds,
>    Thy grand and soul-impassioned muse was hurled
>    Upon thy memory of a scoffing world;
> Yet wilt thou live beyond the pigmy creeds;
> And as the thunder-riven storm-cloud feeds
>    The famish'd land, thy soul's great harvest will
> Flow onward through all time. Even now it leads
>    Full many a toiler up Mind's rugged hill.
> Few were thy years, yet sage wast thou in song,
>    Immortal in thy pure mortality;
> Bold and defiant in thy hate of wrong,
>    Quenchless as Etna, mighty as a sea.
> While the soul-incense from the funeral pyre
> Balmed the creations of thy prostrate lyre.[10]

The paradoxical 'immortal in thy pure mortality' suggests the suspension of temporal restraints, and a note of repentance, almost a plea for forgiveness, creeps into the defiant promise that Shelley will become a spiritual leader in spite of all the abuse he had to suffer. Although the classical allusions in the poem are robustly obvious, they are couched in terms more obviously Biblical than Hellenic. The Messianic figure or the prophet is difficult to miss, and the note of respectful homage parallels the image. Echoes of Moses leading Israel out of Egypt towards the promised land can be detected, too, in a speech that seems to invite or expect no response. This is the homage of a devoted follower, one who celebrates the migration into a better land, one who will take the lead from and be content with following his wise leader. Exploration, individual perceptions and a dialectic reading process have no place in this statement. Shelley is too exalted for this to happen.

Robert Buchanan's 'On Shelley' abandons the most private and intimate suggestion of dialogue and strikes the note of a declaration of faith offered to a wider audience of fellow believers, present and future. His poem works with the full range of prophetic roles:

> He's gone! The music of his voice is gone!
> He who was wisdom's highly favour'd one!
> In whom thought, feeling, fancy, all combined
> To form the essence of a mighty mind;
> A meteor of the air – a burning light –
> 'Midst the world's darkness, brief as it was bright;
> A spirit purged from dross, and deeply fraught
> With all the subtle elements of thought;
> Whose vast expansive mind did boldly scan,
> With eagle eye, the destiny of man;
> Who pass'd the breach that narrow souls confined,
> And left the world a century behind.
> Led on by truth, he scaled the dizzy height
> Of proud philosophy, and from the bright
> And lovely things of Nature he did cull
> The fairest flowers, to render beautiful
> Those great imaginings of man's high fate
> That fill'd his ever active brain. Elate
> With splendid visions of the high behest
> That waits the good and virtuous, his warm breast
> Harbour'd no selfish feeling; he did live
> Not for himself, but that man might receive
> The richness of his wisdom. But no more
> Will he illumine the world! The blaze is o'er!
> Yet, wide the seeds are spread, and taking root,
> Which soon shall fill the world with choicest fruit;
> And ages yet to come will fondly bless
> His name – a boon denied in this.[11]

Beginning at the point of loss, the poem gradually establishes a new existence for Shelley. The meteor image of superhuman power, of unstoppable natural force, of light takes the poem into a perception of Shelley as a 'spirit purged from dross,' existing above the conditions of the temporal world. This is the ideal condition for his role as a prophet and a seer, whose extraordinary insights provide man with new opportunities. He lived 'Not for himself,' but sacrificed his own comfort to help man to new understandings. The rhetoric of the final lines confuses meteors, flowers, and seeds in an attempt to establish a sense of hope that his work has taken on a different existence and will continue to live a life of its own. The awkward mixture of figures of speech captures, quite inadvertently no doubt, the essentially irrational nature of this hope, making it akin, again, to a religious faith that accepts the presence of mysteries in man's life that surpass all understanding, but at the same time leaves the process of continued hope open to all.

In 1840, *Tait's Edinburgh Magazine* published a poem signed E.T. It progresses from the dialogue of mourners to the direct address.

> That hand, that once did wake the poet's lyre
> To strains of sweet and magic witchery,
> Is powerless now: and quenched the heavenly fire
>     Which once did animate his spirit high,
> And taught it from its mortal coil to fly.
>     No more he'll soar aloft on fairy wing,
> Nor his soft spirit with the mourner sigh;
>     For now with angels he holds communing
> On themes sublimer far than e'er did poet sing.
>
> And thou wast hated and accursed of men,
> Thou, gentle spirit, and yet them did bless,
> Thy love extended to each denizen
>     Of earth; nor on them smiled'st thou the less,
> Though they blasphemed thy name, made thy distress
>     Their sport, and mocked when thy wan face
> Did look on them. But soon shalt thou possess
>     A fame coeval with the human race;
> For hearts of men shall be thy memory's dwelling-place.[12]

The apostrophe of the second stanza casts Shelley in the mould of the long-suffering, persecuted prophet who was always prepared to turn the other cheek, whose aspirations took him beyond the sorrows of an earthly existence. The tone suggests a wish to offer atonement, a humble recognition that man has not yet fully appreciated the offers of insight that Shelley could make. The easily recognisable religious overtones of 'blasphemes' merely echo the same thought.

The apostrophe could sometimes be used even more overtly and irrationally to deny the reality of Shelley's death.

Then thou art gone to thy rest; yet we will not deplore
    Thy fate so untimely – the sea be thy tomb!
For thy spirit had dwelt there thro' long years before
    Thy body sank under the green water's gloom.

'Twas there thou didst weave those magical spells
    That chained the minds which they stole among;
'Tis there eternal melody swells
    Mingled with strains of thine own sweet song.

Thine was the spirit that wandered far
    From its earthly clay – thro' Heaven's blue dome;
And the midnight earth, and the twinkling star,
    And the deep sea were its constant home.

And the spirits that animate Nature's forms,
    The soft blue lake and the Appenine,
And the waving wood and raging storms
    Ever claimed kindred thoughts with thine,

Thou didst dwell in them and they in thee;
    And neither seemed to be sprung from earth;
But in love, and beauty, and poetry,
    Alike they had their heavenly birth.

And Ocean knew his poet brother,
    And opened its emerald breast;
And the billows sung to one another,
    To welcome thee to thy bed of rest.

Calm be thy slumbers and happy their breaking
    When the destined time for oblivion's sped,
When all from their deep sweet sleep are waking,
    And the earth and sea restore their dead.[13]

Shelley's death merely allowed him to continue an existence in surroundings already familiar and agreeable to him. There is a sense of gradual metamorphosis promising to end in universal resurrection of which Shelley's fate seems a precursor. Until the day of resurrection, the dialogue with Shelley is still possible, but in this poem there is little sense of a balanced dialogue, more a suggestion that we may watch Shelley and cherish the thought of future resurrection.

The implications of resurrection are present in John Alfred Langford's sonnet 'To Shelley.'

> Thou wronged and childlike spirit! – oft have I,
> Enraptured, pondered o'er thy living page
> Then turned indignant to the bigot age, –
> That basely on thy head heaped calumny,
> And spat its sland'rous venom on thy name.
> Thou loving heart and earnest! – it is well
> For us and for the world, that such have been,
> Who dared to raise their voice above the swell
> Of tyrant shouts, – despising scorn and shame.
> How in thy bosom burned Truth's holy flame,
> When mock religion in the church was seen!
> Then came thy song resounding full and free,
> In praise of justice, right , and liberty, –
> Which yet shall win its meed – a deathless fame![14]

This is the celebration of the naive courage, almost of a Christ-like quality, which will receive its just reward eventually.

The lyrical mode offered perceptions of Shelley quite different from those of prose discussions. It offered the perfect format for perceptions that emphasized personal, unselfish commitment to moral and social reform. The open-ended dialogue drawing on perceptions of Shelley as a Messiah, a saviour and a prophet in some special relationship with the world around him created an opportunity to encompass the extremities of his critical reputation. Just as widely different moral and social convictions could meet in the belief that reform presupposed personal commitment, so the poetic lament could accommodate widely different perceptions of Shelley. The broadly shared belief that good unselfish deeds would somehow lead to new and better social and moral conditions accommodated mysteries and contradictions that were beyond the reach of analytical prose. The lyrical laments of the mid-nineteenth century were uniquely suited to making Shelley and his poetry agreeable to the general reading public.[15]

## Notes

[1] The most comprehensive collection of contemporary criticism of Shelley remains Newman Ivey White, *The Unextinguished Hearth: Shelley and His Contemporary Critics* (Durham, NC: Duke University Press, 1938). It also includes some obituaries

and poetic tributes published immediately after his death.
2. As a result, very few of these texts have been subjected to critical analysis. One exception is Thomas Lovell Beddoes, 'Lines Written in a Blank Leaf of the "Prometheus Unbound"' discussed in Michael O'Neill, '"A Storm of Ghosts": Beddoes, Shelley, Death, and Reputation",' *The Cambridge Quarterly* 28 (1999), pp. 102-15.
3. For a comprehensive list of these texts, see Karsten Klejs Engelberg, *The Making of the Shelley Myth* (London and Westport, CT: Mansell Publishing Limited and Meckler, 1988).
4. F. 'Elegy on the Death of Shelly [sic],' *The Bard*, vol. 1, [no.5] (16 November 1822), pp. 38-40
5. For details on all writers mentioned in the article, see the *DNB*. Alexander Baillie Cochrane appears under the name of Cochrane-Baillie.
6. This essay does not allow for detailed discussion of the complex interrelationship of these moral and social ideals, but numerous studies exist, e.g. Richard D. Altick, *Victorian People and Ideas* (New York: W. W. Norton and Company, 1973), and Walter E. Houghton, *The Victorian Frame of Mind: 1830-1870* (New Haven and London: Yale University Press, 1957).
7. Accounts of these periodicals remain scarce, but *Chambers's Journal* and *Tait's Edinburgh Magazine* are included in *British Literary Magazines: The Romantic Age: 1789-1836*, ed. Alvin Sullivan (Westport, CT, and London: Greenwood Press, 1983) and in *The Wellesley Index to Victorian Periodicals: 1824-1900*, ed. Walter E. Houghton et al., vols 1-5 (Toronto: University of Toronto Press, 1966-1989).
8. See Alexander Baillie Cochrane, *The Morea* ([London], 1840), pp. 81-82.
9. It was first published anonymously in one of Leigh Hunt's journals: *The Tatler*, vol. 2. No. 191 (14 April 1831), 763. Then in Thomas Wade, *Mundi et Cordis: de Rebus Sempiternis et Temporariis: Carmina* (London, 1835), p. 120.
10. See *The Beacon: A Weekly Journal of Politics and Literature*, no. 10 (28 December 1853), p. 159.
11. See *The New Moral World*, vol. 4, no. 170 (27 January 1838), p. 112.
12. E. T. 'Shelley,' *Tait's Edinburgh Magazine*, vol. 7, no. 81 (September 1840), p. 594. E.T. may be the initials of Emily Taylor, a dissenter who joined the Church of England under the influence of Frederick Denison Maurice. See *DNB* for more details.
13. D. 'To Shelley, (Who was drowned in the Mediterranean.),' *Chambers's London Journal*, vol 3, no. 113 (22 July 1843), p. 232.
14. See *Cooper's Journal*, vol. 1, no. 21 (25 May 1850), p. 328.
15. This accommodation came at a price, though, as Matthew Arnold recognized in his later characterization of Shelley as 'a beautiful and ineffectual angel beating in the void his luminous wings in vain.'

# VICTORIAN ANGLES ON BLAKE: READING THE ARTIST'S HEAD IN THE LATE NINETEENTH CENTURY

Lene Østermark-Johansen

When eventually Walter Savage Landor (1775-1864) died, he had outlived most of his Romantic contemporaries. For the last many years of his life he had been 'the mad old poet,' abandoned by his family, but cared for by the Brownings and other Anglo-American expatriates in Florence. Landor's mental derangement was generally known in England, and shortly after his death readers of John Forster's life of the poet could read the following meditations on madness among the Romantics:

> [In 1836] At an old bookseller's in Bristol he [Landor] picked up some of the writings of Blake, and was strangely fascinated by them. ... He protested that Blake had been Wordsworth's prototype, and wished they could have divided his madness between them; for that some accession of it in the one case, and something of a diminution of it in the other would very greatly have improved both.[1]

One wonders, of course, whether grammatically 'his madness' refers to Blake's madness or to Landor's own, but the term may well have been left deliberately ambiguous. In 1869, when Forster's life of Landor was published, William Blake's reputed madness had long been the subject of some debate. Ever since 1785 Blake's works had occasionally been described as the works of a madman,[2] but it was the publication of Alexander Gilchrist's *Life of William Blake* in 1863 which more than anything brought the issue of artistic madness to the fore.[3] Gilchrist's biography initiated the enthusiastic late-Victorian Blake cult in which the artist soon emerged in such new disguises as a veritable Swinblake, an art-for-art's-sake-Blake, or as one of Yeats's Irish visionary predecessors.[4] A defence of Blake against the allegations of madness was obviously a major concern for Gilchrist; apart from dealing with the issue in a separate chapter with the somewhat categorical title 'Mad or not Mad?' Gilchrist began his book with a quotation from Wordsworth:

> Yet no less a contemporary than Wordsworth, a man little prone to lavish eulogy or attention on brother poets, spoke in private of the *Songs of Innocence and Experience* of William Blake, as 'undoubtedly the production of insane genius',

(which adjective we shall, I hope, see cause to qualify), but as to him more significant than the works of many a famous poet. 'There is something in the madness of this man,' declared he (to Mr. Crabb Robinson), 'which interests me more than the sanity of Lord Byron and Walter Scott.'[5]

The authority of Wordsworth is here invoked to justify Gilchrist's (and our) inquiring into the madness of Blake, which – of course – is more interesting than the sanity of Byron and Scott. It is the sanity of Wordsworth's voice that gives credibility to Gilchrist's project. Writing at the time when Henry Maudsley, the mid-Victorian lunacy debates and asylum reforms were at their height, when the sensation novels of Charles Dickens, Wilkie Collins and Mary Elizabeth Braddon were just beginning to raise questions of medical authority and definitions of madness, Gilchrist was touching on a matter of topical relevance. Every major late-Victorian monograph on Blake after Gilchrist would start out by defending Blake's sanity in the voice of the amateur quack or the fellow artist, better equipped than anyone else for understanding the full range of the artistic mind. Thus Swinburne's critical essay (1868) is rooted in the dialectic between what other people saw in Blake and Swinburne's own profound understanding of artistic genius:

> In a time of critical reason and definite division, he was possessed by a fervour and fury of belief; among sane men who had disproved most things and proved the rest, here was an evident madman who believed a thing, one may say, only insomuch as it was incapable of proof. He lived and worked out of all rule, and yet by law. He had a devil, and its name was Faith. ... People remember at this day with horror and pity the impression of his daring ways of speech, but excuse him still on the old plea of madness. Now on his own ground no man was ever more sane or more reverent.[6]

In the long introductory memoir to his edition of Blake's poetical works of 1874 William Michael Rossetti posed the question of Blake's madness on page 12 and left the reader in great suspense for another 75 pages, before finally introducing such terms about him as 'an enthusiast,' 'a queer fellow' and concluding with great caution, well aware that he was treading on sacred ground:

> To call Blake simply a madman would be ridiculous and despicable; even to call him (as some have done) an inspired madman would be most incomplete and misleading. But it may, I think, be allowable to say that he was a sublime genius, often perfectly sane, often visionary and *exalté* without precisely losing his hold upon sanity, and sometimes exhibiting an insane taint.[7]

When in 1893 Edwin Ellis and the young William Butler Yeats published their monumental three-volume edition of Blake, they printed for the first time Blake's text of *The Four Zoas* and devoted the major part of their critical discussion of Blake to an exploration of his symbolic system. Indeed, in their preface, they proudly heralded *The Four Zoas* as the 'guarantee of his sanity.' Dismissing, with youthful arrogance, the works of Gilchrist, Swinburne and Rossetti as useless, as empty myth-making, not founded in a proper reading of Blake's own words, Yeats and Ellis saw their book as contributing to an entirely new understanding of Blake's texts and ideas: their Blake is both a medieval mystic and a great modern symbolist poet. Well aware of writing at the end of the century Ellis and Yeats looked with great optimism into the future of Blake studies, a future that would liberate Blake from the absurdities of the madness myth: 'Fresh material comes in from time to time, and now that readers are relieved of their discouraging inability to prove that they are not studying the life or works of a madman, it is probable that much will be done in the near future.'[8]

This brief survey of the haunting myth of Blake's madness serves primarily as an overture to the real subject of this essay: William Blake's head and the Victorians' attempt to establish a visual image of the Romantic poet that fully corresponded to their own complex myth of him. Elsewhere in this volume Peter Simonsen has convincingly demonstrated Wordsworth's concern with controlling the image of the author in the frontispiece portraits to his 1836 and 1845 volumes of poetry, but biographies also traditionally contain frontispiece portraits of their subjects. As biographies usually made their appearance after the death of their subject, the desire to control one's afterlife was a major Victorian concern, as so much of the recent literature on the subject has pointed out. Destruction of material, authorized biographies and autobiographies were all ways of attempting such control, at avoiding Judas the biographer while playing Christ the martyr.

The biographer and the portrait painter share the important role as interpreters, as intermediaries between the subject and an audience. In fact, very few biographies are written without some form of publication in mind, and most visual portraits are undertaken with a viewer in mind. The oscillation between human subject and art object embodied in the very genre of the portrait necessarily incorporates a viewer's gaze. It is the viewer who establishes the relationship between the representation of the self in the real world and its analogue in the world of art; indeed, the mimetic aspect of both portraiture and biography connect them closely. Without some element of likeness to the original, to the life of the subject, there would be no portrait or biography. Richard Brilliant describes portraiture as 'an art of deception in which artist and subject are both accomplices,[9] and it is in the complex coming together of self-representation and artistic representation that the whole genre of portraiture resides. Provokingly, Brilliant suggests that 'portraiture is such a calculating art of (mis)representation that no beholder can be completely innocent,'[10] yet despite this awareness of misrepresentation, the genre of portraiture is also characterized by the notion of 'correctness,' 'faithfulness' to the original.

Which is the best portrait of Blake? What does it mean that something is 'a good portrait'? A quick glance at the frontispieces of the major Victorian monographs on Blake soon reveal that there is not much agreement on the matter. Although Blake never rivalled Wordsworth when it comes to the actual number of different portraits of the artist taken during his lifetime, Geoffrey Keynes's catalogue lists some forty different portraits of the artist, done by himself or artist friends.[11] By the mid and late nineteenth century many of these portraits would have been known to Blake's biographers and editors as a figural record of the subject over the years: Blake in youth, in middle age, as an old man; seen by himself, in earnest, in caricature, formally posing or captured in informal situations in quick sketches by artist friends. Quite a few of Blake's artist friends who had painted portraits of him, such as John Linnell (1792-1882), George Richmond (1809-1896) and Samuel Palmer (1805-81), were still alive with major private collections of Blakeana, made accessible to Gilchrist, the Rossettis and Swinburne. Thus although Blake was distinctively of the past, it was a just tangible past that could be reached through these survivors.

If portraiture is an 'art of deception in which artist and subject are accomplices,' it is, of course, not insignificant that in the Blake portraits both sitter and painter are artists: most portraits of Blake consequently become statements by fellow artists about being an artist, about being Blake *the* artist. The constant focus on Blake's head, seen in profile, en face, in three-quarters or from above, makes it quite obvious that these are all images of a great mind, of an artist with an unusual faculty of imagination, to speak in phrenological terms. Where contemporary portraits of such other Romantic poets as Byron and Wordsworth certainly allow for inclusion of the poet's body in the painting, Blake is all head.[12] Blake the artisan, with his hands deep down in etching fluids and water colours, appears to have been completely neglected even by his artist friends for whom – in their artistic representation at least – Blake the Romantic artist was entirely a brain worker. As such, most of these portraits become metaphysical, rather than physical portraits; there is an artistic attempt to capture the essence of Blake's great mind and soul through a repeated focus on his skull, the very skull which in

Yeats's and Ellis's words seemed 'almost a muscle of the mind.'[13] This image, highly suggestive of all the strength, energy and activity with which Yeats and Ellis associated Blake, also attributes an almost plastic quality to Blake's skull. Could one actually see his great mind at work simply by looking at his skull?

A very large number of the Blake portraits are profile portraits. The profile is an interesting form of reductive sign: the sitter cannot see his own profile, right and left profiles are seldom identical, and it takes an 'other' to verify the 'correctness' of a profile portrait. When we study these profile portraits of Blake, we see him, in other words, from an angle from which he could never have studied himself; we immediately impose the gaze of an 'other' upon Blake and are aware that we do not see the full face, that one half is hidden from us. Ever since the late eighteenth century, Lavater and generations of physiognomists after him had recommended the profile view as the basis for a physiognomic reading of people's heads; in its reductive and rigid formality the profile provides a certain generalization of individual and particular features, and makes them comparable to a whole physiognomic system of foreheads, noses and chins.

We do not know exactly what was the interplay between Blake and his artist colleagues when they painted portraits of him. Did they settle on the profile view by mutual agreement, or do these profiles reflect Blake's own keen awareness of physiognomical representation?[14] Was he so highly conscious of the unusual shape of his skull, with its extraordinarily high forehead, that he deliberately wanted to invite a reading of his own head from any future audience by letting himself be portrayed as the subject of a physiognomical reading? According to Lavater, 'the peculiar delineation of the outline and position of the forehead' was the 'most important of all the things presented to physiognomical observation.'[15] In Lavater's taxonomical hierarchy the forehead came out top as the seat – together with the eyes and eyebrows – of the intellectual life of man:

> The form, height, arching, proportion, obliquity, and position of the skull, or bone of the forehead, show the propensity, degree of power, thought, and sensibility of man. The covering, or skin, of the forehead, its position, colour, wrinkles, and tensions, denote the passion and present state of mind. – The bones give the internal quality, and their covering the application of power. The forehead bones remain unaltered, though the skin be wrinkled, but this wrinkling varies acording to the various forms of the bones.[16]

There is an interesting tension between the static and the fluctuating in Lavater's description of the bone structure of the forehead and the skin that covers it. It is the tension between being and becoming, between inborn qualities and a plastic film which allows for the expression of emotions and a recording of the passing of time. It is, in fact, in the very same interface between the constant and the momentary that most portraits exist; while trying to express a certain constancy of character in the sitter, portrait painters also frequently attempt to capture a momentary, yet 'characteristic,' facial expression to give an air of vividness and immediacy to the portrait. The frozen moment captured in portraiture is often intended to sum up a life, most especially, of course, in portraits of people in old age, and in the summing up of a life, the genre of portraiture resembles that of the biography. Indeed, the representation of Blake in the frontispieces of the late Victorian monographs of him all suggest this parallel between the image and the life: the Blake we see, before we read about him, is a mature or an old man, sometimes serene and composed, sometimes full of the ardour and fury that Yeats would invoke in his late poem 'An Acre of Grass' from *Last Poems* (1940):

> Grant me an old man's frenzy,
> Myself must I remake
> Till I am Timon and Lear
> Or that William Blake
> Who beat upon the wall
> Till Truth obeyed his call;
>
> A mind Michael Angelo knew
> That can pierce the clouds,
> Or inspired by frenzy
> Shake the dead in their shrouds;
> Forgotten else by mankind,
> An old man's eagle mind.[17]

It is the 'old man's eagle mind' which is the subject of inquiry in most of these frontispiece portraits. Blake himself appears to have used the serene figure of Socrates as his alter ego or ideal of aged wisdom. Henry Crabb Robinson's famous diary entry for 10 December 1825 about Blake in old age, frequently quoted by the Victorians, evokes some of the complexity of Blake's identification with Socrates:

Shall I call him Artist or Genius – or Mystic – or Madman? Probably he is all –
He has a most interesting appearance [.] He is now old – pale with a Socratic
countenance and an expression of great sweetness but bordering on weakness
– except when his features are animated by expression [.] And then he has an
air of inspiration about him ... ['] What resemblance do you suppose is there
between your Spirit & the Spirit of Socrates?[' '] The same as between our
countenances [.'] – He paused & added – ['] I was Socrates.['] And then as if
correcting himself: ['] A sort of brother – I must have had conversations with
him – So I had with Jesus Christ – I have an obscure recollection of having
been with both of them [.']¹⁸

The same trio of Blake, Socrates and Jesus Christ recurs in Blake's Notebook in one of the fragments of 'The Everlasting Gospel.' The Notebook is the socalled 'Rossetti Manuscript,' bought by D. G. Rossetti in 1847 from Samuel Palmer's brother, and one of the most important pieces of Blakeana to the Pre-Raphaelites, stimulating much of the interest in Blake that was to follow.[19] Rossetti proudly wrote on the flyleaf the price and provenance of the Notebook, together with one of its chief assets: 'Among the sketches, there are one or two profiles of Blake himself.'[20] On p. 33 of the Notebook we read the following poetic discourse on visions, noses and the dialectics of Heaven and Hell:

> The vision of Christ that thou dost see
> Is my Visions Greatest Enemy
> Thine has a great hook nose like thine
> Mine has a snub nose like to mine
> Thine is the Friend of All Mankind
> Mine speaks in parables to the Blind
> Thine loves the same world that mine hates
> Thy Heaven doors are my Hell Gates
> Socrates taught what Melitus
> Loathd as a Nations bitterest Curse
> And Caiphas was in his own Mind
> A benefactor to Mankind
> Both read the Bible day & night
> But thou readst black where I read white.[21]

David Erdman has explained Blake's image of Christ's snub nose with a reference to a prose note some 30 pages further into the Notebook:[22] 'I always thought that Jesus Christ was a Snubby or I should not have worshipd him if I had thought he had been one of those long spindle nosed rascals.'[23] From Crabb Robinson's diary entry, Blake's poetic fragment and his prose note emerges an image of a poet highly aware of the significance of physiognomy and of constructing a myth of self. By placing himself as an intermediary between the moderns and such myth-ridden figures as Christ and Socrates, Blake joins their ranks, not unlike the way his great hero Michelangelo had constructed an elaborate Socratic and Christlike myth of self.[24] One wonders whether Crabb Robinson would have described Blake's countenance as 'Socratic' if Blake had not himself suggested a similarity between his own appearance and that of Socrates in the mini-dialogue reported by Crabb Robinson. The recurrence of the word 'countenance' in the diary entry suggests a certain connexion in the diarist's mind between dialogue and description.

As for Blake's 'being Socrates,' he appears to have explored this in the profile self-portrait (drawn before 1809) in the Notebook (plate 4) which actually reveals a forehead which 'is very similar to the almost snubby Socrates in Lavater's *Physiognomy*.'[25] Blake's own nose in this self-portrait is, however, anything but a snub, and although he would not have been able to see his own profile, none of the portraits of him painted by other artists depict him with a Socratic snub. Another profile self-caricature as 'Cancer,' dating from around 1819-20 (plate 5) and presumably intended for John Varley's *Zodiacal Physiognomy* (1828), shows Blake with quite a different kind of high forehead. It does, however, depict him with a distinctive *nez retroussé*, and Blake's visionary head of Socrates of much the same date (plate 6) gives the ancient philosopher a forehead like the one in Blake's 1809 self-portrait and the conventional snub nose.[26] Did Blake's nose shrink with age as he was becoming increasingly Socratic? All three portraits depict their subjects from the left profile with prominent foreheads and protruding eyes glancing heavenwards, but noses vary. So what, indeed, did Blake look like? And what did Socrates look like?

The countenance of Socrates had been one of the great challenges in Lavater's physiognomic system. If, in the well-ordered Christian world, there was supposed to be a direct correspondence between man's inner qualities and their manifestation in his outer appearance, how could one of the greatest thinking minds of antiquity have been so reputedly ugly? Lavater devoted an entire chapter in the first volume of his work to an exploration of the case of Socrates and provided no less than 9 different illustrations of the great philosopher's head.[27] Distrust in the visual source material was one of Lavater's first ways of tackling the problem: 'What painter, however good, is accurate in his foreheads? Nay, where is the shade that defines them justly?

Plate 4

William Blake, *Self-portrait caricature* pencil, before 1809.

Plate 5

William Blake, *Self-caricature as Cancer*, pencil, 16.5 x 11.4, c. 1820.

Plate 6

William Blake, *Socrates*, pencil, 31.1 x 20.2 cm, c. 1820.

How much less an engraving from the last of a succession of copies?'[28] Another was of course to attribute a special kind of expert gaze to the physiognomist; all the ancient rumour mongers who had declared that Socrates was ugly did not know the full significance of a forehead such as his: 'Whoever considers this forehead as the abode of stupidity has never been accustomed to observe the forehead. ... In these high and roomy arches, undoubtedly, the spirit dwells which will penetrate clouds of difficulties, and vanquish hosts of impediments.'[29]

Lucy Hartley and Sally Shuttleworth have pointed out the importance given to the gaze in eighteenth- and nineteenth-century physiognomy: it is through the eyes that human beings differentiate people from each other and form judgements on them; in one's reading of another's face, it is also the other's eyes that reveal the highest degree of intellect and character.[30] Through careful observation, by means of his expert gaze, the physiognomist could discriminate the familiar from the unfamiliar and see the general in the particular. Although not denying Socrates his uniqueness, Lavater was also placing him amongst a particular category of foreheads whose vaulted arches testified to their intellect and spirituality. And in the architectural structure of the face, the nose was, of course, a crucial building stone:

> I hold the nose to be the foundation, or abutment, of the brain. Whoever is acquainted with the Gothic arch will perfectly understand what I mean by this abutment; for upon this the whole power of the arch of the forehead rests, and without it the mouth and cheeks would be oppressed by miserable ruins.[31]

The nose of Socrates thus prevented his formidable forehead from collapsing into ruins, and as an index of character his snub suggested a patient sufferer.[32] Indeed, from Lavater's description of the characteristics of the snubnosed, one begins to see why Blake 'always thought that Jesus Christ was a Snubby':

> There are, indeed, innumerable excellent men with defective noses, but their excellence is of a very different kind. I have seen the purest, most capable, and noblest persons with small noses, and hollow in profile; but their worth most consisted in suffering, listening, learning, and enjoying the beautiful influences of imagination; provided the other parts of the form were well organized. ... Boerhave, Socrates, Lairesse, had, more or less, ugly noses, and yet were great men; but their character was that of gentleness and patience.[33]

In Blake's private myth-making, Jesus, Socrates and Blake all shared the fate of being the victims of false accusations. When Leigh Hunt and his two brothers Robert and John had attacked Blake's pictures and his sanity in *The Examiner* in 1809, Blake depicted these three in the figures of Anytus the tanner, Melitus the Poet, and Lycon the orator, the three accusers of Socrates in Plate 93 of his *Jerusalem* (Plate 7).[34] Inscribed on their pointing, but noseless, bodies are the words: 'Anytus Melitus & Lycon thought Socrates a very Pernicious Man[.] So Caiphas thought Jesus[.]'

Plate 7
William Blake, *Jerusalem*, plate 93.

There can be little doubt that Blake knew his Lavater; he had engraved 4 plates for his book on physiognomy and had annotated his *Aphorisms on Man* carefully. In Blake's copy of Lavater's *Aphorisms*, now in the Huntington Library, the title page reveals Blake's affection for the Swiss physiognomist. None other than Gilchrist drew his readers' attention to this particular annotation: 'On the title-page occurs a naïve token of affection: below the name Lavater is inscribed "Will. Blake" and around the two names the outline of a heart.'[35] Anne Mellor has pointed out how several of the anecdotes about Blake in Gilchrist's biography provide examples of the poet's physiognomical observations on himself and others,[36] and she analyses a series of Blake's *Visionary Heads* from the point of view of early nineteenth-century theories of physiognomy and phrenology in order to demonstrate Blake's fascination with the reading of heads. All the strange bumps on several of his *Visionary Heads*, drawn around 1820, certainly suggest that he was deeply involved in the 'bumpological mania' which swept over England in the 1820s and which both acquired serious followers, such as Flaxman, Coleridge, Mill, Martineau, and Bulwer-Lytton, and provoked elaborate satires with such enticing titles as *The Craniad: A Serio-Comic Poem* and *Travels in Phrenologasto*.[37]

Gilchrist's many references to Blake as a reader of heads follow the reader's own initial reading of Blake's head on the cover of the book and on the frontispiece. In 1861, a year before the death of Gilchrist, John Linnell had made a watercolour copy on paper of his portrait of Blake on ivory of 1821, presumably with the intention of letting it form the basis for the engraving by C.H. Jeens which now serves as the frontispiece to Gilchrist's book (plate 8).[38] Embossed in gold on the cover and facing the title page, Blake's profile head invites a reading before the ensuing life of this 'pictor ignotus.' The highlight of almost divine inspiration illuminates the forehead from the right and reveals a series of remarkable bumps. Equipped with any of the phrenologcal manuals in circulation in mid-Victorian England, the reader could discern which faculties were particularly well developed in the great artist's head.

Plate 8
Engraving by C. H. Jeens after John Linnell, *Portrait of William Blake* (1861).

A. C. Swinburne substituted his own reading of the frontispiece to Gilchrist for any frontispiece to his own book on Blake of 1868, a book which originally started out as a review of Gilchrist, but soon expanded beyond the review. Although lavishly illustrated, Swinburne's monograph contains no visual portrait of Blake, but the ekphrastic powers of the author's opening pages evoke Jeens's engraving after Linnell in a manner as suggestive as Walter Pater's prose description of Leonardo's *Mona Lisa* of 1869.[39] Indeed, for anyone acquainted with Pater's *Mona Lisa* it is difficult not to see a clear precursor in Swinburne's Blake. Both these verbal portraits 'grow' upon the observer by the subtle means of a hypnotic prose rhythm, through their strangely smiling subjects who somehow transmit their seductive souls to the reader. Although lengthy, Swinburne's prose portrait deserves quoting in full:

> We have now the means of seeing what he was like as to face in the late years of his life: for his biography has at the head of it a clearly faithful and valuable likeness. The face is singular, one that strikes at a first sight and grows upon the observer; a brilliant eager old face, keen and gentle, with a preponderance of brow and head; clear bird-like eyes, eloquent excitable mouth, with a look of nervous and fluent power; the whole lighted through as it were from behind with a strange and pure kind of smile, touched too with something of an impatient prospective rapture. The words clear and sweet seem the best made for it; it has something of fire in its composition, and something of music. If there is a want of balance, there is abundance of melody in the features; melody rather than harmony; for the mould of some is weaker and the look of them vaguer than that of others. Thought and time have played with it, and have nowhere pressed hard; it has the old devotion and desire with which men set to their work at starting. It is not the face of a man who could ever be cured of illusions; here all the medicines of reason and experience must have been spent in pure waste.[40]

Swinburne's Blake is an ecstatic singer, much like Swinburne himself. Indeed, his very face is transformed into a piece of music, melodious rather than harmonious, in which those strange bumps and depressions become ascending and descending notes. The 'look of nervous and fluent power' suggests the almost mesmerizing powers projecting from Blake's head, and the 'strange and pure kind of smile' makes him both experienced and innocent, both adult and child. Blake's rapture is Swinburne's own; Swinburne's electrified – and melodious – prose and his enthusiasm for his subject provide the book with a tremendous flow of energy. And like Pater's *Mona Lisa* – 'older than the rocks among which she sits' – a woman whose beauty is 'wrought out from within upon the flesh,' 'thought and time' have played with Blake's features 'and have nowhere pressed hard.' Swinburne's decadent Blake may have a forehead which is the precursor of Yeats's and Ellis's 'muscle of the mind,' but it has a spiritual and aesthetic delicacy to it, without much muscular energy.

Shortly after the publication of Swinburne's critical essay, another review of Gilchrist appeared in the January issue of *The London Quarterly Review* for 1869. James Smetham, a minor Pre-Raphaelite poet, began his lengthy essay by a reading of the Linnell portrait of Blake as a landscape. Swinburne's reference to Blake's thoughts as pressing gently on his head from within and thus moulding his skull suggested some underlying phrenological ideas. Smetham's mapping of Blake's head certainly also suggests the mapping of the mind of Victorian phrenology. Through their dissolution of the mind into a collection of heterogeneous elements the Victorian phrenologists allowed for an acceptance of 'the double man within you,' of a series of competing energies and faculties within man that made him not one, but many, as complex as Swinburne's innocent and experienced artist. Where inner forces had worked their way outwards in Swinburne's reading of the Linnell portrait, Smetham sees Blake's head as a landscape, sculpted from the outside by the forces of nature:

> The great landscape painter, Linnell – whose portraits were, some of them as choice as Holbein's – in the year 1827 painted a portrait of William Blake, the great idealist, and an engraving of it is here before us as we write. A friend, looking at it observed that it was 'like a landscape.' It was a happy observation. The forehead resembles a corrugated mountainside worn with tumbling streams 'blanching and billowing in the hollows of it;' the face is twisted into 'as many lines as the new map with the augmentation of the Indies:' it is a grand face, ably anatomised, full of energy and vitality; and out of these labyrinthine lines there gazes an eye which seems to behold things more than mortal. At the exhibition of National Portraits at South Kensington there was a portrait of the same man by Thomas Phillips; but very different in treatment. The skin covers the bones and sinews more calmly; the attitude is eager, wistful, and prompt. Comparing the two so fine and so various portraits, you are able adequately to conceive the man, and in both you feel that this awful *eye*, far-gazing, subduing the unseen to itself, was the most wonderful feature of the countenance.[41]

The Phillips portrait was painted in 1807, and popularised through Schiavonetti's engraving included as the frontispiece to the 1808 edition of Blair's *The Grave*. It appears to have become the rival image to Linnell's likeness of the poet in the late Victorian quest for the best portrait of Blake. The painting had long been surrounded by a wonderful myth; in 1833 Allan Cunningham had published Phillips's entertaining account of Blake's sitting for his portrait and the conversation which had produced this expression of visionary rapture in the sitter. Provoked by Phillips's claim that Michelangelo was not as skillful a painter of angels as Raphael, Blake had entered into a long discourse about how he had been visited by none other than the arch-angel Gabriel who had testified to Michelangelo's superior skills as a renderer of the heavenly messengers.[42] The Phillips portrait (in Schiavonetti's engraving) was used as the frontispiece for W. M. Rossetti's edition of the poems, included as frontispiece to volume two of the second edition of Gilchrist in 1880 (plate 9), even used as the frontispiece to the second edition of Swinburne's essay of 1906. Smetham had seen it at the South Kensington Museum, and in the great Blake exhibition at the Burlington Fine Arts Club in 1876, organised by William Bell Scott, it took pride of place over the mantelpiece, next to a photograph of the Linnell miniature portrait of Blake.[43] When Cunningham's *Lives of the Most Eminent British Painters* was re-issued in 1879, the editor commented in a footnote to the life of Blake:

> The telling of this wild story was just what Phillips needed, for it brought that rapt, intense look upon Blake's face which the painter has caught so well. The portrait of him painted on ivory by his friend Linnell, during the last years of his life, and reproduced in Gilchrist's 'Life', is merely that of a serene, benevolent old man, but that by Phillips, engraved as a frontispiece in Rossetti's edition of his poems, represents the visionary poet.[44]

Plate 9
Engraving by Schiavonetti after Thomas Phillips, *Portrait of William Blake* (1807).

In the Phillips portrait, the artist is dressed up as a gentleman; Phillips's portrait of Byron in Albanian dress, painted a few years later (1813-14), suggests a painter with a certain fondness for theatrical effects. His gentleman Blake may be both a poet and a painter; the pencil in his hand depicts him in the act of drawing or writing – on his cuff? – and the strong light that hits his forehead from above suggests the artist's communication with divine powers. Fortunately his protruding eyes – large as those of fairytale dogs – do not face the spectator; the three-quarter, rather than the full-face angle, prevents a direct confrontation with this man and his daunting gaze, and as we gaze at Blake, we can rest secure that he will not gaze back at us, busy as he is communicating with the arch-angels.

Smetham began his essay with a reading of two existing portraits of Blake; he concluded his piece with the erection of an imaginary hall of fame to Blake in a rarefied, Pre-Raphaelite universe with walls frescoed by Burne-Jones, Ford Madox Brown, William Bell Scott and D. G. Rossetti. At the centre of the hall would be what appears like a marble counterpiece to Haydon's famous portrait of Wordsworth brooding on Helvellyn, a Miltonic Penseroso:

> At the inner end of this hall of power there should be a marble statue of Blake, by Woolner –
>
>> 'His looks commercing with the skies,
>> His rapt soul sitting in his eyes.'
>
> He should be standing on a rock, its solid strength overlapped by pale, marmoreal flames, while below his feet twined gently the 'Serpent of Eternity.' The admission should be by ticket – the claim to life-tickets founded upon a short examination passed before a 'Blake commission.' None who could not pass this examination satisfactorily should be admitted to those sacred precincts. The trees should whisper, the brook should murmur in the glade, for the delectation of those who had earned their title to enter; and the lodge-gates, kept by 'a decayed historical painter', should never open to any one who would be likely to laugh at the 'queer little figures up in the air,' which are the symbols of heavenly realities in the little grey or dark designs we have been endeavouring to describe.[45]

By the end of the 1860s the Blake cult would appear to be very carefully enshrined and controlled within a Pre-Raphaelite universe: admission only after careful examination! As Shirley Dent and Jason Whittaker have pointed out, the power of sight, of seeing with or through the eye, was tremendously important to the Pre-Raphaelite Blake cult. In a letter to Anne Gilchrist of 1862, Samuel Palmer had pointed out that 'Talent *thinks*, Genius *sees*; and what organ so accurate as sight. Blake held this strongly.'[46] While on the one hand concerned about representing Blake as a seer, as a visionary, Gilchrist and his followers were also deeply engaged in making the public see Blake, in opening the readers' eyes to Blake. Many of the publications on Blake are extremely lavishly illustrated with Blake's own images, and Gilchrist is constantly asking his reader to 'look' at Blake.

It is so much the more striking, of course, that the Blake portrait which by the late 1880s and 1890s gained great cult status, was the only portrait of the artist with his eyes closed. In a short illustrated article in the *Century Guild Hobby Horse* for 1887 Herbert Horne publicized George Richmond's copy of the phrenologist James Deville's cast of Blake's head (see plate 11).[47] Earlier that year Alexander Gilchrist's son Herbert had recounted his visit to the ageing Richmond who had shown him Blake's life mask and told the story of its making. In 1823, the amateur phrenologist James Deville had desired to make a cast of Blake's head 'as representative of the imaginative faculty.'[48] If one reads the obituary of Deville in *The Phrenological Journal* for 1846, it would appear that he was the leading phrenological cast maker in London in the 1820s; in close contact with both Spurzheim and Gall, Deville was building up an impressive collection of original skulls and casts to prove the theories of these phrenologists, a collection which at his death counted some 2450 specimens, out of which some 1500 had been taken by Deville himself in his house in the Strand. Sadly, the obituary makes no explicit reference to the cast of Blake's head, but it may well be included in the following passage: 'There is a very interesting series of casts from the heads of remarkable characters, together with casts of the exterior and interior of their skulls. Some of these were insane and idiotic, some of them poets, and the others desperate highwaymen.'[49]

Thus convicts, aborigines, and remarkable men all found their way into Deville's collection in his desire to map the full extent of the human mind on the skull. George Richmond did, however, point out to Herbert Gilchrist that although the plaster cast gave posterity an exact copy of Blake's skull, the facial expression captured in the cast was very un-Blakean:

> 'That is not like dear Blake's mouth, such a look of severity was foreign to him – an expression of sweetness and sensibility being habitual: but Blake experienced a good deal of pain when the cast was taken, as the plaster pulled out a quantity of his hair. Mrs Blake did not like the mask, perhaps the reason being that she was familiar with varying expressions of her husband's fine face, from daily observation: indeed it was difficult to please her with any portrait – she never liked Phillips's portrait; but Blake's friends liked the mask.'[50]

Herbert Gilchrist did not illustrate the object of his conversation with Richmond, and his visit to the old painter was just one of many incidents in the book. But Herbert Horne reproduced the mask in photogravure and wrote a brief article in which he celebrated it as the only reliable portrait of Blake, after having dismissed both the Phillips and the Linnnell portraits as 'records of contrary moods.' The only other portrait mentioned in Horne's essay is the Sudarium, the Holy Face. According to legend, on his way to Calvary, Christ wiped his face with the towel handed to him, and the features of his face remained on the towel. The frontal icon has been one of the most influential in Christian art since the Middle Ages.[51] Both the Sudarium and Blake's life mask are examples of what modern artists would call 'body art'; Christ's perspiration on the cloth, the imprint of his own face, the use of his own body in the artistic process add new dimensions to the image of his face. Such an image is not entirely artificial – it contains pieces, or fluids, emanating from the Holy Body. In comparing Blake's life mask to the Sudarium, Horne was partly alluding to Blake as a Man of Sorrows, as a man much misunderstood, and as a man inspired by a divine inner light, in touch with God. Furthermore, the Sudarium traditionally depicts nothing but the Holy Face; the life mask gives us Blake's head, completely severed from his body. In Horne's paraphrase of Richmond from Gilchrist, he even suggested the existence of some valuable Blake relics: 'Much of the forced expression of the nostrils, and more particularly of the mouth, is due to the discomfiture which the taking of the cast involved; many of Blake's hairs adhering to the plaster until quite recently.'[52] What happened to those hairs? one wonders. Amongst the true devotees of the late-Victorian Blake cult, such pieces of the artistic body would undoubtedly have sold at high prices.

Soon after Horne's article, the life mask featured as the frontispiece to volume two of Ellis and Yeats's edition of Blake (1893). This book printed Tatham's double portrait of the young and the old Blake as the frontispiece of volume one (plate 10), as if to suggest an entirely new Blake, liberated from the Linnell and Phillips portraits which had been so closely associated with the Pre-Raphaelite Blake of the 1860s, 1870s and 1880s. The double portrait also suggested Blake as an artist with double vision, a man for whom allegory and symbolism were the natural means of expression. Doubling soon became quadrupling when in 1907 Ellis had separated himself from Yeats (and vice versa) and published his own *The Real Blake: A Portrait Biography*. The portrait, the only portrait, in this biography, is the frontispiece which shows the life mask from four different angles (plate 11). These four different angles partly help us certify that Blake's snub nose belonged entirely to the realm of myth, but Ellis used the cast for further myth-making. Yeats had invented the legend that Blake was of Irish ancestry, and Ellis started out by commenting that 'No one can study the cast of William Blake's head made for Deville the phrenologist without seeing that he was an Irishman.'[53] 'Four' recurs in the book, with references to Yeats's attempts to construct an Irish mythology based on the figure four, to *The Four Zoas* which Ellis and Yeats saw as the key to Blake's own mythology, and Ellis concluded his book by a celebration of Blake as somebody who could experience the world in its fourth dimension:

> We must not rashly consider that this occult mental power, which Blake called 'Imagination,' was like our ordinary imagination, though it had a kinship. It exceeds it sometimes as the fancied fourth dimension of space exceeds the usual three, has its own *here* and *there*, its own *before* and *after*, a Time where successivity does not rule, and a Space where Place has other laws. So he called it Eternity, and by it the Real Blake is yet with us, his posterity, as he was with Catherine, his widow.[54]

Plate 10
Tatham, *William Blake in Youth and Age* (1830).

Is the real Blake still with us, almost a century after Ellis and only 24 years away from the bicentenary celebrations of his death in 2027? It would certainly appear that the Deville mask has stood the test as one of the 'best portraits' of Blake. It is also the only portrait of Blake in Shirley Dent and Jason Whittaker's book on Blake's influence and afterlife from 2002, and just like their nineteenth-century predecessors, the authors begin their book with a reading of Blake's head. They place it, however, in the context of twentieth-century body art, more specifically the modern sculptor Marc Quinn's reworking of the Deville mask in his series of self-portraits from the 1990s, simply entitled *Self*, and they hail it as a complex celebration of the imaginative and inspirational powers of William Blake:

> By pointing to the appropriate part of Blake's skull, Deville believed that he would be able to demonstrate immediately why Blake was a visionary artist. This mask, seen by other artists such as Francis Bacon and Anthony Gormley, as well as Quinn, has been the catalyst for their own artistic production in a variety of materials, including paint, bronze and blood. This plaster cast has become the spark for other instances of art that do not simply copy the original (as did Deville) but translate it into new media: reading *Self* forces us to re-read Blake. Deville's attempt to capture the original artist's inspiration succeeded in a way that he could not, ironically, have imagined and what we see in the life mask is Blake's major piece of performance art, centered on his own body, and the myth of his life as an imaginative artist.[55]

The relation between original and copy is particularly complex in the case of the Deville mask: Blake himself appears to be the 'Original,' and part of the almost sacred aura of this portrait is its supposedly exact copy of the original, when it comes to permanent form rather than temporary expression. We have, in other words, a copy of Blake's head with an entirely uncharacteristic facial expression, but that does not seem to pose any major problem to Blake devotees. As an artefact, it appears to have been multiplied even in Blake's own lifetime: of the two existing nineteenth-century plaster copies, the one in the National Portrait Gallery and the other in the Fitzwilliam Museum, art historians still do not exactly know which was the 'original.' The fragility of the plaster made curators in the National Portrait Gallery desire a bronze copy to be made some years ago, to be sure that they would always preserve a copy of Blake's head. However, in the newly refurbished Regency Galleries in the NPG, opened to the public on 20 May 2003, only the Phillips portrait meets the visitor keen to see some likeness of

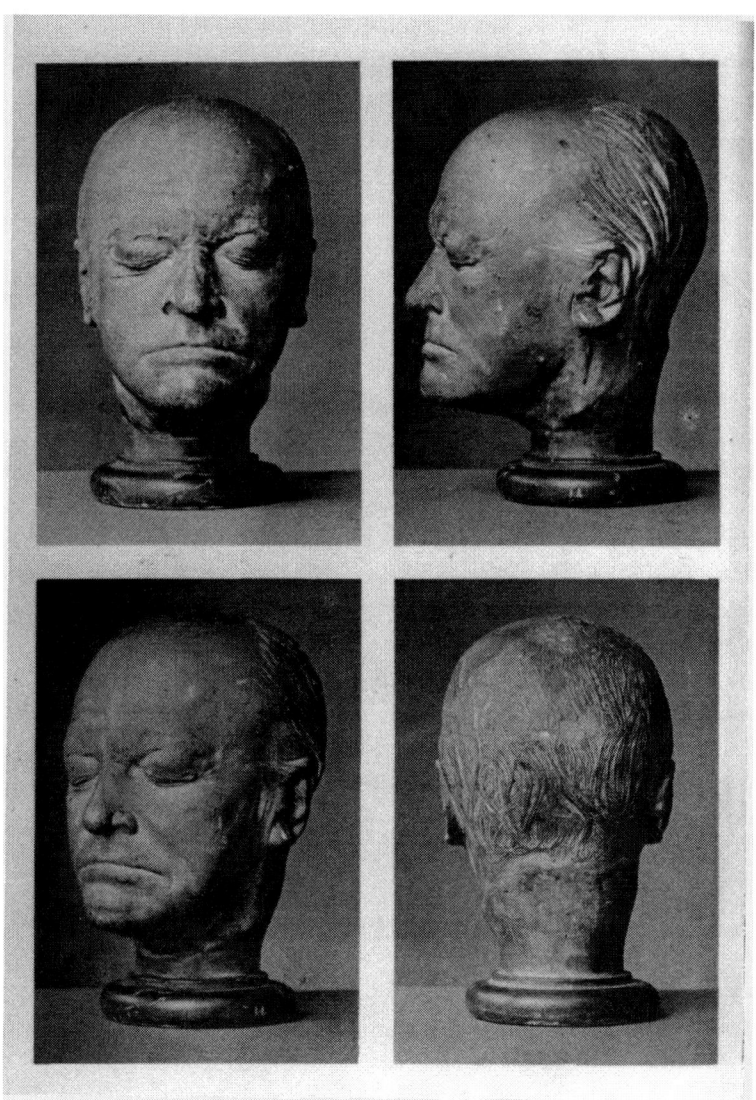

Plate 11

James Deville, phrenological cast of William Blake's head (1823).

William Blake. The Linnell miniature and the Deville mask are no longer on display, but emerge from the computer screen of the NPG database, if the visitor is keen enough to tap in the letters 'William Blake' on the keyboard. If not, he can always buy his own copy of the life mask from the NPG shop at the bargain price of a mere £95. Seeing Blake, even with closed eyes, would appear to be no less popular today that in the nineteenth century.

## Notes

1. John Forster, *Walter Savage Landor: A Biography*, 2 vols (London: Chapman and Hall, 1869), vol. II, pp. 322-23.
2. For a very brief account of this complex issue, see G. E. Bentley, Jr, *The Stranger from Paradise: A Biography of William Blake* (New Haven and London: Yale University Press, 2001), pp. 379-82. A glance through the thousands of titles in Geoffrey Keynes, *A Bibliography of William Blake* (New York: The Grolier Club, 1921) reveals how pressing an issue Blake's madness was in the many nineteenth-century publications on the poet.
3. Alexander Gilchrist, *Life of William Blake, 'Pictor Ignotus.'* With Selections from his Poems and Other Writings, 2 vols (London and Cambridge: Macmillan & Co., 1863).
4. The standard work on Blake's posthumous nineteenth-century reputation is Deborah Dorfman, *Blake in the Nineteenth Century. His Reputation as a Poet from Gilchrist to Yeats* (New Haven and London: Yale University Press, 1969). More recently, the subject has been dealt with from a somewhat different perspective in Shirley Dent and Jason Whittaker, *Radical Blake: Influence and Afterlife from 1827* (Basingstoke and New York: Palgrave Macmillan, 2002).
5. Gilchrist, vol. I, pp. 1-2.
6. A. C. Swinburne, *William Blake: A Critical Essay* (London: John Camden Hotten, 1868), pp. 4-5.
7. *The Poetical Works of William Blake, Lyrical and Miscellaneous*. Edited, with a prefatory memoir, by Wiliam Michael Rossetti (London: George Bell and Sons, 1874), p. lxxxix.
8. Edwin John Ellis and William Butler Yeats, *The Works of William Blake. Poetic, Symbolic, and Critical*, 3 vols (London: Bernard Quaritch, 1893), vol. I, p. x.
9. Richard Brilliant, *Portraiture* (London: Reaktion Books, 1991), p. 84.
10. Ibid., p. 35.
11. Geoffrey Keynes, *The Complete Portraiture of William and Catherine Blake* (London: Trianon Press, 1977).
12. See the chapter on 'Byron and the Romantic Image' in David Piper, *The Image of the Poet: British Poets and their Portraits* (Oxford: Clarendon Press, 1982), pp. 91-145.
13. Ellis and Yeats, vol. I, p. 16.

14 For this complex subject, see Anne K. Mellor, 'Physiognomy, Phrenology, and Blake's Visionary Heads' in Robert N. Essick and Donald Pearce (eds), *Blake in his Time* (Bloomington and London: Indiana University Press, 1978), pp. 53-74.
15 J. C. Lavater, *Essays on Physiognomy; for the Promotion of the Knowledge and the Love of Mankind*, trans. Thomas Holcroft, 3 vols (London: Robinson, 1789), vol. III, p. 164.
16 Ibid., p. 163.
17 'An Acre of Grass,' stanzas 3 and 4 in W. B. Yeats, *Collected Poems* (London: Macmillan, 1984), p. 347.
18 Crabb Robinson quoted from G. E. Bentley, Jr, *Blake Records* (Oxford: Clarendon Press, 1969), pp. 309-10.
19 See Dorfman, pp. 59-63.
20 David Erdman and Donald Moore (eds), *The Notebook of William Blake. A Photographic and Typographic Facsimile* (Oxford: Clarendon Press, 1973), p. 2.
21 Ibid., [N33 transcript].
22 David V. Erdman, '"Terrible Blake in his Pride": An Essay on *The Everlasting Gospel*' in F. W. Hilles and H. Bloom (eds), *From Sensibility to Romanticism. Essays Presented to Frederick A. Pottle* (New York: Oxford University Press, 1965), pp. 331-57.
23 *The Notebook of William Blake*, [N64 transcript].
24 See Paul Barolsky, *Michelangelo's Nose: A Myth and its Maker* (University Park and London: Pennsylvania State University Press, 1990).
25 *The Notebook of William Blake*, [N67], note (a).
26 See Robert N. Essick, *The Works of William Blake in the Huntington Collections. A Complete Catalogue* (San Marino: The Huntington Library, 1985), pp. 75-80.
27 See Lavater, trans. Holcroft, Vol. I, pp. 209-29.
28 Ibid., p. 219.
29 Ibid., pp. 218-19.
30 See Lucy Hartley, *Physiognomy and the Meaning of Expression in Nineteenth-Century Culture* (Cambridge: Cambridge University Press, 2001); Sally Shuttleworth, *Charlotte Brontë and Victorian Psychology* (Cambridge: Cambridge University Press, 1996).
31 Lavater, trans Holcroft, Vol. III, p. 185.
32 For a lengthy discourse on the snub nose in its eighteenth- and nineteenth-century context, see my essay 'The Tragedy of Recession: Broken, Simian and Syphilitic Noses in Nineteenth-Century Art and Physiognomy' in Victoria de Rijke, Lene Østermark-Johansen and Helen Thomas (eds), *Nose Book: Representations of the Nose in Literature and the Arts* (London: Middlesex University Press, 2000), pp. 201-21.
33 Lavater, trans. Holcroft, vol. III, pp. 186-87.
34 See Bentley (2003), pp. 312-13.
35 Gilchrist, vol. I, p. 62. See also Robert N. Essick (ed.) (1985), p. 181. The title page is reproduced in Carol Louise Hall, *Blake and Fuseli: A Study in the Transmission of Ideas* (New York and London: Garland Publishing, 1985).

36 See Mellor p. 57.
37 See Roger Cooter, *The Cultural Meaning of Popular Science: Phrenology and the Organization of Consent in Nineteenth-Century Britain* (Cambridge: Cambridge University Press, 1984).
38 See plates 26-28 in Keynes (1977).
39 Pater's essay on Leonardo was first published in *The Fortnightly Review* 6 for November 1869 and subsequently included, with alterations, in his book *The Renaissance* of 1873. For the *Mona Lisa* passage, see *The Renaissance: Studies in Art and Poetry*. The 1893 text ed. Donald L. Hill (Berkeley: The University of California Press, 1981), pp. 98-99.
40 Swinburne pp. 1-2.
41 James Smetham, 'William Blake,' *London Quarterly Review* 21 (Jan. 1869), pp. 265-311, p. 265.
42 Allan Cunningham, *The Cabinet Gallery of Pictures* (1833). Phillips's account is reprinted in Bentley, *Blake Records*, pp. 182-83.
43 See *Burlington Fine Arts Club Exhibition of the Works of William Blake*, curated by W. B. Scott (London: Spottiswoode & Co, 1876).
44 Allan Cunningham, *The Lives of the Most Eminent British Painters*, rev. ed. Mrs Charles Heaton, 3 vols, Bohn's Standard Library (London: George Bell and Sons, 1879), vol. I, p. 421.
45 Smetham p. 310.
46 Letter from Palmer to A. Gilchrist 2 July 1862; quoted from Dent and Whittaker, p. 30.
47 The mask has since 1937 been on loan to the Fitzwilliam Museum, Cambridge. See David Bindman (ed.), *William Blake: Catalogue of the Collection in the Fitzwilliam Museum, Cambridge* (Cambridge: Heffer and Sons, 1970), pp. 58-60. There is another copy of the mask in the National Portrait Gallery, inv. 1809.
48 Herbert Gilchrist, *Anne Gilchrist: Her Life and Writings* (London: T. Fisher Unwin, 1887), p. 59.
49 James P. Browne, M.D., 'Memoir of the Late Mr James Deville,' *The Phrenological Journal and Magazine of Moral Science* XIX (1846), pp. 329-44, p. 339.
50 George Richmond quoted in Herbert Gilchrist, pp. 59-60.
51 See Moshe Barasch, 'The Frontal Icon: A Genre in Christian Art' in *Imago Hominis: Studies in the Language of Art* (New York: New York University Press, 1994), pp. 20-35. One of the illustrations in Barasch's essay even happens to be a fifteenth-century Holy Face from the Casa Horne in Florence.
52 Herbert Horne, 'The Life Mask of William Blake,' *Century Guild Hobby Horse* 2 (1887), pp. 28-30, p. 30.
53 Edwin J. Ellis, *The Real Blake: A Portrait Biography* (London: Chatto & Windus, 1907), p. 5.
54 Ibid., p. 438. Italics in the quotation are the author's own.
55 Dent and Whittaker, pp. 5-6.

# BOOK REVIEWS

Lis Christensen, *Elizabeth Bowen: The Later Fiction* (Copenhagen: Museum Tusculanum Press, 2001), 224 pp. £22. ISBN: 87-7289-624-8

Elizabeth Bowen (1899-1973) is increasingly recognized as one of the major English novelists of the twentieth century; among her best-known novels are *The House in Paris* (1935), *The Death of the Heart* (1938) and *The Heat of the Day* (1949). About her later novels there remains much critical disagreement. Established by 1939 as a writer of subtle and even intellectual sensitivity, Bowen was often rated as a finer analyst of passions and their intricacies than contemporaries such as Rosamund Lehmann; she was even regarded as a successor to Virginia Woolf. As a commentator on manners and morals Bowen displays an incisive wit comparable to that of Edith Wharton. There was hostile criticism, that her work lacked spontaneity, that its effects were over-strained, but after the success of *The Death of the Heart*, there was a consensus that Bowen was one of the major novelists and short-story writers of her generation.

That estimate was consolidated by her next novel, eleven years later, *The Heat of the Day*, with its haunting evocation of bombed and bomb-threatened London, its uncanny and mesmerising sharpness of vision whether in sunlit glare or during black-out. Its descriptive and tonal qualities more than compensated for the somewhat implausible narrative of deception in love and espionage. Yet it was her tone, aristocratic and mannered, and her ornate and eccentric syntax, that would become objects of disdain in the 1950s, when the English novel was to be represented by less mannered writers such as Kingsley Amis, John Braine and Alan Sillitoe.

Bowen's late novels were therefore published in an unsympathetic atmosphere, and were themselves increasingly contrived and intricate in both tone and structure. In this, as in other respects, Bowen's career as a writer followed Henry James's: the late work is the most daring and the most challenging. *A World of Love* (1955) is the most delicately inflected of all Bowen's novels; to her devoted admirers it marks a step forward. But for critics of the day, its allusiveness and indirection, and the ostentatious artifice of its prose led to accusations that Bowen had lapsed into self-parodic excess.

What Bowen was doing, however, as Lis Christensen shows, was not to attract a contemporary readership but to test an earlier one. Her novels of the 1930s had been narrated by an immensely authoritative voice: portentous comments on the characters' feelings and actions, assured generalizations about love and other matters, all seemed designed to infiltrate and control the reader's own response. This sustaining device is used less and less, until in the later novels, *The Little Girls* (1964) and *Eva Trout* (1969), one can, as a reader, breathe quite freely. We are no longer manipulated and led; instead we are perplexed by abrupt shifts in intonation, evaluation and narration. Bowen's strategy in the late novels is explained thus by Lis Christensen:

> Foregrounding the textual surface as she does may well have the effect of drawing attention to all that is not said in her fiction, or not said immediately, or not said in so many words: and the suppression of information by the narrator brings our imaginations into play – to fill in the gaps in the storyline ... or constantly to re-assess our understanding....

The subsequent detailed examination of the four post-war novels explores how the devices work, and how the reader is involved in the construction and understanding of the story. Christensen is attentive not only to the narrative but to the ways in which Bowen establishes patterns of dialogue. She is particularly responsive to Bowen's use of repeated word-clusters and recurrent phrases; her studies of each novel demonstrate convincingly that it is deliberate artistry that underpins these works that, on first or casual reading, might seem wayward, arbitrary and opaque.

The main limitation of this critical work can be ascribed to its deliberately narrow field of study. The author's concentration on verbal detail prevents her from offering a broad assessment of Bowen's achievement in these late novels. Attention to her early novels, notably *The Hotel* (1927) and *Friends and Relations* (1931) with their relative freedom of narratorial comment, might have suggested that *The Little Girls* and *Eva Trout* are not entirely new in their methods; in some respects they revert to an earlier practice. Even within the terms of Christensen's concentrated field of inquiry, Bowen's eccentricity of vocabulary and syntax calls for a fuller treatment of social and comic registers than is provided here.

None the less, this is a book that Elizabeth Bowen herself would surely have appreciated. Its meticulous, loving scrutiny directs one's attention to the details in the verbal texture of these extraordinary novels. The illustrations are imaginatively chosen, and emphasize the visual, even pictorial nature of Bowen's imagination. The cover design (unattributed) depicts a half-open door with a glimpse of book-laden shelves beyond. One wants to push that door open, of course, and walk in. Bowen's novels are inviting, they give us glimpses, but the threshold of the door can symbolize the surface of the text, through which, as this study shows, there is no easy passage.

Glen Cavaliero

Russell Duncan and David J. Klooster, eds, *Phantoms of a Blood-Stained Period: The Complete Civil War Writings of Ambrose Bierce* (Amherst: University of Massachusetts Press, 2002), pp. xvi + 352. $60.00 hardback, $19.95 paperback. ISBN: 1-55849-328-x

In its immediate aftermath surprisingly little imaginative literature tried to deal with the Civil War, but the decade of the 1880s – when Ambrose Bierce began mining his extensive combat experience for essays, poems, and stories – saw many American authors trooping belatedly to the colors afforded by warfare. The spate of writing they inaugurated has scarcely slackened since. Histories of the conflict form a reliable staple of American publishing, pumped out to satisfy legions of Civil War buffs whose enthusiasm for the subject leads some to don blue or grey uniforms and re-enact battles. The American Civil War has by now inspired legions of authors; indeed an entire sub-genre of 'war literature' is generally regarded as being initiated by Stephen Crane's *The Red Badge of Courage*, no earlier than 1895.

Within this communal festival of collective memory where exactly is Bierce's place? The editors of Bierce's war writings, Russell Duncan and David J. Klooster, note the national need for a mythology of reconciliation to succeed the harsh and vindictive treatment at first accorded the defeated South under Reconstruction. Regimental histories by the hundreds poured from the presses, and Grant was only the most notable commander among the scads who authored memoirs that were often exercises in self-justification. Memorial monuments sprouted in town squares across the land, stressing a heroicized and romantic vision of the ultimate sacrifice offered by so many American youths.

It was a vision that comported ill with Bierce's own experiences as an eighteen-year-old who was the second in his Indiana county to enlist. Youthful idealism for freedom may have brought him in, but that was soon superseded by duty (though perhaps not by strong bonds of military comradeship: virtually all the soldiers in his stories are loners), a sense of adventure, and perhaps even a perverse fascination with death. His story 'George Thurston' describes an officer whose unnecessary displays of flamboyant bravery seem efforts to master a constitutional tendency to run away, while 'A Tough Tussle' describes another with a military record resembling Bierce's who can hardly tolerate the sight of corpses and thus 'was a braver man than anybody knew, for nobody knew his horror of that which he was ever ready to incur.' Like several other figures in Bierce's fiction both officers commit suicide in order to master their fear. So many of Bierce's postwar friends took the same route (contemplated also by Bierce himself, as several essays on suicide attest) that his own mysterious disappearance in 1913 has sometimes been attributed not to the hostilities of the Mexican Revolution but to the final execution of a long-matured plan, much like Hemingway's.

Whatever existential turmoil underlay the conspicuous gallantry that Bierce displayed, he received fifteen commendations for bravery under fire in campaigning that saw him rise rapidly from a private through thinned ranks to topographical officer with the grade of lieutenant. He fought in most of the bloodiest battles of the Western theater, from Shiloh, Stone River, Chickamauga, and Missionary Ridge through Pickett's Mill, Kennesaw Mountain, Franklin, and Nashville, leaving the army only after a near-fatal head wound caused him to suffer dizzy spells. If ever an author were qualified to write honestly about battle it was Bierce.

With pardonable zeal Bierce's editors urge the merits of his stories as unprecedentedly convincing treatments of battle, as rebukes to Whitman's claim that 'the real war will never get in the books.' And indeed Bierce excels in rendering violence as grotesquerie ignored by the era's patriotic hagiography. 'Chickamauga' memorably dramatizes the bloody aftermath of battle by presenting it through the uncomprehending eyes of a child to whom the crawling casualties seem red-faced clowns ready to play horsey for him. But the surreal effect is rather cheaply purchased by withholding the crucial information that the child is a deaf-mute incapable of hearing their cries, and the surprise ending is achieved only with the help of misleading statements that make the story's third-person limited point of view seem closer to omniscience than it is. Perhaps more satisfying is 'A Horseman in the Sky,' where a Confederate officer, his mount shot while overlooking a steep cliff, leaps off, and presents – to a startled Federal a thousand feet below – a grandly grotesque image that seems to herald the Apocalypse.

In the 1870s Bierce had industriously composed horror stories, but his war fiction is weakened by sporadic attempts to blend in the supernatural, as in 'Three and One are One,' 'Stone's River,' 'The Other Lodgers' and 'Two Military Executions.' A postwar poem declares a 'cold inclemency of light/ More dreadful than the shadows are,' and one can only agree with that finely phrased maxim insofar as military ghost stories are concerned. Likewise too many stories compromise the verisimilitude of their battlefield settings with implausible melodramatic plots where soldiers wind up killing parents, killing wives, killing children, killing old friends, or killing themselves, in compensation for killing acquaintances, for showing fear, or for being jilted by sweethearts. Bierce's efforts to defend the realism of such fiction seem misplaced though sometimes such creaky ironies do help render the fog of war in which isolated military automata must act in ignorance of the larger import of their actions.

For all Bierce's stylistic prowess his stories do not necessarily gain from being collected; as Edmund Wilson noted, there is something fatiguing about reading this relentless ironist in quantity. But perhaps the chief service of this edition is that by amply displaying the virtues and limitations of Bierce's fiction it calls into question our tendency to privilege fiction over the essay as the superior form of imaginative literature. For Bierce the two forms were often hard to distinguish, his fiction incorporating autobiographical elements, his essays not always straightforward military reportage. In 'What Occurred at Franklin' and 'The Crime of Pickett's Mill' the topographical officer's desire for accuracy, for unvarnished historical truth, acquires a passionate intensity. Bierce's experiences as a young recruit in the early West Virginia campaign are detailed with sardonic humor in 'On a Mountain,' and nothing in his fiction matches the grotesque horror of the ending when, returning with his company past some corpses whose sunken faces had earlier inspired fear, they discover that the corpses no longer have faces, their flesh having been devoured by a herd of wild hogs. 'What I Saw of Shiloh' is a remarkable rendering of battle as experienced by one confused sergeant, not readily paralleled in Civil War literature. 'Four Days in Dixie' is a riveting and amusing account of how on a reconnaissance mission undertaken as a foolhardy lark Bierce was captured by Confederates and marched toward prison, then managed to escape from them the next night and return to his own lines. With comic brio '"Way Down in Alabam"' describes his experiences during Reconstruction when as a U.S. Treasury agent charged with confiscating Confederate cotton bales he was exposed to as much danger from irate Southerners as he faced on the front lines. It would be hard to pick ten stories from this volume that impact the reader as powerfully as these ten essays, that represent the many sides of war so variously, or that lay as strong a claim to aesthetic distinction.

Though they accept rather too uncritically Tim O'Brien's Vietnam-inspired view that the truest literary descriptions of real war are surreal, the editors have done a fine job, organizing their selections to trace the chronological progress of the war and providing introductions to each section plus useful military glossaries for the Civil War novice. Annotation is on target though in some case perhaps too sparing. However, readers in need of assistance, or inspired to further reading, can now consult Robert L. Gale's *An Ambrose Bierce Companion* (2001).

Michael West

Justin D. Edwards, *Gothic Passages: Racial Ambiguity and the American Gothic* (Iowa City: University of Iowa Press, 2002), xxxiii, 145 pp. $34.95. ISBN 0-87745-824-3

In this study of antebellum and postbellum gothic narratives, Justin D. Edwards analyzes the genre and the development of the American gothic, along with nineteenth-century discourses of 'passing,' and representations of racial ambiguity and hybridity. Edwards poses the following questions: 'How are the categories of "race" and the rhetoric of racial difference tied to the language of gothicism? What can these discursive ties tell us about a range of social boundaries – gender, sexuality, class, race, etc – during the nineteenth century? What can the construction and destabilisation of these social boundaries tell us about the development of the U.S. gothic?'

Edwards draws on both literary texts and historical sources in his exploration of racial landscapes of terror, as well as on nineteenth-century popular 'science' concerning race and identity formation. The book investigates what it calls a 'racial gothic' discourse that 'employed striking and metaphoric images to filter and give meaning to the social hierarchies of racial domination and subordination.' Nineteenth-century writers gothicized mixed-race and passing figures, who were delegated to a 'demonization' of difference and thus contributed to the nineteenth-century social project of marginalizing and demonizing the other. *Gothic Passages* uncovers, in short, the anxieties relating to social, sexual and racial transgression.

The first part of the monograph, 'Creating a Self in Antebellum Gothic Narrative,' includes analyses of Edgar Allan Poe's *Narrative of Arthur Gordon Pym of Nantucket* (1838), Herman Melville's *Benito Cereno* (1855), and William and Ellen Craft's *Running a Thousand Miles for Freedom* (1860). The second part, 'Exploring Identity in Postbellum Gothic Discourse,' focuses on Frances E. W. Harper's *Iola Leroy* (1892), William Dean Howells's *An Imperative Duty* (1892) and Charles W. Chesnutt's *House Behind the Cedars* (1900). Edwards obviously moves with ease on both sides of the literary colour line and juxtaposes canonical writers with lesser-known figures in surprising and refreshing combinations.

In dismantling the conventional categories of gender and race, *Gothic Passages* converses with the flurry of mixed-race autobiographies that have come out since the 1990s. A new group of American writers, such as Rebecca Walker (*Black, White and Jewish: Autobiography of a Shifting Self*, 2000), Judy Scales-Trent (*Notes of a White Black Woman: Race, Color, Community*, 1995), Gregory Howard Williams (*Life on the Color Line: The True Story of a White*

*Boy Who Discovered He Was Black*, 1995), and Scott Minerbrook (*Divided to the Vein: A Journey into Race and Family*, 1996) have sought to define a space for themselves and other mixed-race Americans or 'New People.' A recent work, M. Giulia Fabi's *Passing and the Rise of the African American Novel* (University of Illinois Press, 2001), discusses texts also taken up by Edwards, such as Chesnutt's *The House Behind the Cedars*, and shares Edwards's interest in themes such as subversive mixed-race figures, race travel, 'New People,' and critical trespassing. The subterranean gothic themes that crop up in these works take centre stage in Anne Goodwyn Jones and Susan Donaldson's much-praised collection *Haunted Bodies: Gender and Southern Texts* (University Press of Virginia, 1997), surely a precursor for Edwards's gendered and racial readings of the American gothic. With essays by many of the finest scholars in the field, this work deserves a place in Edwards's bibliography. One contributor to that volume, Patricia Yaeger, has in *Dirt and Desire* (University of Chicago Press, 2000) uncovered the racial and gendered bodies that litter southern fictional landscapes. Though she focuses on a period later than Edwards's, her throw-away figures and grotesque gargantuans also seek to redefine southern interpretations of racial and gender demarcations. A work of a more general nature, Michael Kreyling's *Inventing Southern Literature* (Univeristy Press of Mississippi 1998), shows the influence of these critical concerns in stimulating new discussions of literature and literary history. Though Edwards mentions none of these works in his otherwise full bibliography, he implicitly participates in this discussion among scholars within American and Southern studies.

Edwards has uncovered an impressive range of works and sources, much of it little-known nineteenth-century material. He skilfully combines genre criticism, commentary on nineteenth-century scientific discourses, recent theories of identity formation, and close textual analysis. *Gothic Passages* reveals not only an unusual sensitivity to issues of gender and race but also an interest in recent developments within literary and cultural theory. Edwards's work contributes significantly to various debates within American Studies and will offer to scholars and students within the discipline many an interesting angle, a fresh perspective on canonical writers and an introduction to more obscure ones, all presented in intelligent and readable prose.

Clara Juncker

# ABSTRACTS

**Andrew Bennett**: Poetry and Ignorance

In this paper I suggest that Romantic and post-Romantic poetics may be conceived in terms of a particular emphasis on the poet's ignorance – that, in Jean Laplanche's terms, the poet's 'address is enigmatic' to the extent that the poet himself 'does not entirely know what he is saying,' since he is 'other to himself.' What Romanticism brings into focus is the fact that one can neither know to whom one addresses a poem nor, in part because of this ignorance, the entirety of what one is saying. The essay focuses in particular on a reading of Wordsworth's troubled thinking of thinking on the one hand, and on recent debates concerning authorial intention on the other.

**Ian Duncan**: Hume, Scott, and the 'Rise of Fiction'

This article explores the philosophical matrix for the 'rise of the novel' provided by Humean empiricism. By designating the imagination as the cognitive faculty that structures experience, Hume releases fiction from traditional associations with the falsification of a metaphysically guaranteed reality or truth, and grants it epistemological legitimacy as a representation of 'common life.' Fiction acquires its modern categorical autonomy – as the discourse defining a particular genre, the novel – in the era of Romanticism, in Scott's dialectical combination of fiction with history.

**Karsten Engelberg**: Poetic Laments of P.B. Shelley: Conventions, Familiar Mysteries, and Critical Responses

The poetic laments of the 1840s and 1850s lifted Shelley out of the polarized controversy that had shaped his reputation ever since his first publications had attracted critical attention. The intimacy of the lyrical mode and the traditional Christian thinking of the elegy provided a vehicle for broadly Evangelical and radical perceptions of Shelley. The laments reconciled polarized views by shifting the perceptions away from rational thinking and moral, political argument towards individual expressions of admiration celebrating existential mysteries and transcendental striving.

**Charles Lock**: Those Lips: on Cowper (*Ekphrasis* in Parentheses)

There is an iconic aspect to every text, indeed to every letter. The demarcation between text and image, affirmed in the very practice of *ekphrasis*, finds itself exposed by a degree of textual and punctuational self-consciousness. William Cowper's poem 'On the Receipt of My Mother's Picture out of Norfolk' initiates a series of nineteenth-century ekphrastic poems. After Cowper, ekphrasis sees its task as providing not a substitute for the plastic work that has been or will eventually be lost (such as the Shield of Achilles), but a supplement, a match, for a work that remains extant.

**Peter J. Manning**: Home Thoughts From Abroad: Wordsworth's 'Musings Near Aquapendente'

This poem purports to be a spontaneous rumination. Stephen Gill characterizes it as Wordsworth's 'last of many poems of friendship and his last substantial elegy,' but the treatment of Walter Scott reveals the poem as motivated by the intrinsically comparative nature of literary reputation, less a product of Wordsworth's 1837 Italian travel than a reflection on the inseparability of Wordsworth from Scott and Byron in contemporary critical discourse. In it the poet strives to configure his own place in literary history.

**Robert W. Rix**: William Blake and the Prophetic Marketplace

Blake is often seen as the archetype for the Romantic artist who willingly accepted a limited audience, writing mostly for himself with the audience as merely eavesdroppers. The article revises such commonplace notions by opening up Blake's works to an understanding of them as public art. Aspects of Blake's self-confessed mission as an artist and his attempt to make art a concern of great national importance are here brought into focus. The article also examines the disparity between the 'prophetic' aspirations of Blake and the grim reality of the eighteenth-century book market.

**Peter Simonsen**: Self Generations: On Wordsworth's Frontispiece Portraits

An account is provided of Wordsworth's decision in 1836 and again in 1845 to publish with a frontispiece portrait. The frontispieces are contextualised in terms of their meanings and implications in a theatrical and spectacular Romantic material culture. They are ways to mark a poet's achievement of fame and immortality, strategic signs to enhance communication, and means to increase the commercial value of a book, thus signalling the commodification of the author's image. By attending to how Wordsworth generates images of himself as author, we may recuperate his neglected later work as well as reach a better understanding of the complexities that inform his career and work as a whole.

**Pernille Strande-Sørensen**: Authentication of National Identity: Macpherson and Burns as Editors of Scottish Ballads

Macpherson and Burns have much in common regarding the editing and treatment of traditional vernacular poetry: both carried out their works on Scottish balladry within the parameters of the Enlightenment, and both operated with an editorial rationale which relied on the concept of authenticity for its validation. They place authentication of national identity as the validating factor of their contributions to Scottish balladry. However, where Macpherson is firmly embedded in an eighteenth-century linear mode of thought, Burns's ideas of national identity and its authentication challenge the linearity of empirical, representational thought.

**Lene Østermark-Johansen**: Victorian Angles on Blake: Reading the Artist's Head in the Late Nineteenth Century

The shape of William Blake's head was the object of continued scrutiny, both among Blake's contemporaries and his late-Victorian editors and biographers. This essay examines frontispiece portraits of Blake from Gilchrist (1863) to Ellis (1903), from profile engraving to sculptural life mask, and links late-Victorian readings of Blake's head with the increasingly complex myth of the artist and his inner vision.

# NOTES ON CONTRIBUTORS

**Andrew Bennett** is Professor of English at the University of Bristol. His publications include *Keats, Narrative and Audience: The Posthumous Life of Writing* (1994), *Romantic Poets and the Culture of Posterity* (1999), and *Katherine Mansfield* (2003); with Nicholas Royle he has published *Introduction to Literature, Criticism and Theory* (1995), and *Elizabeth Bowen and the Dissolution of the Novel: Still Lives* (1995); he is also the editor of *Readers and Reading* (1995).

**Ian Duncan** is Professor of English at the University of California, Berkeley. His most recent publications include an edition of James Hogg's *Winter Evening Tales* (2002) and a co-edited collection of essays, *Scotland and the Borders of Romanticism* (forthcoming from Cambridge University Press). Currently he is completing his second book, *Scott's Shadow: The Novel in Romantic Scotland*, and co-editing an anthology of eighteenth-century travel writing.

**Karsten Engelberg** is an Associate Lecturer in English at the University of Copenhagen and teaches at the Copenhagen International School. He has edited *The Romantic Heritage* (1983), and he is the author of *The Making of the Shelley Myth* (1988) and of articles on Romantic poetry and nineteenth-century periodicals.

**Charles Lock** is Professor of English Literature at the University of Copenhagen. Among his forthcoming publications are articles on *The Cloud of Unknowing*, Thomas Hardy, Joyce Cary and Geoffrey Hill.

**Peter J. Manning** is Professor and Chair of the English Department at Stony Brook University. He is the author of *Byron and His Fictions* (1978) and *Reading Romantics* (1990), and the editor, with Susan Wolfson, of the Penguin editions, *Lord Byron: Selected Poems* (1996) and *Selected Poems of Thomas Hood, Winthrop Mackworth Praed and Thomas Lovell Beddoes* (2000), and the Romantics volume of *The Longman Anthology of British Literature* (2nd edition 2003).

**Robert W. Rix** is Visiting Fellow at Clare Hall, Cambridge University. He has published on William Blake and aspects of eighteenth-century politics and religion in several international journals. He is currently completing a monograph on Blake entitled *The Bibles of Hell: William Blake and the Discourses* *of Radicalism*, while also editing the radical satirist Charles Pigott's *A Political Dictionary explaining the True Meaning of Words* (1795).

**Peter Simonsen** received his PhD from the University of Copenhagen in 2003 and is currently teaching at the Universities of Southern Denmark and Copenhagen. He has published essays on Wordsworth's ekphrasis, black letter typography in Hardy and Wordsworth, the Romantic period problem, and Baudelaire. He is currently working on late Romantic/early Victorian poetry in relation to the problem of literary periodization.

**Pernille Strande-Sørensen**, PhD, teaches at Copenhagen Business School and is currently engaged in a project on Robert Browning and *The Ring and the Book*.

**Lene Østermark-Johansen** is Associate Professor of English Literature at the University of Copenhagen. She is the author of *Sweetness and Strength: The Reception of Michelangelo in Late Victorian England* (1998), co-editor of *Nose Book: Representations of the Nose in Literature and the Arts* (2000), and is currently editing a volume of essays on Victorian and Edwardian Responses to the Italian Renaissance and writing a book on Walter Pater and sculpture.

Book Reviewers:

**Glen Cavaliero** is a member of the English Faculty at the University of Cambridge. Among his many books are studies of *John Cowper Powys* (1973), *The Rural Tradition in the English Novel 1900-1939* (1977), *E. M. Forster* (1979), *Charles Williams* (1983), *The Supernatural and English Fiction* (1995) and *The Alchemy of Laughter: Comedy in English Fiction* (2000). He has also published five volumes of poetry.

**Clara Juncker** is Associate Professor in American Literature, Center for American Studies, University of Southern Denmark. She has published widely within the fields of American Literature, Southern Literature, African American Studies, Composition, and Film.

**Michael West**, Professor of English at the University of Pittsburgh, is the author of *Transcendental Wordplay: America's Romantic Punsters and the Search for the Language of Nature* (2000), for which he received the Christian Gauss Award in 2001.

# FORTHCOMING ISSUES

- Literacy and Vocabulary in Foreign Language Acquisition
  2004
  Editors: Dorte Albrechtsen, Kirsten Haastrup and Birgit Henriksen

- Angles on Shakespeare
  2005
  Editor: Niels Bugge Hansen

- Studies in Translation
  2006
  Editor: Ida Klitgård

- 1707-2007: The State of the Union
  2007
  Editors: Jørgen Sevaldsen and Jens Rahbek Rasmussen